Philosophers in Depth

Series Editor
Constantine Sandis
Department of Philosophy
University of Hertfordshire
Hatfield, United Kingdom

Philosophers in Depth is a series of themed edited collections focusing on particular aspects of the thought of major figures from the history of philosophy. The volumes showcase a combination of newly commissioned and previously published work with the aim of deepening our understanding of the topics covered. Each book stands alone, but taken together the series will amount to a vast collection of critical essays covering the history of philosophy, exploring issues that are central to the ideas of individual philosophers. This project was launched with the financial support of the Institute for Historical and Cultural Research at Oxford Brookes University, for which we are very grateful.

More information about this series at
http://www.palgrave.com/gp/series/14552

Gregg D. Caruso
Editor

Ted Honderich on Consciousness, Determinism, and Humanity

palgrave
macmillan

Editor
Gregg D. Caruso
Corning Community College
Corning, NY, USA

Philosophers in Depth
ISBN 978-3-319-66753-9 ISBN 978-3-319-66754-6 (eBook)
https://doi.org/10.1007/978-3-319-66754-6

Library of Congress Control Number: 2017963363

Printed on acid-free paper

This Palgrave Macmillan imprint is published by Springer Nature
The registered company is Springer International Publishing AG
The registered company address is: Gewerbestrasse 11, 6330 Cham, Switzerland

Preface

Ted Honderich is Grote Professor Emeritus of the Philosophy of Mind and Logic at University College London and a leading contemporary philosopher of mind, determinism and freedom, and morals. This collection assembles a world-class line-up of philosophers to provide the most comprehensive critical treatment of Honderich's philosophy, focusing on three major areas of his work: (1) Actualism, his theory of consciousness; (2) his extensive and ground-breaking work on determinism and freedom; and (3) his views on right and wrong, including his Principle of Humanity and his judgments on terrorism.

The collection begins with a comprehensive introduction written by Honderich. It provides a start-of-the-art summary of his current views and outlines his main thinking in the three areas. Fourteen original chapters separated into three sections follow the introduction. The first section addresses Honderich's work on consciousness—including his Actualism theory, his conception of the physical, and his approach to unconscious mentality. The second section explores Honderich's extensive contribution to the free will debate, including his views on determinism, freedoms, life-hopes, and punishment. The third section addresses various aspects of Honderich's Principle of Humanity and discusses a number of moral and political concepts, including distributive justice, the right to self-determination, the justification of violence, and terrorism. Each section concludes with a set of remarks by Honderich, which address the contributions in that section and provide further insights into his views.

I would like to acknowledge that this collection is the result of an event at the Senate House, University of London, organized by the Royal Institute of Philosophy on February 9, 2016, celebrating the three independent parts of the philosophy of Ted Honderich. The event was presided over by Anthony O'Hear and James Garvey and the presenters included Noam Chomsky, Gregg Caruso, Tim Crane, Paul Gilbert, and Paul Snowdon. At that event, I had the idea of putting together a collection containing pieces by various philosophers on Honderich's philosophy. Thanks to Palgrave Macmillan, and especially Constantine Sandis and April James, the project found a home in the *Philosophers in Depth Series*. This especially pleases me since Ted Honderich is the first living philosopher to be included in the series.

I would like to thank Ted Honderich, the Royal Institute of Philosophy, Constantine Sandis, April James, Brendan George, and all the contributors for making this book possible.

Enjoy!

Corning, NY Gregg D. Caruso

Contents

Notes on Contributors

Gregg D. Caruso is Associate Professor of Philosophy at State University of New York (SUNY) Corning and Co-Director of the Justice Without Retribution Network housed at the University of Aberdeen School of Law. He is the author of *Free Will and Consciousness* (2012) and the editor of *Neuroexistentialism: Meaning, Morals, and Purpose in the Age of Neuroscience* (co-edited with Owen Flanagan, 2018), *Science and Religion: 5 Questions* (2014), and *Exploring the Illusion of Free Will and Moral Responsibility* (2013). His research focuses on free will, moral responsibility, criminal punishment, philosophy of mind, cognitive science, and applied moral, legal, and political philosophy.

Noam Chomsky is Institute Professor (retired) at Massachusetts Institute of Technology (MIT), where he has been on the faculty since 1955. He has also taught at many other universities and lectured widely around much of the world on a wide range of topics. He is the recipient of many honorary degrees and other awards, and is the author of numerous books and articles on linguistics, philosophy, cognitive science, intellectual history, international affairs, and social and political issues. He is a member of the National Academy of Sciences, the American Academy of Arts, and many other learned societies in the USA and many other countries.

Paul Gilbert is Emeritus Professor of Philosophy at the University of Hull. After graduating in Moral Sciences and Research at Oxford, he taught Philosophy at Hull from 1967 to 2007. His main research interests are in philosophy of mind and in social and political philosophy. His principal publications include

Human Relationships (1991), *Terrorism, Security and Nationality* (1994), *The Philosophy of Nationalism* (1998), *Philosophy of Mind* (with K. Lennon and S. Burwood, 1998), *Peoples, Culture and Nations* (2000), *New Terror, New Wars* (2003), *The World, the Flesh and the Subject* (with K. Lennon, 2005), *Cultural Identity and Political Ethics* (2010), and *An Introduction to Metaphilosophy* (with S. Overgaard and S. Burwood, 2013).

Alastair Hannay He is Emeritus Professor of Philosophy at the University of Oslo. He studied at the University of Edinburgh (M.A. Hons.) and received his Ph.D. in Philosophy at the University of London (University College) under the supervision of A. J. Ayer and Bernard Williams. He has been a visiting professor at the Universities of Stockholm and California (Berkeley and San Diego). For many years, he was the editor of *Inquiry*. He has translated several works of Søren Kierkegaard and is the author of *Human Consciousness* (1990), *Kierkegaard* (1999), *Kierkegaard: A Biography* (2001), *Mental Images* (2002), *On the Public* (2005), and *Kierkegaard and Philosophy* (2006). He is a Fellow of the Royal Society of Edinburgh, and Member of the Royal Norwegian Scientific Society of Science and Letters and the Norwegian Academy of Science and Letters.

Ted Honderich is a British philosopher; Grote Professor Emeritus of the Philosophy of Mind and Logic, University College London; visiting professor at City University of New York Graduate Center, Yale; and so on. His work has been mainly about three things: consciousness and mind, including subjectivity, the mind-brain relation, and personal identity; determinism, its truth, and its consequences for freedoms and our human standing; and right and wrong, including his Principle of Humanity, its possible proof, and its bearing on democracy and terrorism. Other writings have been on the political tradition of Conservatism, supposed justifications of punishment by the state, and problems in logical analysis and metaphysics, including the nature of time, the definition of truth, and Russell's Theory of Descriptions. He has lectured in British, continental European, Irish, American, Canadian, Asian, Russian, and African universities. He is the author or editor of many books and also of a philosophical autobiography, *Philosopher: A Kind of Life*.

Barbara Gail Montero is Associate Professor of Philosophy at the College of Staten Island of the City University of New York (CUNY) and the CUNY Graduate Center. She is the author of *Thought in Action: Expertise and the Conscious Mind* (2016) and has received research fellowships from the National Endowment for the Humanities, the American Council of Learned Societies, the Andrew Mellon Foundation, and the Cambridge New Directions in the Study of Mind Initiative. She is writing a book on the body side of the mind-body problem (the question of what is matter) as well as exploring ways in which dance can probe philosophical conundrums.

Michael Neumann is Professor Emeritus of Philosophy at Trent University, Canada. He is the author of *The Rule of Law: Politicizing Ethics*, as well as articles on rationality, the morality of terrorism, and utilitarianism.

Richard J. Norman is Emeritus Professor of Moral Philosophy at the University of Kent. His publications include *The Moral Philosophers* (1983 and 1998), *Ethics, Killing, and War* (1995), and *On Humanism* (2004 and 2012).

Derk Pereboom is Stanford H. Taylor '50 Chair and Susan Linn Sage Professor in the Philosophy Department at Cornell University. He is the author of *Living Without Free Will* (2001), *Consciousness and the Prospects of Physicalism* (2011), *Free Will, Agency, and Meaning in Life* (2014), and of articles on free will, philosophy of mind, and the history of modern philosophy. In his work on free will, Pereboom defends the position that we lack free will, defined as the control in action required for attributions of desert, and explores the implications of this view for rational deliberation, ethics, personal relationships, and treatment of criminals.

Paul Russell is Professor of Philosophy at the University of British Columbia and the University of Gothenburg, where he is also the Director of the Gothenburg Responsibility Project. He has held visiting positions at several universities, including Stanford, Pittsburgh, and North Carolina at Chapel Hill. His publications include *Freedom and Moral Sentiment: Hume's Way of Naturalizing Responsibility* (1995); *The Riddle of Hume's Treatise: Skepticism, Naturalism, and Irreligion* (2008); and *The Limits of Free Will* (2017).

Saul Smilansky received his D. Phil. from Oxford University in 1990, and since 1991, he has been teaching in the Department of Philosophy at the University of Haifa, Israel, where (from 2003) he is a Full Professor. He is also Chair of the department. Smilansky works primarily on normative ethics and on the free will problem. His first book, *Free Will and Illusion*, was published in 2000 (paperback 2002). A second book, *10 Moral Paradoxes*, came out in 2007. Translations of this book have already come out in Finnish, Hebrew, Korean, Polish, and Portuguese. He has also written over 70 papers in philosophical journals, among them *American Philosophical Quarterly*; *Analysis*; *Australasian Journal of Philosophy*; *Ethics, Law and Philosophy*; *Midwest Studies in Philosophy*; *Mind*; *The Monist*; *Philosophical Studies*; *Philosophy*; *Philosophy and Phenomenological Research*; and the *Proceedings of the Aristotelian Society*.

Barry C. Smith is the Director of the Institute of Philosophy at the School of Advanced Study, University of London, and Founding Director of the Centre for the Study of the Senses. He is a philosopher of mind and language, who has also written empirical and theoretical articles on taste, smell, and flavor. He is the editor (with Ernest Lepore) of *The Oxford Handbook of Philosophy of Language.*

Paul Snowdon read Philosophy, Politics, and Economics at University College, Oxford, followed by a B.Phil. there. In 1971, he was elected a Fellow and Tutor in Philosophy at Exeter College, Oxford, and in 2001, he became the Grote Professor of Mind and Logic at University College London (UCL) (a post earlier occupied by Professor Honderich), from which he retired in 2014. He has written about the philosophy of mind, especially the philosophy of perception, metaphysics, and the history of philosophy. In 2014, his book *Persons, Animals, Ourselves* was published, which defends Animalism, and in 2016, he co-edited, with Professor Stephan Blatti, *Animalism: New Essays on Persons, Animals, and Identity*. In 2018, he will bring out a book collecting his papers on perception entitled *Essays on Perceptual Experience.*

Kevin Timpe holds the William Harry Jellema Chair at Calvin College. His work on free will includes *Free Will: Sourcehood and Its Alternatives*, 2nd edition (2012) and *Free Will in Philosophical Theology* (2013). He has also written on issues in the philosophy of religion, moral psychology, virtues ethics, and the philosophy of disability. His work has been published in *Philosophy Compass, Res Philosophica, Journal of Ethics, Faith and Philosophy, Canadian Journal of Philosophy*, and *Philosophical Studies.*

Mary Warnock was educated in Winchester and then at Lady Margaret Hall (LMH), Oxford. She was Fellow and Tutor in Philosophy at St. Hugh's College from 1949 to 1966; head of the Oxford High School GDST from 1966 to 1972; research fellow of LMH and then St. Hugh's; and a lecturer at Christ Church, Oxford, until 1984 when she became Mistress of Girton College, Cambridge, until 1991. She chaired two Government Inquiries into legal and moral issues and was a Crossbench member of the House of Lords from 1985 until 2015.

List of Tables

1

Introduction

Ted Honderich

1.1 Consciousness and Mind: Actualism

Actualism, if it is as much a workplace as a final theory of consciousness and mind, is indubitably also a long way from two main fairy tales still told or remembered.

One fairy tale is that consciousness is just physical—physical stuff or anyway a physical fact. A little more clearly, if not much, consciousness is objectively or scientifically physical. Is that more declaration or even declamation than explanation?

Anyway, it's said to be material stuff in your head, soggy grey matter as the philosopher Colin McGinn contemplated. Only *neural networks*, however wonderfully related within and between themselves or to other things. Somehow not different in kind from the stuff or kind of thing, the nature, of the chair under you, or that growing aspidistra plant in the pot over there, or the London bus that got you here.

T. Honderich (✉)
University College London, London, UK

G. D. Caruso (ed.), *Ted Honderich on Consciousness, Determinism, and Humanity*, Philosophers in Depth, https://doi.org/10.1007/978-3-319-66754-6_1

The second fairy tale is that consciousness is ghostly stuff, as in the old, old Greek philosophical theory of *mind-brain dualism*—Plato and all that. To use the term "mind-brain dualism" that way, incidentally, is to go on misusing it—for there being two things with one of them not physical at all and somewhere somehow floating above or around the other.

Or, to forget the ancient Greeks, and come right up to date with this dualism, consciousness is the entirely similar ghostly stuff, said to be "an abstract sort of thing," in the *abstract functionalism* of very much twenty-first-century cognitive science, in what can also have the name of being *computerism* about consciousness.

It's not good enough that abstract functionalism like the ancient dualism makes consciousness *different* from everything else, which it does and which any decent theory absolutely has to. It doesn't help, either, by the way, that abstract functionalism is tied to and owes a lot to the more than uncertain proposition of what is called multiple or variable realizability or realization. That is, to the effect that *exactly and precisely* the same conscious thought or hope or whatever can go with *different* brain states. That's why it's not identical with any one of them. It's a good step towards making the floating thought or hope unreal, of course. But we don't have to go into that.

Abstract functionalism also seems to have among its various shortcomings another one, close enough in my mind to making it nonsensical. The somehow non-physical consciousness itself—however it is somehow tied to what is underneath it or what it's said to be supervenient on—is itself what philosophers call *epiphenomenal.* That is to say that unlike what somehow just goes with it, it itself doesn't cause anything. It never has any ordinary physical effects at all. Yours wasn't in any way causal, and wasn't in that way explanatory, with respect to where you are right now, which, you may willingly agree, in good American English, is nuts.

Maybe we do not have to wait for an Einstein of consciousness in order to try to do better than the two fairy tales. And we do not have to join a lot of pessimists in our setting out to solve the problem of consciousness right now. Is it really all that hard, by the way? The hardest problem of all?

Some say so. Maybe if they're not fully acquainted with other problems in philosophy? Is it as hard as the problem of truth, of what the truth of a proposition is or comes to—maybe the roles in it of what is called correspondence to fact and coherence with other propositions? Is consciousness as hard as right and wrong? As hard as justifying inductive reasoning from past to future? As hard as the nature of time—say the relation of the temporal properties of past, present, and future to the temporal relations of earlier than, simultaneous with, and after?

Anyway, with consciousness, there is something we can start with. This is not just a good idea, which some philosophers get one morning. Quite a few have got one about consciousness.

We can start with a rich *database* on consciousness in the primary ordinary sense, the main sense in a good dictionary. We can start with this admittedly figurative or metaphorical database, derivable from the language of philosophers, scientists, and others, including you: about 40 items. Owed to their holds on their own consciousnesses, and I trust to yours. Owed to remembering what it was to think something a moment ago, and so on. No stuff there about introspection, inner peering, which led to a lot of dubious psychology in the nineteenth century.

The database includes our taking being conscious in this sense as being *the having of something*, if not in the literal way you have ankles or money. It includes being conscious as something's *being right there*, its being *open*, its being *transparent in the sense of being clear straight-off*, its *not being deduced, inferred, constructed, or posited* from something else. Also its being *given*, its *somehow existing*, its being what issues in a lot of philosophical talk of *contents* or *objects*. The database includes something's being *present*, its *being presented*, its being *to* something, its being what McGinn speaks of as *vividly naked*, and so on.

The database, I say, of which I didn't make any of it up, does what none of five leading ideas of consciousness do—even if their owners contribute to the database. They are the five ideas about what are called qualia, something it's like to be a bat, subjectivity, intentionality or aboutness, and phenomenality, whatever it is. The database, that is, *adequately initially identifies* the subject of primary ordinary consciousness—makes sure that people around here seeming to be disagreeing about consciousness are really answering the same question, not talking past one another. There's a lot of that in both the past and present of philosophy and science about consciousness. It has a lot to do with disagreement and pessimism about consciousness.

The database, we can say, lets us sum up primary ordinary consciousness or anyway label it satisfactorily as being *something's being actual.* As its being *actual consciousness.*

This consciousness, by the way, is not all of *the mental* or *the mind.* It is not that greater stream than the one in William James's still-cited talk of a stream of consciousness, not the greater one that includes more than consciousness in our sense or any ordinary sense. The mental or the mind includes in it, say, standing or ongoing dispositions or capabilities that enable me right now to do what is different from them, *think* for a moment of my age or *have the feeling* that time is passing. And the mental or the mind includes an awful lot more in neuroscience and such related inquiries as linguistics.

The figurative or metaphorical database, with some significant help, including contemplation of various shortcomings of various existing theories of consciousness, and thus the assembling of a specific set of *criteria* for a good theory, sure leads somewhere—as in many different cases in the history of science itself, including hard science. The figurative database leads to an entirely *literal* theory, an account of the nature of something, saying what it is, what it comes to, or comes down to: the theory that is *Actualism.*

The whole theory, as you might expect, given the database, will consist in due course in very literal answers as to (1) *what* is actual and (2) what its being actual is.

More particularly, the theory in its first section is of *what* is actual in each of the three different sides of consciousness—perceptual, cognitive, and affective, which roughly means consciousness in seeing etc., consciousness that is thinking, and consciousness that is wanting or feeling or that latter two of those together. Actualism is therefore very unusual, as good as unique, in the philosophy of *consciousness in general,* complete theories of all of consciousness taken together. It is different in respecting the differences of those three sides, which you may and definitely should find reassuring. Seeing etc. really isn't like believing—or wanting etc.

The second answer in Actualism, as I say, is of course to what *being actual* is in the three cases, the three sides of consciousness, what the data comes to in that respect. Not all the same in all cases.

Of course, Actualism is *a* dualism in the sense that any sane theory of anything is. It makes a difference between consciousness and the rest of what there is. As you will be hearing, that isn't to say it puts consciousness *above* anything else, whatever facts there may be that call for or tempt us to such talk.

The database itself, at least most of the pieces of data, seems to have something to do with something's being *physical*—maybe or maybe not in the standard sense in science and philosophy, which is to say objectively or scientifically physical.

So too does physicality come up somehow with virtually all theories of consciousness in history. Starting with the denial of physicality in ancient dualism and continuing through a ruck of theories, including materialisms and naturalisms, say Dan Dennett's, that are to the effect instead that consciousness is somehow objectively or scientifically physical. Presumably, all the theoreticians weren't ninnies in that preoccupation.

Why not spend some real time getting really straight what being objectively physical is? Why not act with respect to the situation implied quite a while ago by the admirable paper by Tim Crane and Hugh Mellor, "There Is No Question of Physicalism"? It was so titled out of the conviction that no adequate conception of the physical was available, certainly none to be got by exclusive reliance on science.

Could it be that a second source of disagreement and pessimism and worse about the subject of consciousness in philosophy and science, a source in addition to no adequate initial clarification of a subject matter, has been no concentration on the separate question or questions of the physical?

Why not, without following any philosopher's or scientist's leap or flight to a generalization, just ask what characteristics the physical world has? Proceed pedestrianly, walk over the ground, work through a subject? Put together a checklist? Didn't Einstein plod in order eventually to do some leaping, by the way?

Anyway, here is a comparative table, a summary table, a table of physicalities in general. You can more or less satisfy yourself, I say, that this objective or scientific physicality has 16 characteristics. They are the ones in the left-hand column under the heading "Objective Physical World" in the table. An enlarged version to which we will come of this table of physicalities in general, incidentally, will include an additional column—this having been prompted if not suggested by Noam Chomsky's chapter in this book (Table 1.1).

I'd better say that putting the whole table in here is in a way putting the cart before the horse or letting the whole cat out of the bag. The table as a whole from the top heading down has all of it been a kind of

Table 1.1 Table of physicalities in general

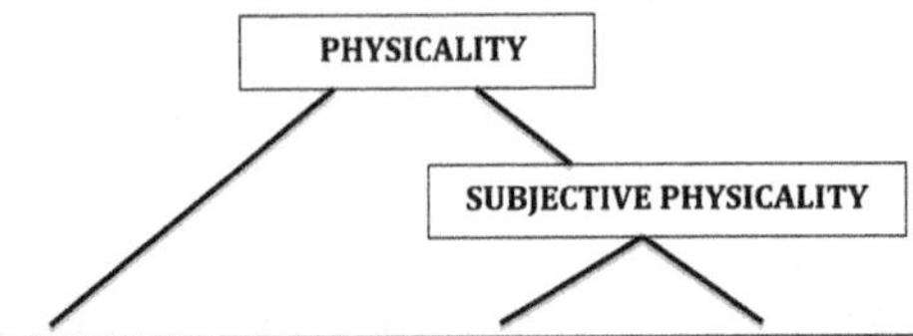

	OBJECTIVE PHYSICAL WORLD	SUBJECTIVE PHYSICAL WORLDS: Perceptual Consciousness	SUBJECTIVE PHYSICAL REPRESENTATIONS Cognitive and Affective Consciousness
	ITS PHYSICALITY	*THEIR PHYSICALITY*	*THEIR PHYSICALITY*
1	in the inventory of science	in the inventory of science	in the inventory of science
2	open to the scientific method	open to the scientific method	open to the scientific method
3	within space and time	within space and time	within space and time
4	in particular lawful connections	in particular lawful connections	in particular lawful connections
5	in categorial lawful connections	in categorial lawful connections, including those dependency-relations with (a) the objective physical world and (b) the conscious thing as neural	in categorial lawful connections, including those dependency-relations with (a) the objective physical world and (b) the conscious thing as neural.
6	a matter of ordinary world or macroworld or perception but microworld deduction	dependent subjective physical worlds *constitutive* of macroworld perception	not perceived, but dependent importantly on macroworld perception
7	more than one point of view with macroworld	more than one point of view with perception	no point of view at all
8	different from different points of view	different from different points of view	no differences from points of view
9	primary and secondary properties, whatever they are	primary and secondary properties despite (5b) above?	no primary and secondary properties at all
	ITS OBJECTIVITY	*THEIR SUBJECTIVITY*	*THEIR SUBJECTIVITY*
10	somehow separate from consciousness	not somehow separate from consciousness	not separate from consciousness
11	public	private	private
12	common access	some privileged access	some privileged access
13	truth and logic, more subject to?	truth and logic, less subject to?	truth and logic, still less subject to?
14	open to the scientific method	open to the scientific method despite doubt	open to the scientific method, despite doubt
15	includes no traditional self or unity or other such inner fact of subjectivity inconsistent with any of the above properties of the objective physical world	each subjective physical world is one element in an individuality that is a unique and large unity of lawful and conceptual dependencies including the above dependency-relations of subjective physicality	each representation is one element in the individuality that is a unique and large unity of lawful and conceptual dependencies including the above dependency relations of subective physicality
16	hesitation about whether this objective physicality includes consciousness	no significant hesitation about taking the above subjective physicality as being that of actual perceptual consciousness	no significant hesitation about taking this subjective physicality as being the nature of actual cognitive and affective consciousness

summary of the Actualism theory of consciousness as a whole—to which we're on the way. But so what? This isn't a detective story or murder mystery. Our use of the table right now is just for its column summing up of what objective or scientific physicality comes to.

Can that understanding of objective physicality somehow lead us to an answer or rather answers to what ordinary consciousness in its three sides comes to? Maybe different answers with perceptual consciousness as against cognitive and affective consciousness, and somewhat different answers with the last two?

But think now about the database that preceded the table and that first question of *what* is actual with a part or side of consciousness, perceptual consciousness in particular. What is actual right now with your own perceptual consciousness? I give you the answer free. You'd give it to me if you were asked. It's the place you're in, probably *a room*. A room out there. No other answer is possible. No other kind of answer.

And what is it for a room to be actual? I suppose the response that will come to you is that the data in the database at least in good part must bring to mind the idea that things being actual is their being *physical*.

Objectively physical? Not if you spend time thinking, walking around here too. The response has to be that a room's being actual is that it has characteristics related to but different from the characteristics of the objective physical world. A room's being actual is that it is having the run of 16 characteristics in the middle column of the table.

The most fundamental or crucial characteristic, you may say, is indeed number 5—that a room's actuality consists in its existing dependently on two dependencies—its existence depending on the objective physical world and also on the perceiver neurally. But all of the 16 characteristics are important for the understanding of perceptual consciousness, relevant to the question of its nature.

They're obviously related to the ones in the first column, those of the objective physical world, but different. They answer the question of what it is for a room to be actual. It's for it to be, as there are reasons of likeness and difference for summing it up, *subjectively physical*.

So in perceptual consciousness, consciousness in perceiving against the consciousness that is thinking and wanting and so on—*what* is actual is indeed *subjective physical worlds* out there. Or rather, more carefully, stages of them, often stages of rooms. These worlds and their stages, if your intellectual personality of realism and down-to-earthness are already kicking in suspiciously—yes, these are myriad in number, and mostly fleeting. But, I answer, no more than piles of objective things in science.

Now cognitive and affective consciousness, and the first question there. *What* is actual in the variety of cases of thinking, wanting, and so on is certainly different. What is actual are representations or aboutnesses or signs or images or the like *of* other things, the things we say they *stand for* or *mean* or the like. More particularly, what's actual with cognitive and affective consciousness is representations-with-attitude, taking something as somehow true or somehow good. These representations are definitely not out there in the world, whatever is the case with what they're of.

And to think about the representations of cognitive and affective consciousness—and to ask about *their* actuality, what their being actual is—is to see of course that it is in fact a matter of characteristics also related to those of the objective physical world and related differently to the characteristics of the subjective physical worlds of perceptual consciousness.

All that about perceptual and then cognitive and affective consciousness has been pretty fast progress. But you may also agree that we have at least the guts of an answer or rather answers to what consciousness comes to, what the three sides of consciousness come to. From the metaphorical or figurative table, we've got to a literal understanding of consciousness.

Something else hardly needs adding: (1) objective physical things, (2) subjective physical worlds, and (3) subjective physical representations, the latter two being subjective physicality, make the great category that is simply that of *physicality*—the genus physicality in general. This is the fact, or these are the facts, and nothing else is, that have led inevitably to concern with physicality in connection with consciousness.

Of course, all that you've heard can do with more distinguishing and noting of questions arising and also objections—more than can be contemplated here.

First is perceptual consciousness. Yes, it does indeed consist most fundamentally in characteristic 5: worlds existing out there in the two dependent ways, worlds being dependent in the two ways. Perceptual consciousness doesn't consist in just the worlds out there themselves, as the good philosopher Crane has been too inclined to object with understandable incredulity.

As also can usefully be kept in mind, as we have, perceptual consciousness also consists in another sense in *stages* of the dependent worlds—just as we can also think and speak, by the way, of the objective physical world and stages in it.

Perceptual consciousness, again, does *not* consist at all in representations or aboutnesses or of-nesses of any kind whatever. No sense data, none of the philosopher-psychologist's mental paint. It does not consist in them, no matter what registration-without-representation, as we can call it, there may be of the objective physical world on a perceiver. Registration with effects on cognitive and affective consciousness. But skip that, along with some other complications.

That my perceptual consciousness now consists fundamentally in a room's dependent existence, you will agree, is happily consistent with the entirely pre-philosophical fact that we don't take rooms to be representations, to be things that literally are about things. They're not signs, not like the pictures on the wall. Just for a start, we don't always walk around in representations.

Our account of perceptual consciousness is a long way from an idea persistent in the history of the philosophy and science of perception, something you may have heard of. Maybe that idea does deserve the name that Freddie Ayer the Logical Positivist gave to it—*Naive Realism*. Other good philosophers, like the definite but diplomatic Mike Martin, of both University College London and the University of California in Berkeley, and Heather Logue at the University of Leeds, now speak of Common-Sense Realism or Direct Realism and have at least sympathy with it.

What is it? That has not been clear to me—far from it. It seems to have been and to be to the vague effect that in our seeing there is some kind or other of *direct* connection with the objective physical thing seen. That is certainly *not* what we are contemplating; indeed, a lot lot less than what we are contemplating.

To come now to cognitive and affective consciousness, as against perceptual consciousness, they are in our view very different. That, by the way, is very much in accord with all the other parts of the whole history of the philosophy and science of perceptual consciousness as against that of consciousness in general. A reassuring fact. Whether or not those people thought about it, there must have been a relevant big reason they took perceptual consciousness itself as different from cognitive and affective.

For us, cognitive and affective consciousness are indeed different, since they are representations with attitude in here—the two attitudes having to do, respectively, with truth and with good. Still, cognitive and affective consciousness can't be *just* or *only* such representations, of course. Say like other words or images or the like. They're different from just the printed words, lines of type on this page or screen, and so on, which definitely aren't conscious at all. They aren't conscious despite being perfectly good representations, say connected by rules with other things.

Cognitive and affective consciousness, rather, as you've heard, consist in *actual* representations, which is now to say representations that are subjectively physical. That is what is missing from all the useful industries on representation or intentionality in the philosophy of mind and maybe linguistics. The actuality of representations, as literally understood, itself distinguishes Actualism from the rest of the industry on representationism in the philosophy and science of mind, language, and so on.

Was the move OK from the sides of consciousness being actual, being according to the database, to the conclusion in the theory or systematic and full analysis that they are subjective physicality? Is that a leap of the sort mentioned earlier that other people have taken to what objective physicality is? I say no, we've worked our way there. I recommend that response to your consideration.

You'll agree there is none of ancient or contemporary ghostly stuff in the story. Or sense data, or that "mental paint," or the vagueness of "content" or "object." Or some damned thing first discernible in the Cambridge of G. E. Moore if you try hard—you're supposed to discern it while it still remains wholly *transparent.*

Our story doesn't have in it either a theatre of the mind with a spotlight or any other such thing. Let alone the more substantial idea of behaviourism—being conscious *is* behaving—from which Chomsky awakened several whole professions and their fans. And we're not going in for physical functionalism on its own, a thing that's physical, not abstract, being effect and cause—which has more to say for it than abstract functionalism. We might get around to tolerating it as a possible further component in theory, secondary, maybe in our theory, but skip that.

Nor in our story of perceptual consciousness itself is there any vulnerability to the tired old objections from illusion and hallucination—the general lines where you can't tell the difference between seeing and really hallucinating and so there isn't something *real* in the seeing. The objections are thought to finish off Naive Realism's story of a direct relation with objective reality out there. They don't touch Actualism. Nor, by the way, in our story of perceptual consciousness itself, are there any representions so-called elsewhere in the wider category of the mental.

And thinking of objections, philosophers have said of some standard physicalist theories of consciousness that something could be conscious in the sense of the theories and still be what the philosophers call a *zombie*—something going around the place without being conscious at all, anyway in the ordinary sense. Well, I put it to you that something that is conscious in our explained sense is not likely to be taken as such a zombie by you or by anyone else with their head screwed on.

Nor either in Actualism is there the elusiveness of talk of phenomenality, which for the terminologically liberal Ned Block is somewhere or somehow in just thinking as well as seeing. Nor in Actualism is there anywhere any of the circularity of so much utterance on consciousness. Such as in the leading idea consisting in being conscious of what it's like to be something, courtesy of Tom Nagel and Timothy Sprigge. That, I put it to you, comes down to saying, consciousness is what it's like to be conscious.

Nor in Actualism is there any vestige of my own old Union Theory of interdependent effects, also known as psychoneural pairs. Or Donald Davidson's Anomalous Monism, seemingly to the wonderful effect, the news, that you need a lot of very original argument for the astonishingly true conclusion that there is no lawful connection, no such relation, between what only seem to be two things but are really just one. And nor is Actualism Galen Strawson's breathtaking revival of the aspectual theory of panpsychism. "Little minds in lettuce leaves?" as I used to ask the same Sussex panpsychist Sprigge.

And, to be up to date, our theory doesn't have in it entities of the worthy but all-inclusive, blanketing and flattening recent and previous contemporary universal externalisms about consciousness, making *all* of it somehow external—anyway so-named externalisms. It doesn't have in it meanings or individuations or actions or extended minds or whatever is found in *all* of perceptual, cognitive, and affective consciousness—properly unorthodox but to me very resistible theories of Hilary Putnam, Tyler Burge, Alva Noe, and Andy Clark. All worthy of attention, but not here.

And yes, we have in Actualism a solution to the mind-body problem, the problem of how consciousness is connected or related to brains or whatever. The problem of the relation between the neurons and the wondering or the dreaming and all that. That problem is just done for. The connection is just ordinary lawful connection which itself is no mystery, which itself can be made clear and unmysterious. That is, connection to which not too many others than my old pal and public combatant, and now pal enough again, McGinn, are superior to—say in speaking of it as just "brute correlation," seemingly dismissing the mere truck of mere science.

Can you use a good summary of Actualism with respect to perceptual consciousness, an aphorism? Bishop Berkeley said of things out there that for them to be is for them to be perceived—really an inner fact. We say that being perceptually conscious is for something out there in a way to be, an outer fact.

Of course, there are questions about Actualism. Say Chomsky's implied and unsettling question about whether we can have an adequate conception of the physical at all despite science not having really and truly provided an effective one since about as far back as Newton. And, I guess, there is a question on my bringing together science and the rest of our knowledge in that table, including philosophical. Look through the table again. And, of course, there are questions about the relation of consciousness to the rest of the mental—thus, the relation of Actualism to *mentalism* in a very general sense, the running together of the conscious mental and the unconscious mental—or *mentalism* in Chomsky's particular sense.

Maybe a further question is about *where* consciousness is, despite the plain and fundamental, if not further examined, answer we have. Mediaeval philosophers spent a lot of time on where states of affairs or properties of things are, as against the things themselves.

There is no question, I am sure, of whether the story of Actualism about perceptual consciousness somehow reduces to intentionality or aboutness—although I have sensed that question near to the lips of a listener or two. There is the question, of course, not of how well Actualism defeats the fortress of intentionality or aboutness as the nature of all consciousness, a fortress standing since the mediaevals and then since Brentano in the nineteenth century, and newly fortified by Tim Crane.

You've heard enough about that, but there's the additional thought here that well before, indeed always before, we ourselves got to the database and any theory of consciousness whatever, we all knew that perceptual consciousness is different from cognitive and affective—that consciousness in seeing the room is different in kind from thinking of the room on the way up the stairs, having a thought of it, or anywhere wanting to change it or keep it the same.

And is Actualism the very nerve or strength of Searle's lovely and celebrated Chinese Room argument against computerism about consciousness? About the man who gets translations right without understanding Chinese? Could be. I hope so. Reflected glory for us?

And there's still the question regularly avoided about what aboutness is, what it really comes down to. Maybe about how a representation "carries the mind" to something or does whatever makes those few words sound right. Maybe the magic and mystery about all of that reduces a lot when you think of the episode of naming a child and then beginning to use the name. The representing is a case of just remembering a decision or resolution and making use of it? So representing is not simple but not so elusive either? Only about as hard as remembering?

And, finally, the question of whether ordinary consciousness, consciousness in the primary ordinary sense, *actual consciousness*, is the right subject of consciousness? Well, clearly there isn't just one right subject. But ours is *the* necessary one. All others depend on the primary ordinary sense. So they depend on a hold on actual consciousness. The very definition of general mentalism including consciousness, but with the rest of the mental identified by way of the consciousness, depends on it.

And really finally, is Actualism a fertile theory, even pregnant? Good for philosophy and also science? Sure is, as you know already.

1.2 Determinism/Explanationism and Freedom

An old and doubted, and indeed sometimes condescended-to, story I put to you is just true. That's the start and basis of what I have to say here.

All spatio-temporal *events* or *happenings* or *states* or *properties of things* or *things themselves*, of whatever extent or duration without exception, as distinct from anything else, of course, that isn't an event, are *effects or lawful correlates*. That is to say, each has a fundamental *explanation*. It has what may be used to be called a sufficient condition as against necessary conditions. A causal or other lawful circumstance, in the case of the first, is a set of conditions including one usually called the cause.

That is, to be clearer, each event in a very general sense is this: such that if or given a particular causal or other lawful circumstance or set of conditions, whatever else were also happening, the event would still have occurred.

That kind of conditional or "if-then" statement is true of all events as distinct from a lot of other things, including merely logically, conceptually, linguistically, mathematically, or theoretically connected items or stages, say "2+3" and "5," and maybe bits of Quantum Theory. It was a pretty dumb determinist, if there ever was one, who included numbers himself, say 5, as distinct from inscriptions of it, in his effects. Or propositions, where those are different from any expression of them, say any particular sentence or utterance.

Causation and lawful connection in sum is no mystery or problem. It is as plain as that strong or whatever-else conditional statement. Causation includes no "natural necessity" if that is something more than conditional connection as defined. And causation and lawful connection include no metaphysics—say in the usual vague sense of the word or in terms of Freddie Ayer's Logical Positivism.

His Verification Principle of meaning, in fact a principle misnamed since it is about what is true or false rather than about meaning generally, rather than about anything in language that has meaning, is a principle both over-estimated and under-estimated by him. In fact in my own idea it is open to be taken as an empirical generalization from what good science, philosophy, and so on does—what it regards in fact as having a truth value.

Since it is that, by the way, it escapes the hopeful thought that it applies to itself and thus makes itself neither true nor false.

Explanationism, as I myself now am more inclined to call it, in order to avoid the misleading heavy connotations of "determinism," shared with "fatalism," fate, predestination, iron necessity, and all that—explanationism is at least a reasonable assumption, in fact the gravamen of naturalism and empiricism, those general facts of almost all science and of good philosophy.

Explanationism is at least reasonable despite our supposedly revealing personal "I could-have-done-otherwise" experiences after having decided or acted—testimony relied on even by otherwise rationally down-to-earth philosophers like Searle. To my mind, he depends very insecurely on these bits of autobiography—as well as on his very own not only earlier-later causation but also up-down causation.

Like others, he is also impressed by wonderful philosophical and metaphysical rather than really scientific interpretations of the mathematics of Quantum Theory. The interpretations, rightly spoken of as weird, and so on, by their own proponents and by approving reporters, are to me, I admit, about as hopeless as Schrodinger's cat. That aid to understanding of Quantum Theory, you may remember that famous thought-experiment, is to the effect that the cat in a box is both alive and dead until it is observed by somebody.

Also in favour of explanationism, I remind you of the absence of real chance in roulette wheels and of the absence of levitating spoons at breakfast and the absence of any such indubitable wonders in machines and what-not, including all the rest of science outside of Quantum Theory and so on. Thinking of the rest of science, indeed the rest of physics, say engineering informed by it, why don't we occasionally discover that bridges fell down really for no reason at all?

And another connected thought. It is necessary, if we turn to the brain or whatever, to suppose either that there isn't indeterminism down below in the microworld rather than the ordinary macroworld or that if there is, then it doesn't translate upward or sideways to where it would count, say the level of neurons.

And, it occurs to me to add, explanationism is about a thousand sea miles or couches from Freud and psychoanalysis and other mysteries and mysterianisms and spiritualisms and confidence jobs.

I admit that certainly there are good philosophers who disagree, at least a little. Yes, there is Gregg Caruso, whose name you know, who is what he speaks of as no more than a *sceptic* about there being free will, uncaused choices, and decisions, not a denier of them. And thus necessarily is, I guess, a sceptic too about explanationism. Has he been frightened by the massed ranks of Baptists and Pentecostals and others of fundamentalist religion in his native land? Well, have a look and reassure yourself that that temptation to diagnosis of mine is unkind and false. Read his book.

Explanationism has the support, if not explicit, of all neuroscience except, it seems, when it is being done by retiring members of the profession. There was Professor Eccles, who wrote the book he entitled *The Self and Its Brain*. There is Professor Libet, who relied on by the same Professor Popper who also relied on Eccles. Professor Libet, who first discovered the brain is *before* the mind in time in terms of events, and then discovered, seemingly on thinking that that discovery took away his free will, that it's the mind, whatever it is, that is before the brain.

Are you shocked by me, by this philosopher's standing-up on his hind legs against some science, even minority science? I confess that it seems to me that philosophy can sometimes do that, if pretty rarely. This, in brief, is because philosophy is concentration, more than science's concentration, on the logic of ordinary intelligence—(1) clarity usually by analysis, (2) consistency and validity, (3) generalness, and (4) completeness. Philosophy has or seeks to have those merits.

Well enough described as thinking about facts rather than getting them? Well, science sometimes strays into the thinking about.

Something else about explanationism or determinism: both the historical doctrines of traditional Compatibilism and Incompatibilism about determinism and freedom, after some centuries of philosophical and other attention, have been falsified, demonstrably so. I claim a little old credit here. Hume was wrong in taking our freedom as we understand it to be consistent with causation. Kant was wrong in taking our freedom as we understand it to be inconsistent with causation.

This is the case simply since in our conceiving, as distinct from fact, there is *both* incompatible freedom (origination, free will where it doesn't just mean freedom, lawlessness, and unexplainable control and responsibility) and compatible freedom (voluntariness—choice and action according to desire, embraced desires, not being in jail etc., and thus quite unfated). The two of them are even in our legal systems. So, there is not just *one* idea—which, of course, *would* have to be either inconsistent or not with something else.

There is a related but alternative true-enough story called Attitudinism, about our life-hopes and a lot else, and a connected real problem.

The real problem of determinism has been that of accommodating ourselves to the frustration of certain attitudes—at bottom certain desires, things within Affective Consciousness.

We run up against a conviction owed to reflecting on our own past lives. Reflecting on our own particular actions too, these by the way being definable movements and the like caused and represented by an active intention, historically known as volitions. Actions, you note and agree, not being items located inside the head, not of arms, and so on, as the otherwise sagacious Jenn Hornsby said in striking an early blow for the independence of feminist philosophy.

The conviction we run up against in the real problem of determinism is that an attitude somehow akin to the one tied to Indeterminism, that way of holding yourself lawlessly morally responsible, does have *some or other* basis despite the truth of determinism.

We need to look for a radical escape here, get out of philosophical and religious and other cart tracks that have never got anywhere, be nearly as brave as the daredevil interpreters of the mathematics of Quantum Theory. We need to be brave but with our feet on earth. We need to find a solution as radical but real life here as Actualism is with the problem of perceptual consciousness. Make an escape from dismay and intransigence about our lives and causation into affirmation.

More particularly, about the real problem of determinism of free will or origination or inexplicable responsibility, such astute students as Bob Kane have in fact allowed that in wanting it, we are in fact wanting something you can say without worry is real. A desire for a certain *human standing*. We are wanting to be above nature or at least above the rest of nature.

We won't get this elevation, according to me, in various known ways found in the philosophy of the past. This is about funny powers, new randomness, God's gift to us, religion generally, as well as neuroscience having shown that the mind is after the brain and then helpfully turning out to show, as you've heard, that it's before it.

Nor will we get the elevation by way of what seems to me the pretty absurd argument owed to an admittedly clever philosopher and metaphysician, Peter van Inwagen. That if determinism were true, there would be no sense in which we are in control when we decide to cross the street or leave our wife—because we aren't in control of a train of past causes. See Wikipedia for a start. And remember that there's something called voluntariness, at bottom doing what you want, of which you'll be hearing some more. That's a kind of control.

We need something better for purposes of preserving human elevation. It will have to be very different. It may be somewhere else, as has happened often enough with problems in both science and philosophy. The Actualism theory of consciousness provides this uniquely—as well as truth to our irrepressible conviction of *subjectivity* with respect to consciousness—as follows.

Each of us, you have heard, has the stages of a subjective physical world dependent on her or him as well as dependent on the objective physical world. To be rhetorical, each of us is therefore a god, a kind of creator-god, however petty. I'm serious enough about this. We all register, indeed live, what only some of us express, say in philosophy.

Differently and still more seriously, really and absolutely seriously, each of us is a lawful *unity* of perceptual, cognitive, and affective consciousness. Look back at the table of kinds of physicality in connection with consciousness again. That unity is also an individuality and a personal identity—a further enlargement to the best conception of personal identity, that of John Locke a while ago and his rational improver Derek Parfit recently. That reality mentioned already and known to you—we could say lived in. No inner entity, no such self, no ego, no spook—none of that is the large fact of subjectivity, the referent of your "I," the true content of your use of the first-person pronoun.

Surely the unity that is yourself according to what you have heard of both consciousness and determinism/freedom also does the trick or a trick of giving each of us a little upgrading? More standing? Come to think of it, we need it. Not because of explanationism, but something else. To which you and I now turn. Our moral standing.

1.3 Right and Wrong, Humanity, Terrorism

There is a morality, a principle of right and wrong, to which we are all committed by two things.

The first thing is that this morality is in accord with a particular fact of our affective consciousness. It is in accord with the fact of the great goods in our lives if we enjoy them, the objects of what can be counted as our six great desires. We put them ahead of everything else.

1. We all desire the great good of *going on existing*, which includes within each of us a personal world that is going on longer. We all desire a life of at least 73 years, not 37. We want not to leave life at an age that is just middle age in England or America.
2. We want a kind of existence that has to do with our *bodies*—not to be in pain, to have necessary surgical operations, and so on. Maybe not to be anxious, not to be depressed, not without decent sleep.
3. We want fundamental freedoms and powers generally described, not only political ones. We want not to be coerced by various personal circumstances arranged by others, subjected to compulsion, bullied, unable to run our own lives. We want to be free or to have a right to get and have a working life, a job, such a life providing an independence from others, some independence.
4. We want good *relationship* with those around us, closer relationships to some, say our children. We need, rather than merely want, our children to be okay, to be decently fed, to learn. I can steal food if they're starving, can't I? Not kill to get it, maybe, but certainly at least use what can be called reasonable force. We also want a good sexual and related other important relationships, some of them wider, to many people.
5. We also want *respect and self-respect*. Not the absurdity of being taken as less than human because of country or other place of origin, class, and language of parents learned from them, or the like. I have and make a claim not to be condescended to or cheated because I am brown or black, or have a hooknose, or belong to other supposed visible membership of a race. I have a claim too to be able to come to know things, not to be ignorant, and to come to have feelings that enlarge a life.

6. There are also the distinguishable, if related, *goods of culture*, starting with being able to read. All of us want at least some of the cultural goods. Many of us want the practice and reassurance of a religion, or the custom of a people. Or a homeland if that comes in this category, a homeland out of our real past rather than anybody else's, our people's real past rather than somebody else's partly pretended past.

As I say, these six great goods make and make certain in each of us a moral judgement about ourselves, each of us making such a judgement to the benefit of one's self, in effect an assertion of moral personal necessity. A life with at least a minimum of the great goods in it. The rightness of an undeniable subsistence level, and the wrong of not having it.

Of course, anybody can want a lot more, say more than ordinary distinction or more recognition or profit or fame. There are also individual and indeed idiosyncratic desires. But all that is desire for something other than what I am talking about, what indeed is best spoken of as satisfactions of primal needs.

Speaking as your guide in all these reflections, the one who is running this conversation, it's time for a confession. A confession not large enough to be terrible, let alone fatal. It's a doubt about my list of our great desires, a smallish doubt about what exactly should go into a list of our great desires, our primal needs. Maybe something other than the six? Maybe a running together of some pair of them, or a division into two of one of them? I seem to remember that other philosophers have run up somewhat different lists of great goods, some of them religious philosophers.

I'm not very sure of the list we have—just sure enough. But there's something I'm surer of that is more important.

There is *some* specifiable list of great goods such that we all, or enough of us in our species, share them and such that we put them ahead of the remaining lesser goods. Some list like the one we have. There is that fact of human nature, that fact of evolution, a fact tied up, incidentally, with explanationism and categorical lawful connections. The very best list, if there is such a thing, will have on it things pretty close to the six just listed. It will still be of things better and deeper and so on, than everything else, say better than having more money or the pride of it, or just being good looking, or getting on television, getting good book reviews, all those real enough but lesser things.

You can conduct your own inquiry, your part in the present conversation, in terms of your own best list if it differs from mine. It will have to be in sight of mine, I guess. But the main thing about it has to be that arguably we share the desires in question. That they are fundamental human desires? Or animal? Wider than human? I slide right past that question answered confidently by some vegetarians, my daughter included. I slide past guiltily, but with confidence in being in the neighbourhood of truth.

So much for the first thing that commits us to a morality—each of us claiming a right to satisfactions of the primal needs.

The second thing, which must cut against the self-interest, the self-justifying self-interest, is *our minimal rationality*. That is just the fact of our having *reasons*, including moral reasons, necessarily reasons as general as any other reasons. So we are committed, despite our disregarding it, most of us anyway, to a certain morality of good consequences *for all* by our individual human nature—our basic desires and our reason.

From my own assertion of my own needs, and my giving it as a reason for having things, I come to right and wrong for all like me. This can have the name of being a kind of moral truth, the fundamental moral truth, an accord with the really relevant facts—despite any questions to which we may come. As you will have guessed, what I am on about is close enough to the great ordinary injunctions of morality, starting with the Golden Rule. Or rather, what I am on about is a philosopher's explicit exposition of, and argument for, instances of the greatest of moralities.

I get to a more explicit conclusion, a philosopher's conclusion, which hopefully has the merits of philosophy, by way of a further definition—a definition of *a bad life*. As you will expect, bad lives are to be defined in terms of deprivation of the six great goods or something close enough to them. And so we come to the Principle of Humanity.

The Principle of Humanity is simply that the right or justified thing as distinct from others—the right hope, intention, plan, action, practice, credit, responsibility, punishment, struggle, institution, government, body of law, society, possible world—the right one is the one that according to the best judgement and information is the rational means in the sense of being effective and not self-defeating with respect to the end of getting and keeping people in general out of the bad lives—getting them into or keeping them in the related well-being instead.

Of course, the principle is what philosophers have called a *consequentialism*. It is that type of morality. That is, it takes an action or whatever being right as a matter of its consequences, its effects, not is origins. That is paradigmatically true with punishment and the having of all the means to well-being.

That is not to say, of course, that the principle is the nonsense that an action is right on account only of its consequences in a certain sense. It is not the nonsense, say, that an action's being a killing itself does not have to be taken into account in considering consequences—that you can concentrate just on the revolution to come you are serving or the deterring of possible murderers in your present society. What makes something right for any arguable consequentialism is of course both the ends and the means—the further ends and the immediate effects of the killing itself, say on the victim's family. Again, then, Humanity is not the nonsense that the end justifies the means, as somebody is always ready to say, where the end is only part of the effects. It's a case of the ordinary truth, the truth that is part of any at least half-witted consequentionalism, that it's the end *and* the means that justify the means.

All this is against the veils and the paint jobs over and on the self-concern in which most other morality and politics consists. Say the remarkable but common idea that what is right is what comes from an agent's good intention, say a goodwill. Say Bernard Williams's talk of *integrity*. I have a lot to say there and hereabouts—some other time. But I say right now that good intentions joined to mistakes of fact can make for doing the wrong thing. And, with respect to Bernard, that Hitler could have been, maybe even was, a thing of integrity, true to himself, and so on.

Nor of course is Humanity the tradition of Utilitarianism, which is another consequentialism—that what is right is what produces the greatest total of satisfaction or happiness, the greatest happiness of the greatest number. That when intelligent does take into account all consequences of actions but would and does justify victimization when it works—that is, when it produces the greatest total, say possibly by punishment. The Principle of Humanity, near enough, *is* the principle *against victimization*, the greatest such principle.

To the principle are attached certain policies, several fundamental ones having to do with redistribution of the means to well-being. Starting with redistribution from possessors who have so much that in fact they would not be significantly affected by the transfers.

One thing that will never be added to the principle, contemplated for a moment, is any proposition to the effect that the rational means to its end amounts to or includes about as much deprivation, distress, misery as in our societies, no doubt conceived in anodyne terms of inequality, as we have now. That proposition of the tradition of conservatism, and in a way of liberalism, is remarkable for the inanity lie of it, or the lie of it, or the viciousness of it, or for partaking in all three.

Another smaller policy, relevant at this very moment, and a little before now, has to do with the necessity of escape from restraining conventionality in expression and argument, escape from societally based constraint against moral truth, escape from licenced and profitable vocabulary. We need less academic "balance," less parliamentary language, less moderateness, less philosophical self-censorship and hesitation, less respect, less tolerance of crap, less of giving time to self-interest and its apologists, less of a lot else. We need Chomsky's and his predecessors' disdain for an intellectual and in particular an academic class.

Do you wonder about what might be added to my implicit idea, as you rightly guess it is, of what it is to be held morally responsible for something? My idea that ascribing moral responsibility for a past action is in fact a concern with the future? With future as well as immediate effects. I grant, if less than in the past, that holding a man responsible, say a rapist or a politician, most politicians, is instead in fact significantly acting on a kind of grievance about the past, about what has been done. That, however, is not the rational point of holding responsible. That point has to be about the future. Less rape, less misery, and so on.

The Principle of Humanity, if it has in its history the abolition of slavery, and in the English Revolution Colonel Rainsborough's words "the poorest he that is in England hath a life to live, as the greatest he," and everybody voting, is also consonant with and must take a kind of support, some support, from recent and present *humanitarian* causes. Notably in the appalling conflicts in Syria and in the case of refugees or migrants attempting to cross the Mediterranean to get to Europe. If Humanity is much more than that sporadic humanitarianism, it is related to it and can find a support in it.

Arguably Humanity has been the principle of the Left in politics when the Left has been true to itself. It could not conceivably be the principle of the Right in politics, or a Centre. Or indeed, say, of mere the liberalism started by John Stuart Mill when he said that a society is to leave individuals to themselves as long as they didn't harm another, and then failed to say effectively what harm is.

Could it be that Humanity is the best principle in Christianity and in Muslims, at least before Christians and Muslims got to work at overcoming their decencies?

I mainly remark or remark further, at proper length, that the principle is superior to a whole slurry of attitudes in ethics, politics, international relations, and conflict, and, alas—God should have existed and forbidden it—in ordinary political philosophy. The principle is superior to talk, cant, ideology, and more. In place of a book or rather books of analysis that call out to be written, I offer you, necessarily, just a run of paragraphs.

The Principle of Humanity is superior to talk, cant, ideology, and more on *desert*, as distinct, say, from personal credit of consequentialist use for serving the end of the Principle of Humanity. In particular, the principle is superior to declamation and indeed argument of the form "Right because deserved" which amounts to the circularity "Right because right."

If the principle does not say go to our prisons and open the gates, follow the revolutionary French in the storming of the Bastille, it is more reflectively in just their spirit with respect to offences against property in general.

Humanity is superior too to venerating talk of "the free society," which dimly runs together voluntariness and origination and more in order to conceal a reality. That reality is in fact our *involuntary society*, a society of *compulsion*. So too is Humanity dismissive without a moment's hesitation of mere vapouring on the *fair* and the *just*, fairness and justice, of such use to a wretched public-relations minister in economic depression or recession. What *is* fair and just is only humanity.

Humanity is also superior to talk of and allusions to equality in itself, to the relations themselves, as distinct of course from absolute inhumanity with respect to those towards and at the bottom with respect to the relations—and also the further effects of the relations. Humanity is superior to mere legality and legalism. And to our oligarchic and not merely hierarchic democracy. To free enterprise that makes most of us less free.

Superior too to supposedly okay and excusable omissions as against terrible acts with just the same effects—say with respect to those places where the average lifetime is less than half of ours, a world of enduring misery, a world about as much of our making as of those in it. A world of which we barely have snapshots. Add one to your thinking and feeling right now. Say of a man with river blindness being led around his village at the end of a string by a child, say a child in Uganda who isn't learning to read.

Humanity is also superior to "our values" or "Western values" in the low and some of the less low newspapers. And to opinions in the mere rich men's newspapers, columnists who prate of their boyhood Communism but now know their de facto conditions of employment by *The Times*. Also superior to television interviewers accepting the little ways of the transparent non-answerers of questions, interviewers in fact accepting vicious evasion, that defeat of and affront to moral and other intelligence.

And loosenesses about "the just war" too. And whole inexplicit political traditions such as conservatism. And not only the English liberalism in coalition government with conservatism, the liberalism that is true to John Stuart Mill on the subject of harm, but American liberalism. Say about a hypothetical social contract thought up by one Rawls at Harvard, more particularly a contract by contractors whose first commitment by implicit definition is to private-property liberty. Circularity at best. Also American liberty to get rich, thought up by one Nozick in the same place, about a basketball player, but no liberty to have help to keep on breathing.

And, pretty near the bottom, humanity is superior to economism, that method of adding up or other calculation that also takes into account the colour of the numbers, notably blue or red. Yes, our main economics is mainly a political tradition, in several ways related to the tradition of conservatism.

Does that survey of slurry to which Humanity is superior show you to be in a conversation being led by a perpetual adolescent, an innocent, an unrealist, or worse—a professor of little mind and less logic? Write a book or two then. Try to make use of what you have to suppose may be our shared line of life, the attempt of which you've heard at that logic of ordinary intelligence—clarity usually by analysis, consistency and validity, generalness, completeness.

For me the slurry raises the final question of what to do. There's a lot, I guess, starting with the force and honesty of the mental fight of Chomsky and those who follow him, much of their fight being better than mine. And journalism, journalism of humanity. In my country of *The Guardian* and *The Independent*. And civil disobedience, occupying public spaces, boycott and divestment and sanctions.

We have to end here by thinking a bit about something else, a couple of things. First terrorism. Now inescapable in our language and in our lives. By tolerable definition, putting aside various little juvenile essays, terrorism is prima facie wrong and maybe awful violence, illegal, towards a political and thus social end.

Like the law of the land that issues in legal rights, the moral law that is the Principle of Humanity issues arguably and explicitly in moral rights. For just one example, familiar to readers in the pasts, Humanity issues in *a moral right* for the Palestinians in what is known as their terrorism—against neo-Zionism as certainly distinct from Zionism.

It issues of course in such a right as is also unfailingly claimed inexplicitly by exactly neo-Zionism itself, entirely wrongly, in *its* terrorism against the Palestinians. It's terrorism in its taking of the last one-fifth of the land or liberty of the indigenous people of Palestine. Neo-Zionist terrorism is arguably different, by the way, from that of Zionism itself at least defensible in 1948.

I had better own up in passing what you may well have noted in the newspapers or online that my example of a moral right to terrorism has got me some of the attention well known in all of the ongoing propaganda of neo-Zionism—in this case via a weaker officer of the charity Oxfam. I am well supplied with particular refutations of the charge of anti-Semitism, not excluding the lesser fact of a Jewish wife once.

Remember here of course that the charge of anti-Semitism in this context is indeed a worn tool in the campaign of neo-Zionism, not necessarily only a part of what also exists, the prejudice of pro-Semitism. And that that prejudice and racism, certainly, is distinguishable from the understandable pride in Jewishness that is akin to all-American pride or Little Englandism or French hauteur.

The Principle of Humanity also condemns terrorist war, including our war on Iraq, and certainly condemns the mass murderers Blair and Bush. To revert to Palestine, it of course condemns the ongoing ethnic cleansing by neo-Zionism. Also the particular attack on and invasion of Gaza in 2015 by its army, arguably terrorist war at least more to be condemned than any concerted action of Palestinians at any time.

With respect to history ongoing now in early 2017, that of the militia Islamic State in Syria and Iraq, what is necessary for us is not only to act by force against the barbarism and primitivism but also to keep in mind our own civilized recent killing of a million or so more people than have been killed by the barbarians. Our killing in Afghanistan onwards to Syria. Such a proper orientation, rational moral insecurity, such a denial of self-sanctification, must issue in real negotiation, first of all the effective offer of it, very likely not public.

Negotiation and the offer of it that will give up on things. Negotiation mindful of our now momentarily forgettable Sykes-Picot drawing of self-interested lines in the sand after World War I, and all our subsequent exploitation and toleration of exploitation of peoples, some by our friends the barbaric and primitive ruling family in Saudi Arabia.

Also negotiation mindful of the slurry, and also our realpolitik, and our terrorist air war in destruction of the society of Libya, and our letting the refugees or migrants drown in the Mediterranean, children among them, getting the attention of only the photographers.

Who can pretend that there is no question about our own moral standing, our own form of life, our extent of humanity? Who can really doubt that when we are seeking human standing by getting above nature or the rest of nature, via trying to believe in a funny freedom, or, say, by pretending that our democracy is not a form of oligarchy, we might better do something else—turn our attention to our personal inhumanity?

In England and Scotland we better turn our attention to those who lead us in pretending that we're uniquely okay, those in a manipulating and self-serving political class. Most relevantly and immediately for me are the recent leaders of the party called New Labour, that supposed successor to the Labour Party, that previous party that achieved the civilization of the National Health Service. That New Labour that has been partner to the affective consciousness of Conservatism—a consciousness only minimally cognitive.

In America, of course, certainly some of those who pretend that we're all okay are the uneducated and perhaps ineducable and certainly unawakened members of the Democratic Party. They join with their political adversaries, the Republicans, in being almost as capable of blundering past distinctions, notably the one between communism and democratic socialism, the latter of course being or being close to the political system called for by Humanity. Both lots are more than capable supposing that there is *nothing* to be said on and for the other side or sides in Syria, Iraq, and so on, including Islamic State.

The few signal exceptions in English and Scottish politics at this moment, and American politics, are of course the English and American Corbyn and Sanders. Men who are beacons. There is some hope there.

1.4 Conclusion

In thinking of our three subjects of consciousness and mind, explanationism or determinism and freedom, and right and wrong, especially the last, despite my holding to the necessity of escaping a conventionality in expression and of course feeling and judgement, you are not in the company of a fully confident optimist with respect to the formulation and authority of the Principle of Humanity. Yes there are doubts. With the excuse that a life without self-doubt is a lesser life, often only political.

If I am more confident about consciousness than about explanationism and freedom, and more confident about both than about right and wrong, or and maybe on a bad day what follows from the Principle of Humanity, it is clear you have not been offered proofs. Philosophy in its concentration on the logic of ordinary intelligence, thinking about facts rather than getting them, is too hard for proofs, harder than science. It is more like the practice of the law, if sometimes with less pretence and pretentiousness. It is an offering of argument to what you hope is a good judge. Each of us can also aspire to a judge's role.

Each of the chapters on each of the three subjects is followed by my remarks on the chapter. Being good chapters on large subjects, what could be offered here by me are indeed remarks. They are no more than stimuli to reflection on the part of what should be independent readers of this book. What is other than independent fails to be what is implied by my conception of philosophy, including its consumption.

Last but not near to the least, I am grateful indeed to Gregg Caruso, who had the idea of this book and laboured as editor in its making. His idea was a result of a day of lectures on my stuff arranged by the Royal Institute of Philosophy in Senate House of the University of London. The lectures, presided over by Anthony O'Hear and James Garvey, were given by Noam Chomsky, Gregg himself, Tim Crane, Paul Gilbert, and Paul Snowdon.

Part I

Consciousness

2

Mentality Beyond Consciousness

Noam Chomsky

I would like to discuss what Ted Honderich calls "unconscious mentality" in his very enlightening reflections on consciousness (Honderich 2017), but will use the phrase in a sense somewhat different from his. For Honderich, "unconscious mentality" is dispositional belief—in his words, "an old and known subject to say the least," and not a particularly interesting one. Furthermore, the habit of linking it closely with consciousness, his topic in that study, is "a pretty fundamental mistake."

Instead, I will use the term more or less as Honderich indicates when he defines "mentality" as "Conscious and unconscious states and events that are explanatory of at least behaviour, the unconscious states and events somehow related to consciousness, so as to exclude mere musculature etc." I would like to explore the possibility that the conscious and unconscious states interact so closely in explanation of overt behavior and internal thought that the elements of consciousness cannot be extricated without seriously misrepresenting mental life. Among unconscious states, I think we must include those that are inaccessible to consciousness, which also are interwoven inextricably in our mental acts.

N. Chomsky (✉)
Massachusetts Institute of Technology, Cambridge, MA, USA

G. D. Caruso (ed.), *Ted Honderich on Consciousness, Determinism, and Humanity*, Philosophers in Depth, https://doi.org/10.1007/978-3-319-66754-6_2

To clarify further, I will take Honderich's phrase "mere musculature etc." to refer to what David Marr calls "the hardware level" in his classic three-level analysis of the mind-brain. The most fundamental level, with a privileged role, is the *computational level*, which analyzes the general nature of the systems and the nature of the states, events, and processes that are addressed. The *algorithmic level* then develops the actual method that is implemented (if there is one).[1] Finally, the *hardware level* spells out the realization of the systems under analysis in the internal structure of cells, neural networks, muscles, and so on.

Excluding the hardware level, I understand "mentality" to comprise conscious and unconscious states and events that enter into explanation of overt behavior and of internal events that quite commonly do not issue in observed behavior, but still call for analysis and explanation. Such internal events include probably 99% of our use of language—what is loosely called talking to ourselves, something that we do constantly, night and day, and can only be prevented by a dedicated act of will. Internal speech in this sense is conscious, or at least appears to be, though I will suggest that the appearance is misleading in important ways.

Continuing with assumptions,[2] I will adopt what historians of philosophy call "Locke's suggestion." In his words, just as God added to matter such inconceivable properties as gravitational attraction, he might also have "superadded" to matter the capacity of thought. Replacing "God" by "nature" opens the topic to inquiry, a path that was pursued extensively in the years that followed, leading to the conclusion, developed most extensively by chemist/philosopher Joseph Priestley, that thought is a property of organized matter. As Darwin restated the fairly common understanding, there is no need to regard thought, "a secretion of the brain," as "more wonderful than gravity, a property of matter"—though it's worth bearing in mind that the latter is wonderful enough, a topic that has enough of a connection to my speculations here to merit a few words.

Before turning to that, it is perhaps worth pointing out that the common understanding of the eighteenth-century science and philosophy concerning the nature of mind has been rediscovered today as an "astonishing hypothesis," a "radical new idea," the great discovery of the "new biology," and so on—matters I have discussed elsewhere and will put aside here.

Returning to properties of matter, Locke observed that we remain in "incurable ignorance of what we desire to know" about matter and its effects, and there are no "science of bodies [that provides true explanations is] within our reach." Nevertheless, he was "convinced by the judicious Mr. Newton's incomparable book, that it is too bold a presumption to limit God's power, in this point, by my narrow conceptions." Though gravitation of matter to matter is "inconceivable to me," nevertheless, as Newton demonstrated, we must recognize that it is within God's power "to put into bodies, powers and ways of operations, above what can be derived from our idea of body, or can be explained by what we know of matter." And thanks to Newton's work, we know that "he has done so."

Like the great scientists of the day, Newton himself included, Locke regarded the idea of attraction without contact as an "absurdity" that no one with scientific competence could accept—in Newton's own words. As Hume elaborated, Newton's grand achievement was to have lifted the veil from some of the secrets of nature, while restoring Nature's "ultimate secrets to that obscurity, in which they ever did and ever will remain," referring to the "absurdity" at the heart of his theory. There were solid reasons for these conclusions. What Newton had demonstrated, as soon came to be understood, is that the very concept of intelligibility and conceivability that guided early modern science from Galileo must be abandoned, and that the goals of science must be lowered from intelligibility of the world to intelligibility of theories about the world, a transition in intellectual history of greater significance than often realized. In particular, it came to be understood that "it is inconceivable to me" means nothing in science, a lesson that has not been properly assimilated, I think, in contemporary philosophy of mind, but I will not pursue that line of thinking here.

The eminent historian of science Alexander Koyrė captures the outcome succinctly when he writes that despite his unwillingness to accept the conclusion, Newton demonstrated that "a purely materialistic pattern of nature is utterly impossible (and a purely materialistic or mechanistic physics, such as that of Lucretius or of Descartes, is utterly impossible, too)"; his mathematical physics required the "admission into the body of science of incomprehensible and inexplicable 'facts' imposed up on us by empiricism," by what is observed and our conclusions from these observations. Contrary to what is sometimes argued, contemporary interpretations of gravity in the framework of quantum theory and relativistic space-time only deepen what Newton and his contemporaries regarded as an "absurdity."

Newton and the sharp critics of his "absurdity" (Leibniz, Huyghens, and other prominent scientists of the day) all recognized that Newton's theories were quite intelligible. That was not their objection. Rather, they still adopted the principle of early modern science that its task is to show that the world itself is intelligible to us, that it accords with our modes of cognition. The "mechanical philosophy" that guided science from Galileo through Newton does, probably, capture fairly well our intuitive understanding of what qualifies as an account of the observed phenomena of nature. Its failure tells us something significant about the limits of human cognitive capacity, not overcome but rather bypassed as science turned to less extravagant goals: construction of theories that are intelligible, such as Newton's—and to the extent that we can achieve this goal, theories of various aspects of mentality.

In studying mentality, it is worth bearing in mind other lessons of history of science. Not only is intelligibility (in the Galileo-through-Newton sense of "conceivable to me") irrelevant to the contemporary scientific endeavor, but we also must be cautious about apparent failures of reduction. The history of chemistry is an instructive case. As recently as a century ago, chemistry was widely regarded by respected scientists as hardly more than a method for predicting the results of experiments, not real, because chemical laws "cannot at present be reduced to physical laws," as Bertrand Russell observed in 1927.[3] As discovered right at about that time, chemistry would never be reduced to physics as then understood, because it was inadequate. The quantum revolution led to the unification of chemistry with the radically new physics. The outcome confirmed the good judgment of eighteenth-century chemist Joseph Black that chemists should proceed to develop "a body of doctrine" and "defer accounting for the laws" discovered until inquiry leads to deeper understanding. So chemistry proceeded, in relative isolation from physics, until a new and deeper physics was developed. There are lessons here for contemporary study of mind, and its concerns for accounts in terms of neurophysiology, which is far less developed than physics was when Russell wrote.

A final background comment about what I mean by thought. A good point of departure is Turing's comment in his famous 1950 paper where he raised the question of whether machines can think. The question, he said, is "too meaningless to deserve discussion," an observation too often ignored in what has followed. Turing's imitation game, the "Turing test," had other goals, as he explained—and for reasons I've discussed elsewhere, it is, I think, much less serious than tests proposed in the seventeenth century (see Chomsky 2004).

As far as I know, Turing did not elaborate on why he considered the question of whether machines can think to be too meaningless to deserve discussion. Possibly he had in mind some subsequently published ideas of Wittgenstein's, whose lectures Turing had attended in 1939. Wittgenstein observed that "We only say of a human being and what is like one that it thinks. We also say it of dolls and no doubt of spirits too. … We can only say of a human being and what is like one that it thinks" (1953, pp. 359–360). That is the way the tools are used. Accordingly, to ask whether machines think is as pointless as to ask whether submarines swim or Chinese rooms translate. The reference to dolls and spirits and the phrase "what is like one" allude to what Friedrich Waismann called "open texture," the possible extensions of the use of a term, a topic of considerable interest that bears directly on the matter of interaction of conscious and unconscious thought in humans in ways to which I will return.

Summarizing, then, I will take for granted that all three of Marr's levels of analysis are part of the theory of the physical world (i.e., the world, including the functioning of the mind/brain and its occasional manifestations in behavior). Furthermore, it should not surprise us if we come up against secrets of nature that must be relegated to "that obscurity, in which they ever did and ever will remain"—understanding the concept not in absolute but in organism-relative terms, and adding the observation that humans are organic creatures, not angels, with capacities and traits that have scope and limits, the two closely interrelated.

With just those words of background, and excluding here Marr's "hardware level"—Honderich's "musculature, etc."—let's turn to the states that enter into an explanatory account of overt behavior and internal thought, conscious or unconscious, and in the latter case, accessible or not to consciousness, ignoring here rather peripheral matters as the subliminal perception familiar in advertising.

More significant unconscious states are also a familiar matter. Merely to illustrate with a few current examples, a review by William Braun of a new production of Alban Berg's opera Lulu opens as follows: "Just about everyone who has ever taught a class or given a lecture has had the experience: you are speaking about a subject you know fairly well, and you hear yourself say something that must have been in the back of your mind for some time, but which you have never consciously thought about" (Braun 2015). I suspect, and will suggest later in the chapter, that the experience is far more general, a constant in daily life buried below fragments that emerge as inner speech; and that what is "in the back of the mind" is commonly beyond access to consciousness.

To take just one more example, in reflecting on his intellectual formation, the late Benedict Anderson opens by remarking that, "In my early days at Cornell, use of the concept of 'comparison' was still somewhat limited. I don't mean that comparisons were never made: they were made all the time, both consciously and (more often) unconsciously" (Anderson 2016). That can, I think, be generalized to more complex reasoning, again possibly beyond the reach of consciousness.

To explore the topic, let's begin by considering one of the most ancient problems of philosophy: How can we cross the same river twice? I crossed the Charles River on the way to work this morning, and expect to cross it again tomorrow, but is it the same river? The problem of identity through time runs through the history of philosophy, alongside the problem of individuation: What makes an individual distinct from others? The latter problem disappeared with the rise of corpuscular theories in the seventeenth century. For a corpuscularian, the entity just is what it is—a "distinct portion of matter which a number of (corpuscles) … make up" (in Robert Boyle's words). That leaves the prior question of identity, the one raised by Heraclitus: what makes an entity the same through time despite changes.

In studying the problem of identity, Locke and Hume led a "subjectivist revolution," to borrow the phrase of Udo Thiel in his masterful review of these issues (Thiel 2013). Along with others, they reformulated the question in cognitive rather than metaphysical terms. For Locke, existence is preserved "under the same denomination," in terms of the abstract idea under which we consider the being. Hume interprets our tendency to assign identity through time as instinctive, an act of the imagination that is unique to humans, its nature again an impenetrable mystery, he surmised. In this case, the mystery is at least in part penetrable by exploring the meaning of words and concepts. Consider, for example, "river." A good deal can be brought to consciousness by thought experiments, thus preparing the ground for potential explanation.

Suppose that the flow of the Charles River has been reversed overnight. I will still be crossing the same river. Suppose that what is flowing becomes 95% arsenic because of discharges from an upstream plant. It is still the same river. Ted Hughes (1998) even saw it as "100 per cent proof toxic," but still the Charles River. The same is true of other quite radical changes in the physical object. On the other hand, with very slight changes it will no longer be the Charles River. If its sides are lined with a fixed barrier and it is used for oil tankers, it is the Charles canal, not a river. If its surface undergoes a slight phase change to the glassy state, the surface is roughened, a line is painted down the middle, and it is used to commute to Boston, it is the Charles highway, no longer a river at all.

Exploring further we can determine the contours of the concept and the associated open texture. These appear to be mental universals, or very close to it. Differences among languages and cultures appear to be slight, apart from the mode of externalization.[4] Crucially, the meaning of the word is acquired by children in all of its intricacy, virtually without evidence, as the properties of the acquired concept quickly reveal. We then face the problem of explanation: What are the rules and principles that determine the essential features of the concept and the nature of the open texture? The latter is surely not a matter of Yes or No but rather graded along many dimensions, and only certain dimensions are relevant among the innumerable possibilities that can be imagined. The answers are unknown, and the topic has barely been explored, though it seems to be amenable to productive inquiry. A little thought strongly suggests that the answers lie in mental processes that are not only unconscious but not accessible to consciousness, and that enter directly into thought and action.

There has been some inquiry into these matters, back to classical Greece. Aristotle considered the nature of a house, concluding that it is a combination of matter and form. In his words, we "define a house as stones, bricks and timbers," in terms of material constitution, but also as "a receptacle to shelter chattels and living beings," in terms of function and design; and we should combine both parts of the definition, integrating matter and form, since the "essence of a house" involves the "purpose and end" of the material constitution. Hence, a house is not a mind-independent object. That becomes still clearer when we investigate further and discover that the concept *house* has much more intricate properties, an observation that generalizes far beyond. For Aristotle, this was metaphysics—he was discussing houses, not the word/concept *house*. But pursuing the subjectivist revolution, we can more appropriately rephrase the account in terms of the acts of Humean imagination—our modes of cognition, to which experience conforms, in the classic phrase.

Every term/concept that has been investigated has properties similar to Heraclitus' *river* and Aristotle's *house*: identity is indeed determined by an act of Hume's imagination, in curious and intricate ways, acquired virtually without evidence and hence universal with at most slight variations (see Chomsky 2013). The investigations so far have been shallow, restricted to thought experiments. Deeper inquiry should not be impossible. It has not been undertaken, I think, largely because of prejudice. Though the topics are ancient and have been explored back to classical Greece, in the modern period they have been displaced by a representationalist doctrine that is illustrated in the titles of such basic texts of contemporary philosophy and psychology as W.V. Quine's *Word and Object* and Roger Brown's *Words and Things*. The doctrine holds that the terms of language and thought refer directly to extra-mental things, entities that a physicist could in principle identify without exploring the mind—that is, without exploring Hume's imagination or Aristotle's form, the latter reformulated in cognitive rather than metaphysical terms. The doctrine is simply false for human language and thought. Abandoning it, we can inquire into the interaction of conscious and unconscious processes, including crucially mental acts that are inaccessible to consciousness.

It is of some interest that the terms/concepts of human thought and language appear to have no counterpart in animal symbolic systems. As far as is known, in these there is invariably a one-one correlation between the symbol and some identifiable mind-external event. A monkey's cry, for example, might be elicited by a motion of leaves, warning of a predator; or by a hormonal change, indicating hunger. The evolutionary origin of human concepts is a complete mystery. Specifically, that is true of the terms used to refer in ordinary language use, the terms that link language to the mind-external world, though not by a relation of reference or denotation in the technical sense. The distinction between reference and referring is familiar, but I think its significance has been insufficiently appreciated. And it seems to bear directly on the subtle and intimate interactions between unconscious processes, including those inaccessible to consciousness, and on the fragments that sometimes enter consciousness.

The problems proliferate rapidly as soon as we move beyond words to more complex constructions. Here we find a constant interplay between conscious awareness and unconscious principles of both types: accessible or inaccessible in principle. Consider one of the most fundamental and in many ways surprising universals of language, the principle of structure-dependence: the operations that determine the meaning of expressions keep to structural hierarchy, ignoring far simpler computations involving linear order. Thus, the sentence "birds that fly instinctively swim" is ambiguous: "fly instinctively" or "instinctively swim." The facts are immediately evident, and we can easily become conscious of a superficial explanation based on arrangement of words into phrases in two different ways. Suppose the adverb is peripheral to the sentence, as in "instinctively, birds that fly swim." The ambiguity is resolved. The interpretation is "instinctively swim," the option that is much less natural and that is much harder to compute: linear proximity is trivially computed but structural proximity is a much more complex operation. The operative principle, structure-dependence, holds all relevant constructions in all languages. The principle is applied unconsciously, but can be brought to consciousness. It calls out for explanation, however.

There is only one explanation known—and it is, in effect, the null hypothesis: the principle follows from the thesis that language is optimally designed in a fundamental sense that I will not review here (see Chomsky 2016). The theory is intelligible, but the operations of the mind that it formulates are not accessible to consciousness. The explanation cannot be discovered by introspection, but only by the normal means by which we study objects external to us.

To take another standard example, consider the sentence, "John is too angry to run the meeting." It is ambiguous; either John is to run the meeting or we are. Suppose we question "meeting," forming the sentence, "which meeting is John too angry to run?" It is now unambiguous: John is to run the meeting. The facts are not hard to bring to consciousness, perhaps even the crucial structural distinction concerning the placement of the phrase "to run the meeting." There are plausible explanations, but again, the mental processes they postulate are not accessible to introspection. We can only evaluate the proposed explanations as we evaluate theories of the natural sciences. And again the two kinds of unconscious process are entangled in a complex web.

Do examples like these, which abound, fall under the category of thinking? Are we thinking when we determine and act on the meaning of a sentence? If not, it's hard to see what is left of thinking. There is good reason to believe that our system of thought with language is literally constructed by operations of the kind I just described—that without them, there is no thinking with language at all. And if we do not think with language, the concept of thinking loses its essential content. We would have to abandon even Wittgenstein's observation that people think, maybe dolls and spirits, since he had in mind the use of language in thought.

Traditionally, language is described as sound with meaning, or as audible thought. The latter rendition is closer to accurate. What seems still more accurate is that language is thought, which is occasionally audible—or externalized in some other modality (sign language is remarkably similar in design, acquisition, and use, and even neural representation). More explicitly, each language is a generative process that yields an infinite array of structured expressions with fixed and determinate semantic interpretations, hence in effect a "language of thought," maybe the only such. There is good reason to suppose that it is close to uniform among languages, not only on the basis of the results of inquiry into a wide variety of languages but also because of the crucial fact that these properties of language are acquired, virtually reflexively, with little or often no evidence. Accordingly, they must be among what Hume called the "parts of [our] knowledge" that are derived from "the original hand of nature"—part of our genetic endowment in modern terms, what is called "universal grammar" in contemporary usage.

If this is correct, we expect to find that the observed diversity, complexity, and mutability of languages are restricted to the peripheral externalization process, which relates the internal system that generates a kind of language of thought with sensory motor systems that have their own independent properties and in themselves have little if any relation to language. That appears to be an increasingly plausible assumption.

Returning then to the question of language and thought, these considerations help ground the conclusion that examples of the kind I discussed are paradigm cases of thinking, and illustrate the intimate interplay of processes that are unconscious and, in crucial cases, inaccessible to consciousness.

I might note in passing that all of this is inconsistent with Quine's influential thesis that rule-following reduces either to "fitting," as the planets fit Kepler's laws, or "guiding" by conscious thought. Or with John Searle's closely related "connection principle," holding that operations of the mind must be somehow accessible to consciousness. These principles do not seem to me to withstand analysis, though one could preserve them by narrowly restricting what we decide to call "thought" and "mental processes," a move that seems to me unwise, if only because these processes are such an intimate component of the fragments that reach consciousness.

Other domains also offer examples. One is the discovery of explanatory theories. A plausible approach was outlined by Charles Sanders Peirce, who argued that theory-construction is guided by an "abductive principle" that "puts a limit upon admissible hypotheses," so that the mind is capable of "imagining correct theories of some kind" and discarding infinitely many others consistent with the evidence—in fact, non-denumerably many as can be shown by Nelson Goodman's famous puzzle of induction. That at least restricts to some feasible domain the search for theories that are then subject to reflection, confirmation, and other criteria. Peirce also observes that in a fixed state of scientific understanding, it is common for a number of scientists to converge on the same or similar theories. Whatever the abductive principle is, it must come to us "from the original hand of nature," in Hume's phrase—as part of our genetic endowment. And like other such guiding principles, it is inaccessible to consciousness though interweaving inextricably with what reaches consciousness. And since it is organism-specific, it is not guaranteed to converge on truth, contrary to what Peirce argued on flawed evolutionary grounds.

Universal grammar plays something of the same role for language, and the basic observation carries over for all biological capacities.

It has been known for some time that processes inaccessible to consciousness enter into choice of action, though they do not determine it. A classic demonstration is the Benjamin Libet experiments 30 years ago. They showed that about 500 milliseconds before a motor act, say moving the finger, there is slight cerebral action in the area relevant to the act, while reported awareness comes only about 300 milliseconds later. This has sometimes been studied in the context of freedom of will, though mistakenly I think. Some have argued from the temporal sequence that the initial activation presents random alternatives for selection by conscious choice—a model much like Peirce's abduction. But the crucial question still remains: Why this set of alternatives, not innumerable other ones. We are left pretty much where we always have been—and where contemporary neuroscience is. In a recent view of the state-of-the-art in the study of voluntary motion, two leading neuroscientists, Emilio Bizzi and Robert Ajemian, write that we are beginning to understand the puppet and the strings, but have no ideas about the puppeteer. In this domain, we haven't really come very far from the days when Thomas Willis, one of the leading seventeenth-century pioneers of the concept of "thinking matter," nevertheless held that the immaterial soul remains the "chief mover of the animal Machine" (Willis 1664; as cited by Makari 2015, p. 57).

But whatever one thinks about freedom of will, the results provide further evidence that inaccessible unconscious processes intermingle with what reaches consciousness.

I mentioned that externalization of language is very rare; almost all use of language is internal. Let us now venture into some murky waters, barely explored, so we are limited to introspection and speculation: the matter of inner speech and thought with language. Vygotsky did some work on the topic, but in ways not relevant to our concerns. To think about the matter further, let's go back to William Braun's comments on the ordinary experience of "hearing yourself say something that must have been in the back of your mind for some time, but which you have never consciously thought about." What you hear yourself saying comes out fully formed, often in considerable complexity, with no awareness of planning or reflection. The same is true when you are sitting down to write an article, and don't know how to begin, and all of a sudden paragraphs start pouring out fully formed, from the back of your mind. What has been happening in the back of your mind? It seems that the thoughts were forming, being considered, shaped and elaborated, rejected as on the wrong track, and finally being turned into an articulated form, all without awareness, and with intimate intermingling of processes that are inaccessible to consciousness.

Introspection—which for now is all we have—suggests that much the same is true for what we experience as inner speech. Without conscious reflection, we think to ourselves in words, often in complex and intricate constructions, which quite suddenly appear to consciousness without awareness of any prior reflection. Typically what comes to awareness are scattered fragments, which sometimes are not easy to weld together into well-formed expressions. Quite commonly, we search for the right words and phrases, recognizing that what we are saying to ourselves is not quite what we mean. These efforts seek to attain what we mean, but fail, which indicates that there is something that we mean, but it is inaccessible to consciousness, and we can at most try in various ways to approximate it.

If systematic research into the topic is ever undertaken, it might turn out that the core system of language that forms semantic representations without access to the sensorimotor system is working away, beyond the level of consciousness, constructing thoughts, and sometimes releasing fragments to consciousness that can then be constructed internally as fully formed expressions, and sometimes, though in fact very rarely, is even externalized in some sensory modality, and perhaps used for communication and other interactions—or for no such purpose at all, as when we think or write for ourselves.

To summarize briefly, I have been trying to suggest that the study of certain aspects of consciousness can be carried forward by placing it in a richer setting, taking into account the intimate interactions between what reaches awareness and internal processes of mental computation that are unconscious, often inaccessible to consciousness, and very likely a core feature of fundamental human nature.

Notes

1. For a system of competence, such as knowledge of language or arithmetic, there is no algorithmic level, though there are algorithms for performances accessing this system (in the case of language, an I-language in the technical sense).
2. For sources, see Chomsky (2016).
3. Russell (1927). See Chomsky (2016, Chap. 4) for discussion.
4. For some discussion and sources, see Chomsky (2016) and Berwich and Chomsky (2016).

References

Anderson, Benedict. 2016. Frameworks of comparison. *London Review of Books* 38 (2): 15–18.

Berwich, Robert, and Noam Chomsky. 2016. *Why only us? Language and evolution*. Cambridge, MA: MIT Press.

Braun, William. 2015. A new lulu arrives at the Met. *Opera News* 80 (3).

Chomsky, Noam. 2004. Turning on the "imitation game.". In *The Turing test*, ed. S. Schieber, 317–321. Cambridge, MA: MIT Press.

———. 2013. Notes on denotation and denoting. In *From grammar to meaning: The spontaneous logicality of language*, ed. I. Caponigro and C. Cecchetto, 38–45. Cambridge: Cambridge University Press.

———. 2016. *What kind of creatures are we?* New York: Columbia University Press.

Honderich, Ted. 2017. *MIND: Your being conscious is what and where?* Chicago, IL: Chicago University Press.

Hughes, Ted. 1998. Astringency. In *Birthday letters*. New York: Farrar Straus Giroux.

Makari, George. 2015. *Soul machine: The invention of the modern mind*. New York: W. W. Norton.

Russell, Bertrand. 1927. *The analysis of matter*. Nottingham: Russell Press.

Thiel, Udo. 2013. *The early modern subject: Self-consciousness and personal identity from Descartes to Hume*. New York: Oxford University Press.

Willis, Thomas. 1664. *The anatomy of the brain*. London.

Wittgenstein, Ludwig. 1953. *Philosophical investigations*. Oxford: Oxford University Press.

3

Honderich on Consciousness

Paul Snowdon

Professor Honderich has made major contributions to philosophy, including the philosophy of mind, ethics, and the nature of responsibility, as well as social and political philosophy. His work is always inventive, bold, and challenging. He is also impressively committed to the idea of philosophy as a discipline in which ideas need to be made public to be tested in the resulting debate, a debate in which he will take a characteristically full part, but into which others are invited, and this is, surely, how the discipline prospers and advances. This has been the case throughout his long and very productive career. I am pleased to be able to pay tribute to him by contributing to this volume.

I have chosen here, as my contribution to one of the debates he has stimulated, to focus on some aspects of Professor Honderich's evolving thought about consciousness, relying on his exposition of it in a concise and yet to be published manuscript—*MIND: You're Being Conscious Is What? Where?* Honderich's approach to consciousness, which he calls Actualism, is an evolving theory. It is not all quite nailed down, and it is

P. Snowdon (✉)
Department of Philosophy, London, UK

G. D. Caruso (ed.), *Ted Honderich on Consciousness, Determinism, and Humanity*,
Philosophers in Depth, https://doi.org/10.1007/978-3-319-66754-6_3

complex and extensive. Indeed, during the time I have been writing this paper, aspects of it have changed, some of it significantly. So, the spirit in which I want to engage with it is as something that is not presented as finished. Of course, this reflects the extraordinary difficulty of properly illuminating consciousness. Here the focus has also to be somewhat limited.[1] I aim primarily to scrutinise Honderich's anti-physicalism, plus some elements in his approach to perceptual experience.

I want to spell out at the beginning some of the general features of Actualism—as I read it. First, Honderich divides consciousness into three categories—the perceptual (to do with the five senses), the cognitive (to do with the conscious thinking of thoughts), and the affective (to do, as he puts it, with wanting in a "generic sense").[2] Second, he is impressed by the disagreements, the lack of anything approaching unanimity, in theories of consciousness, and he suspects this reflects, in significant part at least, misunderstandings or differences of focus between theorists. They are focussing on different phenomena. His response is to construct what he calls "a database," listing truths about consciousness that can both anchor our focus on the right phenomenon (or phenomena) and supply data to which appeal can be made in determining the correct characterisation of consciousness. He summarises the database as saying that "consciousness is something being actual" (2017, p. 20). Clearly, no sane person could disagree with that claim, understood as saying that when someone is conscious something is actually going on, but with some of the specific elements on the list it is less obvious that they are correct or helpful, but it would, I feel, be inappropriate to poke around the list at this stage of the discussion.

3.1 The Database

Before considering the resulting account I want to express three thoughts about Professor Honderich's conviction that the list is needed because theorists have been, to some extent, talking across each other. One question is whether there is any evidence that discussions have been infected by misunderstandings. Here is how Professor Honderich puts it when he introduces the idea: "If you spend some time looking into the competing general theories of consciousness, including the two great fairy tales and lots of other theories and also various impulses and ideas … a question may come to your mind and stay there. Is there all this disagreement mainly or partly because theorists are just not talking about the same thing?" (2017, p. 6).[3] Why should we answer this question in the affirmative, as Honderich wants us to? It is, I believe, in this chapter that the case for that is supposed to be made. However, the bulk of that chapter amounts to spelling out a list of five leading ideas that philosophers have advanced about consciousness. They are that consciousness involves qualia, that there is something it is like to be conscious, that consciousness involves subjectivity (i.e., it belongs to a subject or self), that it possesses about-ness or intentionality, and that it possesses phenomenality.[4] As far as I can see, though, there is nothing about this list that indicates that the theorists proposing them are not focussing on the same basic phenomenon, supposedly called "consciousness." What would be needed to make us suspect something of that sort on the basis of the existence of these five ideas? The answer, presumably, is that it is beyond belief that different people could say these different things about the same phenomenon. Against that, it seems reasonable to say that these so-called leading ideas are not, considered as claims, incompatible. One could believe that consciousness belongs to selves, and that it involves qualia, and exhibits a feature captured in talk of what-it-is-like-ness, and that it possesses intentionality and phenomenality too. Moreover, denying that it possesses any of these hardly indicates that a different feature must be being focussed on. The other part of Honderich's reason that I can discern is that two famous writers, namely Ned Block and David Chalmers, use the term "consciousness" for something that seems distinct from the sort of consciousness that we mean when we talk about being conscious or possessing consciousness. Let us suppose that that is true. It does not indicate that there has been a significant degree of misunderstanding in the debate about consciousness, nor does it even indicate that those theorists have not recognised a distinction between *two* sorts of what they think are both called "consciousness" and have offered clearly targeted theories about the one that is central to the standard debate. I think, therefore, that there is no good reason to be persuaded by Honderich's suspicion, in response to which he produces his database.

A second remark, though, is this. If the centrality in the debate of the term "consciousness" does encourage or sustain misunderstandings, then rather than resort to the data list that Honderich provides, it might be wiser to search for an *alternative* term to focus our theorising. The obvious suggestion is that the aim is to determine the nature of experience and of different types of experiences. I myself would be inclined to aid our focus by employing that term.[5]

My third remark, which is not negative or totally alien to the spirit of Honderich's approach, is that although I am unpersuaded that there has been a disagreement as to what the basic phenomenon is, it is true that the question—what is consciousness or conscious experience?—clearly admits of answers that are responding to it in different ways, with different theoretical interests and goals. If this is correct, then it is no surprise that theorists end up with different answers that are not entirely easy to relate to each other. To illustrate this, philosophers have primarily taken this question along the route of the mind/body problem; can consciousness be reduced to physical processes or not? However, it is clear that this is a narrow question and that there are lots of people who want to understand consciousness in much more detail than would be provided by a defensible solution to the mind/body problem. To be told that consciousness is physical is a bit like being told that water has a chemical structure. Most people interested in the nature of water would not stop at that point. They want to know its actual structure and why it has the properties it has. Anyone interested in consciousness in such a richer way would like, surely, some sort of top-down analysis of what it does (or involves) broken down into elements, and also a bottom-up account of the ingredients in nature that actually do this work and how they relate. I myself would add that philosophers are not going to get far in providing this sort of thing. Anyway, the diversity of approaches, which has struck Honderich, is, I want to propose, linked to a genuine diversity of explanatory interests that so-called theorists of consciousness have.

3.2 The Attitude to Physicalism: A Questionable Conviction

With this database as background and as source of evidence, the role of which is not affected by the previous remarks, there emerges the Actualist theory. We can divide the resulting Actualism into two parts. One part is negative. Certain ideas are claimed to be wrong. The other side is positive, with some positive characterisations of consciousness being offered. I want to engage with some elements in both sides.

Turning first to the negative side it would be no exaggeration to say that Professor Honderich does not approve of quite a number of recent ideas about consciousness. When he talks about fairy tales he has in mind both dualism, traditional substance dualism and more modern property dualism, and the view that would be called "physicalism." I want to engage with his attitude to physicalism, because in opposing this, Honderich is opposing the currently most popular view. It would be a conclusion of major significance if he can discredit it.

Honderich makes this negative claim early on in the book. "One fairy tale is that all consciousness really is just objective, scientific or standard physical stuff in your head, soggy grey matter as some say—meat. As many others say more piously, consciousness is just wondrously complex but still only neural networks, networks of cells. In both cases fundamentally the same kind of thing as the chair you're sitting on despite the differences" (2017, p. 5). Now, when I read this remark I wanted to protest that it is a rather unhappy definition of the view being opposed, which is to say physicalism, in at least two respects. First, no one would say that consciousness is a matter or stuff. Being conscious, or possessing consciousness, is a matter of things going on or occurring, or being in a state, and cannot be equated with any sort of stuff. But perhaps this is too rigid a reading of his words. Honderich may be using "stuff" in a very general sense, a sense in which we can say that a lot of stuff has happened (or occurred). But, second, although physicalists would tend to think that the matter in which, according to them, occurrences of consciousness happen is like the matter in chairs in being physical, they would also think that the matter in question is a rather special kind of matter, certainly not the sort present in chairs.[6]

The initial question is, though, why Honderich thinks we can be fairly sure that this popular idea is wrong.

Now, there is one reasons that Ted seems to think there is for rejecting physicalism, which comes out when he is discussing dualism (in its two forms of substance dualism and property dualism) where he says: "All that [i.e., the criticisms of dualism] is not to say that there is nothing to be said for dualism. There is a very large thing to be said for it. It is that it makes consciousness different from something else. That is what we all take it to be. As our dictionaries say, matter or the physical is what is such that mind or spirit is different from it. Here we have another criterion of a decent account of what consciousness is. A decent account really must make it different—somehow different in kind" (2017, p. 39).

Well, I want to register a lack of agreement with this remark. (1) It is not true that this is "what we all take it be." In fact, I'd be inclined to say that since the late 1950s, the majority of philosophers of mind, and scientist with an interest in consciousness, would definitely *not* so take it. (2) If someone has this conviction then they need to supply some more focussed and specific reason to claim the existence of a general difference between consciousness and "everything else," on pain of having to develop some scepticism about their general conviction of a difference. After all, what is there to respect about the highly general conviction that consciousness is different from things that are physical unless a specific difference can be identified? What has to be done then is to locate a candidate feature C about which two things look plausible—first, consciousness possesses C, and C cannot be possessed by anything that is purely physical. Now, I don't know if Professor Honderich agrees with this remark, but he does supply in the course of his discussion candidates for the role of C, which I'll investigate later in the chapter. (3) I want to make another point in connection with this. If we consider one type of case, which is central to Professor Honderich's argument, that of conscious visual experience, we can ask: what value for C might such experiences provide? Well, if I were asked to describe my current visual experience I might say: my current experience is one in which it looks to me as if there is a computer on a desk, on which there are also some books. I could expand the appearance description if required, but what else can I add? Simply trying to describe as accurately as possible what that aspect of my conscious experience is like, no other information about the conscious experience is available to me, or suggests itself to me. If someone requested me to tell them what the nature is of what is going on, what its presence fundamentally consists in, I am in no position to say. Now, it seems to me, there is a severe limitation on the potential values for C, which I can determine are present in virtue of having the experience. What this means is that the whole weight of the argument falls on the claim that an occurrence, which amounts to one in which it looks to me as if there is a computer, some books, and so forth, cannot have a physical nature, and how on earth are we supposed to know that is true? So a general problem for anti-physicalist arguments along these lines is that the values for C we can determine in virtue of undergoing the experience are pretty limited, and it is not obvious how we can know that no physical occurrence can have the property.

Now, one reaction to the claims just being presented would be that we are entitled to believe that one case is actually different from another case even if we cannot pick out a specific difference. Thus, if I am looking at two photos which are very similar, I would be entitled to hold that they were different, if that is how it strikes me, even though I could not locate in what respect they were different. The intended upshot of this observation is that Honderich is entitled to rely on his sense that consciousness is simply different from the physical without being able to locate a specific difference.

There is, I agree, merit in this response. In some situations, a sense of difference between two cases, without a sense of the specific difference, would be a legitimate guide. However, two points need making. The first is that the legitimacy of the general conviction is lost if no specific difference can be located after a very careful search for it. So, even if we can give some weight to the general conviction, that weight is lost unless we find a specific difference. Second, the cases where the general sense seems legitimate are where it is generated in an observational way. We can trust such observational deliverances. However, our case is highly theoretical, and any sense of difference must be grounded in *thinking* about consciousness and the physical. This is quite different from the observational case. I think, then, that we continue needing some defensible identification of a specific difference.

3.3 Some Specific Contrasts

I want, therefore, to turn to the more specific values for C, that is the feature possessed by conscious perceptual experiences but not by physical occurrences, that, as I read Honderich's argument, he is proposing we can identify. At this point, it is useful to look at the table that Professor Honderich has helpfully provided at the end of his book, which, I take it, summarises his approach to the status of consciousness.

We need a little by way of setting out the character of the list.[7] For our purposes, the important ideas are the ones conveyed under two columns in the list. The first column is labelled the "Objective Physical World," meaning the physical world in space and time. The second column is labelled the "Subjective Physical Worlds; Perceptual Consciousness." The easiest way to understand this is that it covers what we would describe as perceptual experiences. Now, when describing this, Honderich builds in the theory of such episodes that he favours, and so his descriptions might not correspond to what we, either as theorists or as naïve people, would be inclined to say. However, that complication can be set aside for the moment, since the features he is appealing to are ones that are not weird to be attributed to perceptual experiences.

I shall start at contrast number 10, since that is where the purported contrasts emerge. According to 10, the objective physical world is separate from consciousness, whereas perceptual experiences are not. Now, it is indeed obvious that there cannot be perceptual experiences without consciousness, whereas there can be a physical world without consciousness. On most people's conception there was a physical world for a massive time before consciousness emerged in the world. The question is: what does this contrast show? The answer is that it shows nothing. The sense in which the physical world is separate from consciousness is that there can be, and in fact have been, physical things without there being any consciousness. If, however, episodes of consciousness have basically a physical nature, which is what physicalists suppose, then it would follow that there are some physical episodes or states of affairs that cannot exist without consciousness being present. They would be the physical episodes, which constitute conscious episodes. Putting it another way, no physicalist should agree in advance that all physical possibilities are separate from consciousness. It is not only that physicalists should not agree with that, but also that if there is to be in this contrast a reason to reject physicalism, we need a reason to think that all physical episodes are separate from consciousness.

The second candidate contrast is called 11. It says that one contrast is that the physical world is public, whereas the world of conscious perceptual experience is private. Ordinary physical things are public, whereas experiences are private. When explaining this, one thing that Honderich says is that physical processes are "dependent on no particular individual" (2017, p.57). In contrast, perceptual experiences are dependent on particular individuals, namely, the ones having the experience. Now, one part of a response to this is to note that physical processes can depend on the existence of particular individuals. Thus, there could not be such a process as the destruction of Mount Everest without Mount Everest existing. Innumerable physical processes are linked to the existence of particular individuals. Perhaps, what is meant is that physical processes cannot be dependent on the existence of particular subjects of experience. This is simply not obvious. If subjects of experience are particular complex physical structures, then the physical processes they undergo will require the existence of those physical structures, which is to say those subjects. One can say, I believe, that the characterisation of the physical world simply begs the question against physicalism, in both 10 and 11.

The third contrast, number 12, is epistemological. A subject of experiences has some degree of privileged access to his or her conscious states, whereas physical states of affairs are not matters of privileged access to any subject.

This is of course complicated, but one response that strikes me as worth exploring is that there is no such contrast. When people talk about a subject having privileged access to a certain state of affairs they seem to have in mind one of two things. The first is that the subject has a route of knowing about something that others lack in relation to the same thing. It does seem plausible to claim that a subject has a route onto their experiences, which others lack onto those experiences. But the same goes for routes onto physical states too. A subject has a route to know about the shape of his or her body at a time which others lack in relation to that information. So one cannot say as a general truth that if a state of affairs is a physical state of affairs, then a subject cannot have a privileged access to it. The second idea is that the privilege consists in the subject being so related to the state of affairs that if it obtains he must realise that it does. This is sometimes called the "self-intimating" nature of psychological states. Now this is a very complex subject, but it is, it seems to me, questionable that we do have such privileged access to our conscious states. Thus, many things can stop us registering such facts about our own minds, such as lack of attention, distraction, terrifying expectations, and stroke damage. So there seems to be no necessity about such knowledge of our own experiences. If what is meant is, what we might call simply de facto privilege, that is, that as things usually are we will know about some aspect of our experiences, then it can be said that we also possess something of that sort vis-à-vis physical things. If I am standing in normal lighting looking straight at a large elephant, it would be, to say the least, surprising if I did not register its presence. If I am standing in the middle of a fierce downpour, it would be amazing if I did not register that. It seems to me true to say that we are creatures to whom certain things are obvious, and if that were not so we would be incapable of knowledge. But what is de facto obvious to us includes physical and mental states of affairs. (In putting it this way, I am not backtracking from my earlier remarks.) This sketch certainly is not the last word in relation to this issue, but I suspect, and am suggesting, that we cannot suppose there is enough here to establish the needed contrast. (Putting it simply, Professor Honderich has not shown that there is any significant epistemological contrast here. Of course, if the reply I have made does not work it would then need to be asked what ontological significance an epistemological contrast has. That is work for another occasion.)

3.4 A Further Contrast and the Treatment of the Perceptual Case

I am arguing that Professor Honderich has not located any features that entitle him to think that conscious episodes cannot have a physical nature. I want to glance at another possible line of thought that he may be tempted to offer. Honderich says:

> One of the worlds, yours, exists partly in that it is lawfully dependent, dependent as a matter of natural or scientific law or necessity, on something else out there—the objective physical world. And also being lawfully dependent in this way on something else, you neurally, or your brain etc.,—Just as dependent. This second dependency is what further identifies and distinguishes a subjectively physical world. So—being conscious in general, all of consciousness, isn't all of it an internal fact, just a cranial fact. … For us in our theory some of consciousness, perceptual consciousness, will really just be an external fact, anyway more external. (2017, p. 13)[8]

Now, the argument that might be close to the surface here is the following two premised arguments. (1) According to physicalism, conscious episodes are the same as neural occurrences in the heads (or cranium) of subjects. (At times, Honderich calls this claim "cranialism.") (2) In episodes of perceptual consciousness, the central element is something that is not in the head at all, which is what Honderich calls the "subjectively physical" world. Premise (2) is related to the claims that Honderich makes later in the book about perception. He says,

> You may be ready to contemplate, now, whether or not with confident complicity, that what is actual right now with respect to your perceptual consciousness is a room or other place. It's something out there in space, as much as anything at all is out there in space. Yours started with your first perception and will end with your last one. God knows my room is not a room in my head, whatever that would be, whatever that loose talk comes to. Anyway, I know my room isn't any such thing. So do you know about yours. You walk around in your room, as I do in mine. Same then with your whole subjective physical world. (2017, p. 62)

Neither premise in this little argument goes without saying. Premise (1) is accurate in saying what practically all physicalists would indeed say. Since the emergence of the psycho-physical identity theory, the main candidates for identification with conscious episodes are neural events. However, strictly speaking, what physicalism requires is that conscious episodes have a physical nature or constitution, and in itself that does not say what the location or extent of the physical events in question is.

The events may be complex, involving cranial processes but also physical extra-cranial processes. So, even if Honderich is in a position to say that perceptual episodes involve things in space outside the subject's head, then that, in itself, is not inconsistent with physicalism as a general idea.

Premise (2) is, however, the premise that is harder to accept. The theory that Honderich is proposing of perceptual experience—say your visual experience of the room you are in—is that there is a subjective room, which itself is in space, outside you. As well, though, there is what he calls "the" room, which is an objective physical structure in which you actually are. There is no identity between the objective room and that thing which is a perceptually presented room. The thing being called "a room" is present before you only because there is the room, but also only because you are neurally active in the right way too. Its existence is dependent on both things.

Now, there are two reasons why the reliance of the argument on premise (2) creates problems. The first problem is that the claim itself has no solid support. We can bring this problem out by trying to follow how Honderich arrives at his original conception. He relies on your sense of what is happening to you when you do what we call see your room. Your sense is that the occurrence presents you with an external room, something outside you in space. As I might myself say—look, there it is, the external room, seen by me. So it is not unnatural to think that the occurrence involves an external room. However, Honderich himself is of the opinion that the room, which we might say is presented in the experience, is not in fact the objective space occupying room itself—it is, rather, a subjective room, a room which he wishes to describe as "subjectively physical." (Why he thinks that is for the moment irrelevant.) This puts the perceiver who is trying to describe accurately what perceiving the world involves or amounts to in the following position. He or she starts with the conviction that perceiving the room involves presentation of the actual external objective room, that is, with something genuinely in space. But she or he is then told that the room presented in the experience is not in fact that room, but another "subjective" room. Given that Honderich accepts that claim, the question that arises is how he, or the normal subject, can tell where what we might call the "presented room" is. The obvious basis for saying the presented thing is genuinely in space is that the presented thing is the actual real space occupying room, and it is known where that is. But if we have to determine the location of the presented room given the information that it is not the actual external room, how can we say? What is there to show where it is? Of course it seems to be in front of the subject, but maybe that appearance is deceptive. One cannot say that it must be there because that is where the actual objective room is, since we are assuming that it is not that room. Appearance alone cannot, it seems, settle the question, and there seems to be no ground for favouring one answer over another. Or perhaps it can be said more accurately that there is no ground for retaining the conviction that it is before you once it is granted that it is not the actual room, which it can be agreed is before you. Employing a term that Professor Honderich employs, we can say that there is no obvious ground for the externalism he endorses in his account of perceptual experience.

The second problem with (2) in the argument is that it is hard to accept the theory of perceptual experience endorsed in that premise. I want here to focus on a few aspects of it that worry me. What, though, according to the theory, is the role and nature of the so-called subjective room? The answer that Honderich gives is that the existence of the subjective room is what we can say the occurrence of the perceptual experience is. Here is one quotation:

> More particularly, what is it that is actual with your perceiving? … The answer in my case, lucky or unlucky, was that what was actual with my being perceptually conscious was the room's being there. In due course, some months later, being a slow thinker, I got round to thinking it might be better to say my being perceptually conscious was *a* room's being there, but that certainly doesn't subtract from its being out there. … Being perceptually conscious is a subjective physical worlds being there. (2017, p. 61)[9]

Now, this conveys two important things. The total account of the occurrence of the perceptual experience itself, as Honderich would put it, its actuality, is that it is the existence of a subjective physical room. About this subjective room, Honderich says three main things. The first is that it is in space. Thus, he says: "God knows my room is not in my head, whatever that would be, whatever that loose talk comes to. Anyway I know my room isn't any such thing. So do you know about yours. You walk around in your room, as I do in mine. Same then with your whole subjective world" (2017, p. 62). Second, he describes it a "subjectively *physical*," where the primary point of that is, I think, to mark the fact that its existence depends causally on elements in the objective physical world. Third, he denies plenty of long-standing characterisations that philosophers can be read as having offered of the "subjective room." It is *not* the presence of a sense-datum, or a qualia, or a representation, nor is it the presentation to the subject of external room (as naïve realists might propose) (see Honderich 2017, pp. 62–64).

The first element here that I wish to query is the claim that the subjective room is located in space, and that it amounts to something around which or within which the subject actually moves. Among the questions this prompts is this: where exactly in real space is the subjective room? Let us suppose that we say that it is where it appears to be. Thus, my subjective room, or at least the part of it I am concentrating on, is a metre in front of me. Call the location L. If L is not the right location, then it is hard to see how we could work out an alternative location. But, one has to ask, what has that thing which is this subjective (facing wall of my) room to do with location L? In supposing it is at L, we are not attributing to the space L anything that would not be true of it without the subjective room being there. The presence of the room there makes, or seems to make, no difference to L. No interaction at L is modified or affected by the room's being there. In fact, it seems that it makes no difference to anything real whether we suppose it is at L or somewhere else. Now, this is strikingly different to normal spatial attributions. If I think the wall of my real room is at L, then I will think that there will be a collision if a rocket should happen to arrive there too. Space occupation normally cannot be supposed to make no difference. As far as I can see, Honderich's way of speaking of the subjective room in space conforms to the following rule—if the room seems to be at L, it is actually at L. But what is added to the agreed fact that in my perceptual experience it appears to me there is a room at L by adding that it is actually at L?[10]

The second element in the account that I wish to focus on is Honderich's categorisation of the subjective room as "physical." Here is a brief presentation by him of his reason for labelling them "physical." He says:

> Subjective physical worlds, even if fleeting, as about as real as the objective physical world, if differently real. … There are plain reasons, in the list that is coming up, for including the species subjective physical worlds along with the species objective physical world in the genus physical world. They are indeed out there. And, as you will be hearing, subjective physical worlds are dependent on several things, one being the objective physical world. … Another, on perceivers neurally. (2017, p. 71)[11]

Now, I have already queried the claim that subjective worlds are "out there." But what point is being made in describing them as "physical" in virtue of their causal dependence on the objective world and the way the subject is neurally? Thus, if someone were to ask—what do subjective worlds consist in, what is their real nature?—you are being told nothing by being told that they are dependent for their existence on aspects of the objective physical world. On hearing that you can still say—yes, but what nature do they have? I am inclined to think that the illusion is being fostered by calling them "physical" that we are being told what nature they have. It seems to me that we are actually told nothing about the nature of the subjective world in the description that Honderich gives. Moreover, it is reasonable to suspect that since Honderich would deny that subjective worlds have a nature which counts as objectively physical, his own position has a strong resemblance to property dualism (or dual aspect theories) of the sort endorsed by, for example, Chalmers. At a general level, Professor Honderich, it seems to me, ends up with a very similar view.

My final comment on the theory relates to a type of argument that Professor Honderich presents for it. Honderich's argument goes along the following lines. He claims it is obvious that no correct account of the nature of the perceptual experience can be based on postulating old-fashioned ideas or impressions beloved by the empiricists, sense-data, qualia, contents, or representations. He summarises his feelings about such theories by saying, "It has to be put to you that with your consciousness in seeing the room what you have, what you are given, what you are directly aware of, what is not deduced or got from something else, what is real and right there and so on, isn't any of this stuff" (2017, p. 63). Now, the problem is not that this verdict is a mistake, but that Professor Honderich has no legitimate reason to affirm it. His reason seems to be that we can just tell in virtue of undergoing the perceptual experience that these theories are incorrect. But this seems to overlook that the concepts that are employed in these theories are not ones that are simply capable of being observed to apply or not. For example, the proposal that what happens when you have a perceptual experience is that you apprehend a sense-datum is not meant to imply that you can simply recognise the experience as having that character. Something that is a sense-datum would not shout at the subject that that is what it is. This is why sense-datum theorists spend considerable energy arguing for their view. In its status, such a theory resembles the proposal that water consists of hydrogen and oxygen atoms—this is not a proposal that someone simply perceiving water is meant to be able to confirm or disconfirm. It is a theoretical proposal. The same is true, I believe of all the approaches on Honderich's list.

3.5 Conclusion

There is a double upshot to this extended discussion of the last anti-physicalist argument that I credited to Professor Honderich. The first is that that argument rests on two premises, neither of which is acceptable. The second is that there are serious problems for the theory of perceptual consciousness that Professor Honderich has advanced.

My overall conclusion is that there is no evidence presented by Professor Honderich that physicalism is unacceptable. In arguing this I aim to respond to the arguments that he has presented, but I also have what might be called a hidden agenda. That agenda is not to defend physicalism. Rather, it is to provide some evidence in support of my own general conviction that philosophers lack the tools to make any real progress with the mind/body problem.[12] Whether or not I have in any way succeeded in that task, I hope that I have conveyed, even though disagreeing with it, something of the richness and ingenuity of Professor Honderich's evolving thought about consciousness.[13]

Notes

1. I discussed an earlier version of Professor Honderich's views on consciousness in Snowdon P. F. (2006). The main change since then is that he no longer wants to treat the actual objective things around as the external components of perceptual experience, but to postulate as components in perceptual experience things which are external in a different sense.
2. I shall not focus on this tripartite division in the body of the paper, but doubts can be raised. One doubt is that the list is not comprehensive—it seems to leave out such experiences as pains, itches, dreams, and after images. Another doubt is what the third affective category is supposed to cover. It would not be true to say that wanting in general is an experience, and so it seems not to belong to what we mean by consciousness, although it might be something of which we are conscious (in one sense of that word).
3. By the "two great fairy tales" Honderich means the views that are standardly called "physicalism" and "dualism."
4. I hope that this rather compressed list makes sense to readers. If it does not, it does not matter for the critical point I wish to make.
5. The suggestion is not that having an experience is equivalent to being conscious, but that to be conscious it is necessary to be having an experience, and the phenomenon that strikes philosophers as puzzling is the more general one of experience, rather than the more limited one of consciousness.
6. There is some resemblance here with what might be called a big mistake that Descartes made in his arguments. Descartes could not believe that anything consisting solely of matter could think. The question this conviction raises is how Descartes could know what things made of matter could do. He has some reason to wonder how things made of matter as he knew it could do this, but he had no reason to believe that he knew much about the real nature of matter. Rather than concluding that material things cannot think, he could have concluded, provisionally at least, that there was matter of a kind he did not know about.
7. The list occurs on pages 102 to 103 of Honderich (2017).
8. I have re-written the passage slightly by eliminating some paragraph divisions in the original.
9. Again, the quotation ignores the presence of some paragraph indentations.

10. Thinking about the spatiality of the subjective room also raises the question as to whether it has three dimensions. It must have if I can walk around in it—but then what are its dimensions? Where does it start?
11. Again I have jumped between paragraphs. It might be said that I have failed to note some of the features that are on the promised list and which ground the description as "physical," and so have failed to realise the full weight in favour of describing them as physical. One element I have not placed any weight on is that subjective worlds are, as Honderich suggests, available for investigation by science. I concede that this is not properly investigated here. I would say though that it is one thing to simply affirm they are available for investigation by science, quite another to indicate and explain what sorts of investigations by science are possible of subjective worlds as they are envisaged.
12. I argue for this in a general way in Snowdon (2015).
13. I am very grateful for Professor Honderich's response to the earlier version of this paper that I read at the conference in London, and also to others involved in that conference, including Paul Coates, Tim Crane, and Barry Smith.

References

Honderich, Ted. 2017. *MIND: Your being conscious is what and where?* Chicago: Chicago University Press. Cited page numbers are to the penultimate draft and not the published version.

Snowdon, Paul F. 2006. Radical externalisms. *Journal of Consciousness Studies* 13 (7–8): 187–198.

———. 2015. Philosophy and the mind/body problem. In *Mind, self and person*, ed. A. O'Hear, 21–38. Cambridge: Cambridge University Press.

4

Unpacking Ordinary Consciousness

Alastair Hannay

Next to his Actualism, naïve realism is identified by Ted Honderich as the hitherto "most natural and defensible theory of perceptual consciousness" (2014, 334). Naïve realism is natural enough; it is what we *un*-theoretically practice in our everyday management of the world, but as theory? Certainly it is hard to think otherwise than that our perceptual ability allows us to pick out phases in a continuous vista that survives interruptions in our or anyone's adverting to it. As voyeurs in a fictional space of personae dramatis, we regularly succumb to naïve realism, or play at it, in the theatre or as filmgoers. But when, in the farce, all the doors onstage or screen are closed and no one has yet appeared, the empty stage we see represents an impossible perceptual experience.

Do we reflect on this? Naturally not! Outside theory, naïve realism "works" and its contribution to the smooth running of life may even earn it a place in evolutionary theory. Yet, the general belief that our senses allow us to perceive the world as it is has been on hold ever since the

A. Hannay (✉)
University of Oslo, Oslo, Norway

G. D. Caruso (ed.), *Ted Honderich on Consciousness, Determinism, and Humanity*, Philosophers in Depth, https://doi.org/10.1007/978-3-319-66754-6_4

Theaetetus. As theory, not only has the naïveté of naïve realism been put under constant threat of, as Hume put it, "the slightest philosophy" (1963, 146), for philosophers themselves it has been a perennial source of embarrassment that finding arguments good enough to justify a natural belief in our occupation of a common space should be so difficult. There have been others who, impervious to the latters' "egocentric predicament," have tackled the subjectivity of perception head on. Social psychologists have focused on situational and other variables involved in our relationship with the world, and can often be found speaking of perception as *inherently* subjective, so much so that "perception" for them has become synonymous with "seeing as." The naïveté of realism here is not one of innocence but a condition that manifests itself in various ways of *failing* to give the subjectivity of perception its due.

Giving subjectivity its due is a principal component in Honderich's Actualism. The arguments in *Actual Consciousness* are directed at both those who deliberately ignore the subjective aspect of perceptual consciousness and those who attend to it but in doing so generate theoretical entities that exclude any assimilation with naïve realism. Actualism, like naïve realism, delivers the world clean, as it were, that is without the mind's interposing sense data, qualia, content, or anything else that gets in the way of, say, the room you are in as you sit writing a book about consciousness. In perceptual consciousness, it is the room itself that is actual.

This result is not one that Honderich expects philosophers will find easy to accept. In the coming compact version (Honderich 2017) of the larger book's argument, he offers his result in the form of a proposition that he suggests readers may find shocking, but then notes that other seemingly anomalous results that philosophers have come up with have gained acceptance in the course of time. The proposition can be summarized in two parts as the claim (1) that a room's being "actual" means that it exists when you are on hand, and (2) that while the room "up here" is still there when you have gone downstairs, its being there is not the same as its being part of the "objective physical world." In other words, taking the room to be actual, seen as is, means that in your absence you may think of it as still being *as it was* (seen etc.) when you *were* on hand. Instead of "here," it then exists "out there" still as that familiar room.

The reason for its not being part of the objective physical world is bound up with whatever the inescapable subjectivity of perceptual consciousness amounts to, for instance dependence on the brain's ability to convert objectively physical light frequencies into the phenomena that fill our visual space.

An implication must be this, that when one's thoughts return to the room in one's absence that thought will be of it as it was or would be when you are present in it. It is a naïvely realistic thought that escapes naïveté only if one reflects that it includes the qualification "if I were there." For those many like me, to whom visualizing comes easy, the proviso would have to be interpreted as in the above case of an audience presented with an empty stage. The imaging corresponds at that moment to no possible perception.

If this makes the room actual enough in Honderich's sense, then I find myself agreeing with his proposition and am not shocked. There is a linguistic point that may even help to alleviate some of any discomfort it may occasion. To be truly objective, the physical world is not happily referred to as a "world." Oddly enough, a properly physical world would be in the same position as that of naïve realism: it stays put whether or not you have it in mind, though with whatever Heisenbergian proviso may be needed regarding attempts to *bring* it to mind too literally; but otherwise it is so well and truly out there that the expression "out there" loses its meaning. It is true that when seen through contrivances that extend the range and depth of normal vision, Honderich's room and his chair dissolve visually into molecules and spaces; and we agree that the physical basis on which their normal appearances depend must somehow remain "out there." But if we manage, as in a Leibnizian limiting case, somehow to hang on to the idea of this shadowy world even when the shadow disappears, there is in reality nowhere beyond the perceptual horizon to which the indicator "there" in "out there" can informatively point.

In its most literal sense a "world" is something we have and inhabit; it is an existential entity where to talk of something being "out there" is to imply some location within a shared world. There is indeed an extended and illuminating, as well as much used, application of "world" in which we talk of circumscribed worlds of sets of practices, as for example those of the physicist. In the present context, one might usefully adopt Dreyfus's suggestion and speak rather of a "universe of interrelated facts" (2014, 222). To call the aggregate of such facts a "world" may be seen as an example of those analogizing tendencies that lead to anthropomorphisms of the kind referred to by the cautionary William James when he wrote that causation is something we grasp from pushing things around, pressing buttons, and so on (1912, 183ff; cf. 158). Since there is no spectral physical world in which Honderich's room somehow but only just retains its familiar features, we can be assured that the room is there along with us in the only space we know by virtue of being in it. This, I take it, is in line with Actualism and speaks for the realism it advocates.

In his dealings through the years with perception, Honderich has tried consistently to clear the mental rubbish out of the way in order to leave us with a clear view of what is genuinely "out there." In perception, the room is to come, as it were, clean. Such theoretical entities as have entered into the discourse (sense data, qualia, raw feels, "what it is like to be …", content) are mental in a bad way in so far as they prevent access to what is really there in this space that we share. Decisive here, it seems to me, is the notion of "content" or logical content, and the following remarks call tentatively for some further explication and even defence of the letter, if not the spirit, of Honderich's Actualism.

I take it that there is support *in* experience for logical content not being an obstacle in the way of the room. Yet notions of meaning and content are hard to omit from any account of perception. First, on Actualism's side, the *fact that* it is a room is not necessarily any part of the experience of your being in the room in a waking state and knowing where you are. In the normal way, being aware of your location is immediate and not a matter of seeing something consciously as this *rather than* that. Only a theorist would think of analysing our innate ability to recognize things in such a way. Just as no pause need occur in the continuing stream of unfolding experience to bring *what* we are experiencing to mind, nor any continuing commentary protocolling the items in a stream of consciousness, so too there need be no under-the-table scanning operations that pull out the right picture or the right words from an archive catalogued in accordance with the perceiver's conceptual scheme. Any such scheme is already activated, or being activated, in the experience; it is part of its "given-ness," to use a term that Honderich likes. We could say, to use an old word, that "sapience" as the ability to think—and not just think well—first comes to light in *saying* (if just to ourselves) what it is that we experience. But then, secondly, the given-ness of green (for example) implies that something is *seen*, and I would be tempted to agree with those that claim that something being seen means, in our case at least, that it is seen *by me* (for example).[1] Neither implication need come to the conscious mind, but that they *can* do so implies a structure already inherent in the experience and which deserves to be called "mental." Far from being an obstacle in the way of the room and the chair, it is part of their being or becoming actual. We might however say that they are nevertheless obstacles in the way of something else, namely of the imperceptible objective physical world in which the call of objectivity carried to excess requires us to drain it of all that is in this sense mental.

Whatever the case here, why not suppose in Kantian style that apart from being shared by a more or less uniform sentient system common to all, our sensory input is also siphoned through a logical structure already embedded in experience and amenable to a supervening language? In the beginning was Logos: not the word, but logic. Let us guess that the structure of thought is latent in the experience. No doubt the degree of structure will be primitive in relation to the requirements of analytic philosophers, but their demands are fixed by a professional duty to chart and systematize relations between thoughts identified only lexically. Such thoughts, referred to purely by their symbols, are necessarily abstractions from real-life experience and, in general, from the thinking that experience gives rise to. But as philosophers we are confined to a world of symbols. Frege himself said that his job was *not* to investigate "minds and the contents of consciousness whose bearer is the individual person" but "Mind" (1967, 35). It was what we can grasp when we get far enough out of our own minds to distil a thought that we share. What we leave behind is a "mode of the individual mind." Because it is a merely psychological event, Frege calls that mode an "idea"; in referring to it, "one must, strictly speaking, add to whom it belongs and at what time" (Geach and Black 1952, 79 and 60). Quite simply, we must separate a thought, since at least Plato the medium of truth, from the psychological frippery surrounding its occurrence. Like the smooth rock over which the constantly changing stream of consciousness flows, a thought stays the same. Of course, for how else could it be conveyed let alone play its part in formal logic? Yet how often, in a normal day, are thoughts really conveyed other than in newspapers, timetables, Twitter, and Facebook? Conveyed whole, that is. What is, after all, a thought? Where do thought and experience elide and where do they separate?

Could it be that the thought is what our individual sentient systems need in order to achieve the sharing we assume from birth, but which seems so fragile as soon as we give way to reflection and theory? Suppose we say that sentience delivers, in phenomenal guise, a universe beyond sense, but that it does so in a way that we can safely assume is much the same for each of us. Sapience, understood simply as the possibility of language, offers another kind of daylight, a radiance in which we can share each other's thoughts but also, with qualifications, through these, also their experiences. Since sentience is however the inescapably individual backcloth of all our structured experience, whatever thoughts emerge are confined just as much to particular instances of their occurrences. But sentience, as we might say, happily bears the watermark of sapience. Except in breakdown, it is a cheque that is never quite blank. And yet in filling it out we do not escape the particularity of our own minds. However certain we are that our minds are for the most part severally and in all essentials the same, in the world as we have it, and which, yes, without doubt we share, what we make of it is how it presents itself to each mind at any particular moment.

Vision has received favoured treatment in philosophy above sound, smell, taste, and touch. Is it because it gets you out of yourself and over to those things "out there"? You might think that touch did better, offering direct contact with the outside. By no means! Or at least only in what Hume calls a popular "universal and primary opinion of all men" (1963, 146) that skims over the question of whether the tactile sense is the object's acting upon me or just my "internal" response to maximal, but otherwise undetectable, proximity in a space as yet unmediated by any brain. Yet, however revelatory of the environment, visual sensation is still the last event in a causal chain. Even when insisting that phenomenal light accurately reflects objective properties out there (e.g. texture, edges, size), we must still acknowledge that "light" in the objective world is a matter of measurable frequencies as yet unrealized in their potentially sensory mode. If, to those who feel able to take the final link to sensation for granted, that seems unproblematic, the reason can be that its effect is extremely reliable. For all scientific and practical purposes, the light is there doing what science tells us it does prior to acquiring that sensory sheen that is the brain's wonderful switch-on bonus. Yet brains are not part of some super-glutinous mass, a biological equivalent of Hegel's *Geist.* There is no common brain in which our own individual brains "partake" and whose grip on the world out there "subsists" and into which we can all enter. But then, in the form of conveyable thoughts, we do after all have Frege's Mind, and the background experiential roots are shareable in the sense that we can in principle and in favourable circumstances cannot help but catch on, that is, if our backgrounds are sufficiently similar or we have good enough powers of empathetic imagination.

Any account of perception must surely include not only the subjective features noted by social psychologists but also some study of the aesthetics of space, or the different faces that our shared space can show. Aside from Kant, there has been a good deal done later in this area by phenomenologists, but space is something to which analytic philosophers have devoted little time *or* space. There have however been some efforts. We have been treated to "primal" space, a "neutral" space, even a "brute" space and a space that "aspects" in many ways that include those of visual art (see Aldrich 1978, 210, 213–214). But true to form, the distinctions are made in terms of logical grammar with no thought to what is implied for our notions of space itself. Any postulation of an indeterminate space behind its several modes of appearance is of course a construction, a deduction, an inference, and a first step towards puzzle-generating theory. Whatever, on reflection, fails to belong among publicly locatable properties has in phenomenological fact nowhere else to be than in our own inescapably "mental" space. Distinctions between what is due to the world "outside" and what to aesthetic or situational variability are made not in any single experience but in reflection. However imaginary the steps behind you as you walk up the lonely lane at night to the house ahead, they are spatially continuous with the light shining from one of its windows. The slight shudder that runs through you in that same space and the slight quickening of your pace are things you feel "in" yourself, all within that same personally inhabited space. It is true that our language leaves little scope for a specifically mental space, but then there is much that our workaday talk fails to take note of, and which, if it did, it would find hard to express.

I offer an example I once used in answer to a talk by Ted Honderich many years ago in which the given-ness of the object of perception was already at issue: On moving to a new city in rainy weather where clouds have for some time been obscuring the sun, I form a belief that the range of hills visible through the window are stretching in the direction of cooler regions in the north, something that gives them a definite projective meaning or value other than that which they would have if I saw them stretching south in the direction of the warmer regions from which I have come. When the sun finally emerges in the "wrong" place, I see my mistake; yet it can take some time for my sense of spatial orientation to adjust to what I now correctly believe.

Supplements of this rarely noticed kind are surely features of every human perceptual experience, or at least of those from which they have not been pathologically drained. Take the experience of things or environments being "familiar." We can say that it is we who lend our surroundings their air of familiarity, but is it not truer to the experience itself to say that the surroundings lend that sense to us? Might it not even be a deep-rooted survival strategy, this gradual investing ourselves with a sense of belonging within an environment as we progressively inhabit it, a sense whose loss we can sense if we replace it with another? Science no doubt will one day detect its own truth in this thought, but we need not wait upon science to see for ourselves that things and places have experiential properties that do not belong to them in a public space. Latent properties of this kind and their linguistic counterparts, those predicates (when and if the latter come to mind and are honoured with a name) are manifestations of the responsiveness of the so-called sensory field (though better conceived as a perceptual surround) to our longer- and shorter-term histories. They are existential contributions to experience; you can only identify them in terms of how it is for someone, some particular one, to be experiencing.

In his wariness about letting the "I" intrude on "ordinary perception," Honderich belongs in a venerable tradition from Hume to Heidegger. One cannot help but feel, however, that the often heralded "failure" to find any "self" answering to the first-person pronoun is reminiscent of Nikita Khrushchev's announcement that his astronauts had so far failed to find God. If God is anywhere let alone everywhere, that "outer" space is not where to look for the Deity. Hume's own failure was programmatic: no single impression could give us the idea we construct of a continuing self. With less apparatus William James found that the expression "it thinks" was closer to the basic facts, with its logical grammar akin to that of "it rains" and "it blows" (1892, Ch. XI). From a wider existential base, Heidegger came up with what one (though contested commentator) calls "egoless, situation-governed comportment" (see Dreyfus and Dreyfus 1992, 122). More recently, Derek Parfit and Galen Strawson have comfortingly encouraged us to think that continuity and persistence in the self are not what matter anyway and being an "episodic" self is to be self enough.

That Honderich's remarks in this area are few and tentative are transparently due to fear that our talk of "worlds" might get too personal, letting the floodgates of subjectivity open to aspects that are not proper to philosophy, or else may, due to "misunderstanding and feelingfulness," set it off on the wrong foot (2014, 242 [original in italic]). But he does allow that the term "world" in "subjective physical world" can count as a "life-place" (2014, 242) and later intimates that in spite of questions of "the idea of living a life" being associated with "tender-mindedness," there may be something of philosophical significance to be said of personal identity as a "counterpart" to the idea of "unity over time" (2014, 342 [italic removed]).

I "personally" believe that this undeveloped and cautiously introduced aspect is something that any adequate account of actual consciousness must deal with. The room, yes, and the chair, but also Ted Honderich sitting in it and writing or tapping out sentences in a book-to-be on actual consciousness. So let me conclude with some brief and less-than-proper philosophical remarks on goals and personal identity.

The question is what comes to mind at any moment, and how to describe it, but also how to connect it with other such moments. No doubt, what comes into conscious focus moment by moment in the conscious mind is too dependent on what goes on "out there" in our shared world to be used in explanation of what someone is up to. Yet the simple linearity of any announcement by myself of what I am doing can mask a passing system of multi-level implication framed by a specific purpose that makes sense of, or "informs" the means. Those means are prone to possible alteration or replacement as relevant phenomena in the environment catch the eye or ear, their relevance determined by, and cast into routines through, past experience. In crossing a street, some will say that anything I might call my conscious self is engaged merely as a co-operative part of a behavioural system. They may even say I am immersed in it, and yet others will claim that what that really means is that there is nothing there, "no one at home," as Daniel Dennett has put it.

A popular way of talking says, as I cross a street many hard-wired routines come into play. Mostly they can be left to themselves just like tying your shoelaces or necktie; thinking how to tie a bow can actually interrupt the routine and stop the performance. Novelty of course requires correction. Visitors to Britain from the Continent have to adjust to a different left-right rule, and when crossing an unfamiliar street, one should perhaps have some experience of the prevailing speed patterns in the relevant built-up area. But even if speeds can vary, traffic is traffic; generally, it sticks to the road and comes in a uniform direction each side of the street divider if there is one. Speed differences can also be tagged to different sizes and types of vehicle, as also braking distances. All this can be routine "knowledge." In its own kind of hierarchy, the information relevant to what I am trying to do occurs at a high enough level to be conscious, but the input required to sustain the routines required by the particular performance can descend to the so-called proto-pathic levels, over whose routines I would never need to exercise control since they just are there, and for which in any case we have no ordinary words. What I say I am doing in such a case merely skims the surface. My presence in this system coincides first in time with whatever factors are brought consciously to bear on what I aim to achieve and the importance of going on, and with the considerations currently working consciously upon the routines enacted to achieve it. Revisions are made ad hoc and certain provisos may be taken into account, even stopping to taking stock before continuing.

But let us hear more from Dennett. In describing the mental processes that manifest themselves in intelligence, and in line with his insistence that introspection will give us no clues to what is really going on, Dennett once described the mind of Alan Turing as "a variegated jumble of images, decisions, hunches, reminders and so forth, out of which he tries to distil the mathematical essence: the bare-bones, minimal sequence of operations that could accomplish the goals he accomplished in the florid and meandering activities of his conscious mind."[2] There is nothing here to indicate what enabled Turing to satisfy his long-term obsession: the devising of an abstract system that can compute what any computer of whatever internal design can compute. Dennett remarks that a commentary on what goes on consciously in a mind tends in any case to produce nothing but a "Joycean" stream of consciousness. But James Joyce's streams were his own invention and we have a better observer in another James, namely William James. He spoke of the stream of consciousness in terms of "pulses" (1892, 399) and of a succession of its states merging into each other, holding hands as it were, and forming a "personal consciousness" that is "sensibly continuous." If the "I think" is a philosopher's fiction that we can do without, there is still the "it thinks." James speaks of the "interest" shown in consciousness "in some parts of its object to the exclusion of others, and welcomes or rejects—*chooses* from among them, in a word—all the while" (1892, Ch. 11).

Returning again to the notion of structure with its basic subject and object opposition, we could say that, in anything we do, the "subject pole" focuses on salient aspects of an "object pole." It is the scenario in which a behavioural system armed with a project is meeting the changing world, one in which that system's projects are at any moment furthered or frustrated. There is a sense in which if any operation at all is going to be successful, drafting an essay, composing a poem, extracting DNA, solving a mathematical problem, or even just going for a walk, it is in terms of some shorter- or longer-term goals or aspirations of which this can be seen as a part. My actions are subject to scales of preferences that, even if I am only rather feebly aware of them, form my active curriculum vitae. The stock I take in and of a situation, or even of what I can recall of my life, is drawn from my own dispositional trademark. You could call it my personal background (about which you and I may know equally more or less), and the more relevant stock I can take or have at my fingertips, the more effectively engaged I can be in my current piece of "comportment," and correspondingly less at the beck and call of my psycho-neurobiological and "mnemic" inheritance. The more reason, accordingly, to say that here we have a form of self-knowledge in practice in which "I" am essentially engaged.

Whether or not he believed in his own diachronic identity, the industrious and level-headed Montaigne was well aware of the error in taking a self to be just one thing. He attacked historians who explain their heroes by, as he says, "select [ing] one universal character"; by "following that model, they classify and interpret all the actions of a great man" (1987, 364). The conclusion he drew was that we should look for ourselves in our diversity: "Our normal fashion is to follow the inclinations of our appetite, left and right, up and down, as the winds of occasion bear us along. What we want is only in our thought for the instant that we want it; we are like that creature that takes on the colour of wherever you put it. What we decided just now we will change very soon; and soon afterwards we come back to where we were: it is all motion and inconstancy" (1987, 364). And read this: "Those who strive to account for a man's deeds are never more bewildered than when they try to knit them into one whole and to show them under one light, since they commonly contradict each other in so odd a fashion that it seems impossible that they should all come out of the same shop" (1987, 373). Does this suggest that a running commentary on Montaigne's conscious life would turn out to be something like Dennett's version of Alan Turing's? No doubt like Hume and his latter-day acolytes, Montaigne had in mind the over-simplifications to which especially philosophers influenced by religion were prone. As for Montaigne himself or his "self," who would think that these lines were written by a man who spent almost ten years writing his essays in the same room in the same tower. But, of course, he is also right. It is not in a sealed envelope to be opened only at death but in the ragbags of a life's diversity that one must look for "the living of a life" and a self that lives it. There need, of course, be no lasting biographical significance in, and certainly no necessary connection between, what Montaigne wrote and where he wrote it. Earlier an inveterate traveller, in altered circumstances he might have written essays in a series of taverns now signposted as targets for tourists. We can also ask for the motives for the writing and what else he got up to.

And yet—yes, that tower in the Dordogne, the essays, the man himself, all these tell of constancy, a keeping going, a project-in-process, and of a location that was a means to its pursuance. On the other hand, metaphorically speaking, are we not each of us embodied in our metaphorical towers as continuing points of view from which we do not escape except in dreamless sleep and death? This mobile tower is unique in terms of its at-the-moment space-time coordinates. Whether I travel or lock myself up in a real tower, and unless some tall stories of possession and multi-personality are correctly told, I am this tower's sole inhabitant, indeed its prisoner just like those medieval virgins though more so. And does that not mean that, in quite normal optimal circumstances, there is something here that is more than a speech-centre able to produce "I" and give it an illusory reference? Here *I* am, there *that* is, and, yes, and then who are *you*? These forms of words express the fact that I know I am here in my tower even when I have no idea where that tower is. It is where *I* am at least in the sense both that I am (in) no other tower and no one else is (in) this, and this fact is so firmly embedded in my mind that it needs no remarking.[3]

I suspect the same can be said of Ted Honderich as he sat in the chair in that room focused on a long-term battle with himself and others on this most complex of questions: the nature of consciousness. The room is actual and it is there, and it is still up there when he goes downstairs. But once the clutter of sense data, qualia, raw feels, and "what it is like to be" has been brushed aside, there is quite a lot more to unpack in actuality than just the chair and the room.

Notes

1. See David Woodruff Smith (1986, 149–156, see 151): "In this experience I see this [green] frog."
2. From a transcript of The Jacobsen Lecture delivered by Daniel C. Dennett at the University of London, 13 May 1988.

3. A proviso must of course be added in qualification of the tower metaphor. It might meet with modest approval from Montaigne's countryman Descartes, who likened the relationship of *res cogitans* to *res extensa* to that of a pilot in a ship. Ships are infinitely more mobile than most towers, but our own sense of mobility suggests a more hand-in-glove relationship, something that it would be hard for Descartes's distinction to accommodate since he requires space to be non-mental and the mental to be non-spatial.

References

Aldrich, Virgil C. 1978. Aesthetic perception and objectivity. *British Journal of Aesthetics* 18 (3): 209–216.

de Montaigne, Michel. 1987. *The complete essays*. Trans. M. A. Screech. London: Penguin Books.

Dreyfus, Hubert L. 2014. Embodied coping and artificial intelligence. In *Skillful coping: Essays in the phenomenology of everyday perception and action*, ed. Mark Wrathall. Oxford: Oxford University Press.

Dreyfus, Hubert L., and Stuart E. Dreyfus. 1992. Towards a phenomenology of ethical expertise. In *Revisioning philosophy*, ed. James Ogilvy. Albany: State University of New York Press.

Frege, Gottlob. 1967. The thought. Trans. A. M. and M. Quinton. In *Philosophical logic*, ed. P. F. Strawson. Oxford: Oxford University Press.

Geach, Peter, and Max Black. 1952. *Translations from the philosophical writings of Gottlob Frege*. Oxford: Blackwell.

Honderich, Ted. 2014. *Actual consciousness*. Oxford: Oxford University Press.

———. 2017. *MIND: Your being conscious is what and where?* Chicago: Chicago University Press.

Hume, David. 1963. *An enquiry concerning human understanding and other essays*, ed. Ernest C. Mossner. New York: Washington Square Press.

James, William. 1892. *Psychology*. Cleveland; New York: World.

———. 1912. *Essays in radical empiricism*. London: Longmans, Green & Co.

Smith, David Woodruff. 1986. The structure of (self-)consciousness. *Topoi* 5: 149–156.

5

Physicalism Without Dependence

Barbara Gail Montero

The physical world, as Ted Honderich points out in his book *Actual Consciousness* (2014), is almost invariably thought of as necessarily objective. What exactly this means is controversial. However, the rough idea might be stated something like this: the physical world, however else it may be, is in principle observable from different points of view. Or, to put it in slightly different terms, to say that the world is physical is, roughly, to say that there is no aspect of the physical world that can, in principle, be experienced by only one person. As such, physicalism would be refuted by irreducible subjective facts—facts, for example, about what my conscious experience of seeing red is like that cannot be fully conveyed in objective terms about light reflectances, the physiology of color vision, and so forth. But is this right?

The conception of the physical as inhospitable to private, subjective experience is one that Honderich pushes against, seeing it as an insidious stumbling block in both the philosophical and scientific quest to understand consciousness. I agree, but, as I shall explain, I am not sure

B. G. Montero (✉)
College of Staten Island of the City University of New York
and the CUNY Graduate Center, NY, USA

G. D. Caruso (ed.), *Ted Honderich on Consciousness, Determinism, and Humanity*, Philosophers in Depth, https://doi.org/10.1007/978-3-319-66754-6_5

if Honderich goes far enough. Consciousness is real, for Honderich. But is its subjectivity real on its own or must its existence depend on other objective features of the world? This is the question I aim to address in this chapter, ultimately arguing for the view that even if our conscious experiences of the world do not depend on objective features of the world, physicalism may still be tenable.

5.1 Physicalism with Irreducible Subjectivity

Although it is controversial what exactly it means to say that the physical world is objective, it is fairly clear that one thing philosophers such as Thomas Nagel and others who hold this view do *not* mean by this claim is that the physical world can have no points of view, or subjective experience. Most physicalists think that the physical world does contain subjective experience; it is just that the subjective experience must be reducible to, or fully explained by, or—if they are being more explicit—fully explained away by aspects of the world that are not subjective, typically by the quarks, leptons, bosons, and so forth.

Does Ted Honderich hold such a view? On the one hand, he might seem to, for in row five of his chart, he claims that consciousness (whether it is perceptual, affective, or cognitive) stands "in categorial lawful connections, including those dependency-relations with (a) the objective physical world and (b) the conscious thing as neural" (Honderich 2017). But, on the other hand, it is not clear that these dependency relations, as he conceives of them, are intended to explain away subjective experience, for he also holds that consciousness is *actual* and by this he means that it is *subjectively physical.* So my first question for Honderich is: Do the dependency relations referred to in row five of his chart imply the type of reduction that leads to the elimination of consciousness, and if not, why?

My second question, however, is: Why do we need row five at all? Why can't there be a theory of consciousness that, as Honderich wants, eschews mystery, a theory that can be investigated scientifically, a theory that can be rightly called physicalistic yet one that depends on neither the stuff of physics nor the neurons in your brain? In other words, why must physicalists—that is, physicalists who want to accept that consciousness is a real feature of the world—maintain that consciousness must depend on entirely objective properties?

The typical answer to this question is simply that it is a matter of definition: that physicalism implies that everything depends on objective properties. But truth by definition is not so easy to come by; in particular, this typical answer seems to admit two responses. The first is to claim that physicalism, though a dependence thesis, does not require that the dependence base upon which everything rests (that is, the stuff of physics or neuroscience) is objective. This is the physicalist-panpsychist route. The second is to maintain that physicalism need not imply a dependence thesis, that is, that it is does imply anything like row five, at all. It is this latter view that I aim to defend.

5.2 Physicalism Without Dependence

Physicalism, I want to argue, is compatible with subjective consciousness that fails to depend on anything objective. And as a first step in making this case, let me present a scenario in which physicalism would seem to be acceptable—to the masses at least—yet does not entail the dependence of consciousness on physics:

> **The Nothing-but-Physics World.** Imagine that our fundamental physics were such that there could be another possible world that duplicates our fundamental physics yet fails to duplicate any higher-level entities or properties. That is, imagine that duplicating our fundamental physics could give us a world with just quarks, leptons, their antiparticles and such like, but, no chemical bonds, no molecules, no cells, no organisms.[1]

Must physicalism be false in a world in which physics fails to determine chemistry? That is, must physicalism be false in a world in which chemistry does, as Honderich puts it, stand in dependency relations with the objective physical world? Although it would be shocking to discover this, there seems no reason to think that such a discovery would or should prompt physicalists to throw in the towel; this is not because physicalists are a stubborn lot and will uphold physicalism come what may (though this may very occasionally be true as well), but, rather, because a chemical bond, they would want to say, is the kind of thing that is physical regardless of its relation to physics. In other words, it already is part of the objective physical world.

Of course, even if chemistry fails to depend on physics, the mental could still depend on the neural, which arguably is not a subjective feature of the world. Hence, one might think that all my Nothing-but-Physics World thought experiment shows is that if our world were like this, then the physicalist's dependence base should expand to include higher-level properties, such as the properties of chemistry. Yet if the failure of chemical bonding to depend on physics does not suffice to make chemical bonding nonphysical, why should the failure of mental properties to depend on the physical sciences suffice to make mentality nonphysical?[2] Why should a dependence relation be necessary for physicalism when it holds between the mental and neural, but not when it holds between the chemical and physics?

5.3 Disordered Worlds and Punctuated Worlds

One can show why physicalism can survive without dependence in another way. Honderich aims to present a theory of consciousness that maintains all of its singular glory yet still fits into a physicalist picture of the world. How can consciousness be unlike anything else in the universe yet still be physical? One way this could occur would be if, to put it paradoxically, everything were special, or to put it nonparadoxically, if there were no dependence relations between any levels of organization, that is, if neither consciousness nor anything else were dependent on lower-level properties. This would be the case in a disordered world:

> **The Disordered World.** Imagine that our world were such that it was not generally ordered by dependence relations, that, for example, neither chemistry nor botany nor bacteriology nor mycology had a dependence base. The mental, in such a world, fails to stand in dependence-relations to the posits of physics, yet, apart from the posits of physics themselves, so does everything else.

In such a world, it seems that the mere failure to stand in dependence relations to physics is no reason to count as nonphysical something as tough as a chemical bond or as innocent as a morel mushroom. Thus, physicalists, in such a situation, should be able to say: "That's just the way the physical world is." In other words, such a disorderly world, albeit inconsistent with the dependence of everything on the objective posits of physics, need not be inconsistent with physicalism.[3]

While rejecting the idea that physicalism entails a dependence principle, such as that of row five in Honderich's chart—a principle that tells us not only what our world is like, but also what any possible world which duplicates our fundamental physics must be like—one could uphold a merely this-worldly dependence principle, such as Quine's principle that "nothing happens in the world, not the flutter of an eyelid, not the flicker of a thought, without some redistribution of microphysical states" (1981, 98). This extremely weak dependence principle is almost certainly true, if only for the reason that microphysical states are in constant flux. However, must physicalism even entail Quine's "special deference to physical theory" (1981, 98)? Or could one be an irreverent physicalist?

Consider the following:

> **The Punctuated World.** Imagine that we were to discover that microphysical processes were punctuated, that there were brief periods of utter stillness at the microphysical level, yet all higher-level processes unfolded in the smooth, seamless way that we have come to know and love.

It seems that in such a world, physicalism could still be true, even if the flutter of an eyelid, the flicker of a thought, as well as the division of cells, the diffusion of dust, and more were to occasionally occur during states of microphysical tranquility.

5.4 Why the Widespread Agreement?

Although there are a few explicit arguments for the entailment from physicalism to something like the type of dependence principle expressed in row five of Honderich's chart, they do little more than assume the truth of the entailment.[4] Moreover, most who accept the entailment do not do so on the basis of explicit arguments; indeed, it would be the rare and beautiful philosophical argument that garnered such widespread agreement about a view. Why, then, do they accept it?

Perhaps the most common way of cashing out the reason behind the dependence reflex is that physicalism is thought to imply that God, as it were, after creating the domain of objective, fundamental physics, rested; and the failure of dependence relations between consciousness and the objective physical world (again, row five) means that there was more work to be done. But why must physicalism imply this?

The idea of physicalism entailing that God had only to set the quantum gambol in motion has roots in Saul Kripke's (1980) figurative description of the relation between pain and C-fiber stimulation. On Kripke's account, in order for us to feel C-fiber stimulation as pain, God had to perform an extra task beyond merely creating C-fiber stimulation, which shows, Kripke argues, that the relation between C-fiber stimulation and pain could not be identity. Believers in the entailment from physicalism to dependence take this one step further and assume that if God had more work to do, or in other words, if consciousness fails to stand in dependence relations to the objective physical world, then physicalism must be false. Yet if we accept that physicalism need not be an identity thesis, why should the failure of dependence have this implication?

Physicalists who accept the "all-God-had-to-do" metaphor do not think that God actually enters the picture. Rather, God is understood as a placeholder for certain unknown forces of nature or chance or whatever it is on nontheological grounds that brought our world into existence. So, as long as God does not really exist, what is wrong with having her do a little extra work? This extra work may appear suspect because it seems to involve further acts of creation, as it were, beyond the initial creation of that extremely hot, swarming soup that emanated from the Big Bang. But if physicalists can accept that nature can take care of the initial creation, it seems that they should be able to accept that, if further work were needed, nature could take care of that as well. How this is done might be rather mysterious to us, at least for now; however, just as with the Big Bang, this need not be a reason to take the results as nonphysical.

Admittedly, if our world does not comply with even a weak dependence principle, then additional laws are needed to account for observed regularities between lower-level physical and higher-level chemical processes, neural processes, mental processes, and the rest. And one might object that these are exactly the type of laws that would hold between the neural and the mental, if dualism were true. This may be, but why should it matter? The law of gravity, for example, would presumably also hold if dualism were true. Yet the law of gravity does not pose a problem for physicalism. Consequently, it seems that the mere fact that a certain type of law would need to hold in a nonphysical world does not entail that any world with that type of law is nonphysical.

Finally, there is Occham's razor to contend with, and a world with additional laws connecting higher- and lower-level properties might seem ontologically profligate. However, in terms of leading us to the true nature of the world, this razor has always been of the disposable variety. When devising a theory, it may be preferable to pick the simpler of two empirically equivalent hypotheses, but the world itself might not conform to the simpler hypothesis. The world, even if physicalism is true, might not be clean shaven. Or, at least, there seems to be no reason to think that physicalism should exclude this possibility.

5.5 What Does a Dependence-Free Physicalism Entail?

What then is the physicalist's heartfelt commitment, if it is not the dependence of one domain of entities on some other domain? I would like to suggest that physicalism should be seen more as a this-worldly principle that tells us what the actual world is like while leaving open whether there are possible worlds that have such things as physics without chemistry or molecules without tables. Perhaps it is not possible to have physics without chemistry, and mind without brain. But, as I have argued, this should not be seen as a core commitment of physicalism. What, then, are the core commitments of physicalism and what exactly does it tell us about this world?

As even I am not willing to go so far as to admit Cartesian minds into the physical realm, I need to say something about what is really at stake in the debate over physicalism. Once stripped of what I have argued are these unnecessary commitments, I think that what is left is a rejection of the idea that God—not the metaphorical one, but the real thing—plays a role in the workings of the world. If God exists, be She a Cartesian workhorse or the highly efficient creator of a mere dependence base, physicalism is false regardless of the fundamental nature of either the wave function or mentality.[5] Furthermore, even if God does not exist, we tend to see theories that strongly suggest a theistic worldview, especially ones which evoke the idea that God created human beings in her image, as incompatible with physicalism. What is really driving the debate over physicalism is not the question of whether the mental is a subjective feature of the world or an objective one. The mind can be, as Honderich seems to want to accept, both a physical and a subjective feature of the world, and consciousness can be entirely different from everything else. However, what physicalists must reject are worldviews that entail, or strongly hint at, a leading role for God.

Notes

1. If our world were like this, the mental would fail to depend on our fundamental physics as long as the mental is not part of fundamental physics.
2. I am assuming that facts about composition, that is, facts about when certain entities compose a further object, are contingent since in the imagined scenario the fundamental entities of physics only contingently compose chemical bonds. Though this is a controversial view, it does have its defenders. See, for example, Nolan (2005) and Cameron (2007, 99–121).
3. Is it reasonable to question the ubiquity of higher- to lower-level dependence relations in the nonmental realm? My sense is that although some philosophers of science question whether we can reductively explain chemistry and other higher-level sciences in terms of physics, they are hesitant to claim that these higher-level sciences do not depend on physics because, after all, the philosophers of mind say that this would mean that physicalism is false! (For arguments against the reducibility of chemistry to physics, see Hendry (forthcoming, Sect. 3) and Jaap van Brakel (2000, 119–150).) However, the possibility of a physically disordered world as well as a nothing-but-physics world suggests that the truth of physicalism does not require the dependence of chemistry and other higher-level sciences on

physics. And once we relinquish this requirement, it is not unreasonable to think that the clues which have led some philosophers to question the reducibility of higher-level sciences to physics might lead these same philosophers to question the dependence of higher-level sciences on physics.

4. See, for example, Witmer (2001). See also Loewer (2001, 39).
5. For a contrary view, see Peter van Inwagen (2009, part 3).

References

van Brakel, Jaap. 2000. *Philosophy of chemistry: Between the manifest and the scientific image.* Leuven: Leuven University Press.

Cameron, Ross. 2007. The contingency of composition. *Philosophical Studies* 133 (1): 99–121.

Hendry, Robin. forthcoming. *The metaphysics of chemistry.* New York: Oxford University Press.

Honderich, Ted. 2014. *Actual consciousness.* Oxford: Oxford University Press.

———. 2017. *MIND: Your being conscious is what and where?* Chicago: Chicago University Press.

Kripke, Saul. 1980. *Naming and necessity.* Cambridge, MA: Harvard University Press.

Loewer, Barry. 2001. From physics to physicalism. In *Physicalism and its discontents,* ed. C. Gillett and B. Loewer. Cambridge, MA: Cambridge University Press.

Nolan, Daniel. 2005. *David Lewis.* New York: Routledge.

Quine, Willard Van Orman. 1981. *Theories and things.* Cambridge, MA: Harvard University Press.

Van Inwagen, Peter. 2009. *Metaphysics.* Boulder, CO: Westview Press.

Witmer, Gene. 2001. Sufficiency claims and physicalism: A formulation. In *Physicalism and its discontents,* ed. C. Gillett and B. Loewer. Cambridge: Cambridge University Press.

6

Consciousness: What Is *It* Like?

Barry C. Smith

Moment to moment there can be sights, sounds, feels, tastes, and smells, informing us of the world around us, and of ourselves. Being conscious encompasses all this and more: we usually know which way is up, where our limbs are without looking at or touching them. We feel confident or uncertain about our decisions; we are irritated or amused, feel pity, or have sympathy for others. It feels different, subjectively speaking, to be alone or in the presence of other conscious minds. We are aware of time passing quickly or slowly: we anticipate what is about to happen, and hold on to what has just happened. We are alert to threat and danger, to exhilaration and dejection. All of this and the thoughts provoked by it can modulate the unfolding pattern of our conscious lives. These are the moment-to-moment items of conscious experience. But what account can be given of them?

Which methods best get at the phenomena of conscious experience and give us insights into its nature? This is one of the greatest challenges we face when studying consciousness. For however vivid the conscious

B. C. Smith (✉)
School of Advanced Study, University of London, Senate House, London, UK

G. D. Caruso (ed.), *Ted Honderich on Consciousness, Determinism, and Humanity*, Philosophers in Depth, https://doi.org/10.1007/978-3-319-66754-6_6

moments of our waking lives are, when we try to contemplate the nature of consciousness itself, it always seems to elude us. Like David Hume searching inwardly for the self, we seem to come up with something else in its place. What we get hold of is not consciousness but something *in* consciousness: a thought, a feeling, an image, a tune going through one's head. Of course, each of these items is consciously known to us, but when we ask what it is to be conscious of such items we are at a loss to say.

At other times our conscious waking minds look outwards and are fully occupied by things in our immediate surroundings with less focus on their workings, or on purely internal states. Right now my gaze takes in a railway carriage with a passing scene outside the window. In this way, our inner lives are shaped, in part, by what goes on in our immediate surroundings within our perceptual reach. Nevertheless, they are also shaped by what goes on in our brains and our bodies for it's not just distal items that preoccupy my conscious attention. I have a persistent ache in my left shoulder, and bodily awareness of my limbs and posture. There's a residual taste of coffee in my mouth, and I feel cold air on my face and hands. All these things impinge on, or inflect the details of my consciousness. And all the while, I am choosing the words that best express my thoughts, as my fingers type them out on the keyboard of my laptop.

What is it to be conscious of each of these things? Can I be conscious of all of them at the same time? Am I conscious of each of them in the same way and to the same extent? They seem to flesh out the continuous and unified details of my current conscious state. But is that right, or do I only become conscious of each thing as I notice it, shifting attention from one thing to another? It's hard to say. And that's because it is hard to get to grips with each conscious moment as it transpires. Yet that's what philosophical reflections on consciousness seem to require. How are we aware of these conscious states? How well can we know them as we undergo them? And can our answers to these questions tell us anything about the nature of consciousness?

These questions bear on the issues that concern Ted Honderich, both in his recent book, *Actual Consciousness* (2014), and in a new short work developing the themes from that work (2017). Honderich is concerned with consciousness as it is, not with how some seek to describe or fashion it for their own explanatory purposes. But this brings up sharply for

Honderich the issue of how he aims to get at the nature of actual consciousness, or consciousness as it is. It's true that if an individual is conscious, at that moment the individual will be experiencing something. But that settles very little. Being in a conscious experiential state is one thing, knowing which conscious experiential state one is in is another.

Do the details of consciousness announce themselves to a creature that is conscious? A creature's consciousness may be very minimal and it may lack the means to make anything of it. So it is not simply being conscious that matters so much as what fills that consciousness and the awareness we have of it. Being conscious turns human beings into subjects of experience with an inner life: inner, not in the sense of a separate realm cut off from reality and representing it, but in the sense of having a first-person point of view or vantage point from which to take in, focus on, and act upon things in the world around us. Our inner lives are shaped, in part, by our interactions with the world and with others, as well as by our bodies and our brains. The task is to say how all of these things collectively give rise to, and give form to, the conscious experiences we enjoy as humans, and how much and to what extent we know about them. All of this needs to be unpacked in any satisfactory account of consciousness. So how are we to study this elusive phenomenon and how does Honderich hope to arrive at insights into the nature of consciousness?

He tells us that, "We need to pay our very own attention to consciousness, some untutored attention" (Honderich 2014, 191). It's a good question what "untutored attention" amounts to. In advocating it, Honderich believes that he is departing from the usual way to study consciousness in science and philosophy. But untutored or not—and Honderich's is certainly not an untutored eye—it is about attending to the phenomena. How does that help us to avoid the dangers of both the philosophical and scientific approaches to the study of consciousness? If we reflect on or think about the conscious states we're in, we are in danger of distorting them, of moving simply to an account of how we think about consciousness rather than how it is. While if we turn to neuroscience to study the cortical and sub-cortical underpinnings that make consciousness possible, we risk changing the subject by leaving out the subjectivity that seems, in part, to constitute being conscious. This is a problem that any attempt to advance our understanding of consciousness should deal with head-on.

The worry is that philosophers often assume that we have uncontroversial access to what is going on in consciousness. They often claim to use their phenomenologically individuated experiences as a basis for judgements, or constraints on philosophical theories of phenomena in consciousness they wish to account for, like perceptions of colour or experiences of pain. And yet, while presuming to consult their experiences, philosophers often diverge in their opinions about how to characterize the nature of those experiences. So is it some immediate access to the phenomena that shapes their views, or is it how they *think* about those conscious phenomena that leads to their preferred philosophical theories?

In other words, is it thought about our conscious states rather than the conscious states themselves that are brought to bear in these discussions? Of course, some have made a virtue of this predicament in their views about consciousness. According to David Rosenthal (1986) and his supporters of a higher-order thought theory of consciousness, it is reflections on mental states that make them conscious, or at any rate consciously known to us. But this view seems to leave out the subjectivity that best characterizes our conscious lives. What is more, couldn't there be aspects of subjective experience that we momentarily overlook and simply fail to think about but which still have an impact on our subjective experience? If so, then the higher-order theory of thought is off-track. This question asks us to take seriously the possibility that there can be aspects of an experience we undergo that escape our notice and yet which are still part of our conscious lives. This possibility will occupy us in what follows along with another big issue: can we be mistaken about the character of some of our conscious mental states?

Could the way we think of, or simply take our conscious experiences to be, get their natures or character wrong? In other words, can how things *are* in conscious experience be otherwise than they *appear* to us? If so how would we know? I think they can be otherwise than how we take them to be, and that's because whenever we have an experience, hot on the heels of it is our *take* on that experience. This is not a reflection, or thought about it: that's too high level. It is simply a way we intuitively take things to be in our experience, like taking a conscious perceptual experience to be a seeing, or a hearing. This identification (or misidentification) of the modal signature of our experiences is so close to the having of the experience itself that we don't notice room for a gap between them and treat them as the same thing. In this way we fail to recognize that another step is required: that of providing a phenomenological taxonomy of our current experiential states, and it is here that we can go wrong. I will suggest that we can use a number of ways to learn about our conscious experiences, sometimes returning to them in mind and revising what we first judged them to be the case, or alighting on a feature of an experience that we had at first overlooked, like a note in a wine that we missed in our own experience till someone pointed it out, or by learning from findings in sensory or cognitive neuroscience how things must be as opposed to how we take them to be. There need be no simple, or single, source of information we draw on to decide how things are in conscious experience at any moment, and it is a mistake to think there can be.

Turning to Ted Honderich's approach to what he calls *actual consciousness*, he takes the data for his theory to be given by assembling reminders of the quirks of our everyday conscious lives. But can we, as Honderich thinks, really pay "untutored attention" to our own consciousness and use that as data for philosophical theorizing? However familiar the moments of our conscious mental lives seem to each of us, and however convinced we are that we have transparent and accurate access to our own conscious experiences, when we scrutinize them, we may alter them, either when we get above them to reflect on them philosophically, or when we get below them to examine them scientifically. Seldom do we really get alongside them.

For as soon as we examine an episode of conscious life, we risk turning it into a different episode. Try attending to the sensations you are having in your left foot right now. You will be aware of feeling something in the foot, but were those sensations there and going on before you attended to them, or are they brought into being by your attending to them? Is it only through an act of thought or reflection that the qualities of conscious experience appear, or are they there all along, filling out our waking lives but somehow unsung? Once again, it's hard to say. Even if the sensations were there all along, and part of your continuing consciousness of the world, and you as part of it, have the sensations changed—intensified maybe—by your attending to them? These seem to be questions that should have definite answers, and yet they also seem to be empirically intractable.

Nor does it help if we switch to how things seem to us phenomenologically as a matter of our own experience. Phenomenology doesn't provide enough to go on here in helping us decide how things are, or how they were, with the foot before and after attending to it. This is not to say, with followers of Daniel Dennett, that there is no fact of the matter about these issues and that the idea of a continuing conscious scene is an illusion; it is just to say that there is no obvious way to know what to say, either by addressing the issue experimentally or experientially. Yet it is an issue concerning our conscious perceptual experience.

One thing this example helps to make clear is that the nature of what's in conscious experience is not just a matter of how things appear to us, as some philosophers have supposed. Those inclined towards a Cartesian conception of the mental treat conscious experience as constituted and exhausted by how things appear to the subject. In experience, how things appear to you is how they are. But when contemplating what to say about our experience of the foot *before* we gave it our attention—in other words, in thinking about whether attention changes what we are conscious of—we recognize the possibility, though some will simply deny it, that how things appear in consciousness doesn't settle how they are and how things appear is compatible with very different accounts of how experience could be.

Another case, where we are tempted, erroneously, to say how things are in consciousness simply on the basis of how they, comes from elite performance tennis players. When we watch players playing championship tennis, we think we know what they are seeing when they react to a serve and return it, and *they* think they know this too, even though there are objective reasons to conclude that it simply can't be the way it seems to them and to us. Take what happens when Roger Federer returns service. Watching Federer, especially when the film is slowed down will make it *seem* to you that he is keeping his eyes on the ball and following it right up to the moment when he takes his return shot. His coach tells him to keep his eyes on the ball and that's what he thinks that he is doing. It's what he appears to be doing. But that can't be what's happening. He simply couldn't *follow* the ball with his eyes. The ball is travelling at over a hundred miles an hour. It is not possible that he is tracking it visually. What he, or the combined visual and motor system, is doing, is pointing his eyes in the direction where his brain predicts the ball will be. This is what his brain has learned do over hundreds of thousands of trials of his eyes watching the ball leave his opponent's racket at a certain angle. The question is: What does he *see*? What does he *consciously* perceive, or take himself to consciously perceive at those moments? It's hard to say. Perhaps it is what he predicts he should see?

What cases like these and others like it show is that we cannot simply rely on how things seem to us, or how we take them to be, to settle what is actually going on in consciousness. Yet some philosophers have thought we can and that there is no appearance-reality distinction in conscious experience.

But why think that? Is what you know, or think you know, about your conscious life, simply a matter of how things are in consciousness for you right now? Do the contents and character of conscious experiences just announce themselves? Or do the contents and character of our conscious experiences come to light by the way I'm thinking about them? Neither the experiences nor the thoughts about them can easily settle this matter.

For example, as I gaze now out the window of the train I think I see green fields and hedgerows. That's how things seem to me in experience, and to some philosophers, whether or not my visual experience gets things in the world right or wrong, I simply can't be wrong about how things *appear* to me in conscious visual experience. That's because, so the story goes, in consciousness, how things seems to the subject is how they are. That's just what it is to have a conscious experience. This view is usually accompanied by promissory notes about picking out determinate moments of conscious experience by talk of what it's like to have such experiences, of say smelling a rose, or tasting a strawberry. The "what it's like" locution is meant to act as a way of uniquely isolating for inspection how things appear to the subject of those experiences

This initially seductive move, masquerading as the merest piece of intuitive common sense, amounts to little more than a philosophical sleight of hand. How much should we include in that experience? Where does it begin and end? Did any emotions suffuse those experiences of tasting or smelling? Was there a feeling of familiarity at the time? Do these scenes remind me of other times in which I've had similar experiences? How detailed were my perceptions? Were those experiences influenced by information from other sensory information, just as my seeing out the window is influenced by the workings of my vestibular system? In simultaneously thinking of my experience as a philosophical example, did I experience the thinking as part of the experience or auxiliary to it? Can I factor out pure looking from the overall experience? Would the looking have been different had I not been thinking of that experience as a part of a philosophical example, or had my mind wandered to think about something else entirely?

It's far from obvious that we know how to answer these questions. No doubt there is some way "the experience" (however it is to be demarcated) is, and this we can agree to, but it doesn't take us very far. There is something it is like to be in that state; but this is a far cry from the attempted pseudo-precisification of what it's like talk. Granted, there is *something* it is like to be that conscious state. What is it like? We are not told. Again, being in an experiential state is one thing, knowing about the state one is in is another.

How unified is our consciousness? We can ask this question at the level of what we are experiencing, the modalities through which we are experiencing it, at the level of experience being integrated smoothly with how we reflect on that experience, or at the level of the subject of experience. How do we decide these issues? However unified any of these things feel to us, we might ask how unified are they really? Impressive empirical and theoretical work by Tony Marcel has put in doubt some of the regularly asserted unity claims (Marcel 1993, 2003).

If there really was something it was like for me to undergo an experience at a moment it's not clear to me that every aspect of what it was like, then or now, would be available to me to answer these questions. To suppose that the interrogative locution "what it's like" simply nets some determinate aspect of my conscious mental life that I can refer to and theorize about as "what it's like to taste the residue of coffee in my mouth" is something of a philosopher's fantasy. I *take* there to be something it was like, something I'm now trying to attend to, but what was it actually like? Am I guaranteed to know?

Thus, the locution "*what it's like* to" smell a rose, to taste a peach, to see the train carriage is best not thought of as a stopping point, a primitive of philosophical theorizing, so much as a way of recruiting common sense to attempt to highlight the initial targets for inquiry. Talk of "what it's like to experience x" is not unanalyzable; it is best treated as a truncated form of "What I *take* it to be like to experience x," where my take on my own experience is so inextricable from the experience itself that I simply don't notice that there is this extra step and room for error.

In *Actual Consciousness*, Honderich rightly has no truck with "what it's like" talk. Nor, does he veer in the opposite direction by supposing there is no fact of the matter about what occurs in the subject's experience but only what we settle for as a verbal response to questions about consciousness elicited by probing at various times in the processing stream. In other words, Honderich doesn't assume with Dennett (1991) that the consciousness we experience moment-to-moment is nothing other than what we are inclined to say about it: a matter of heterophenomenology, as Dennett calls it.

Though if we can neither rest content with supposedly self-intimating talk of "what it's like to X," nor with a deflationary account of conscious in terms of what we say or think about it, where does Honderich propose to find room to operate in order to turn up something useful about the nature of consciousness? What is the best way to study consciousness and get insights into its nature?

We face something of a dilemma. The closer we stick to how we think things are with us in consciousness, the less likely it is that we can square them with what we know from the sciences about what must be going on in the minds of conscious creatures like us. While the closer we get to the mechanisms that explain what happens in us when we are conscious, the further we seem to be from the phenomena we undergo as subjects of experience. Where does Honderich stand with respect to this dilemma? He thinks he can avoid both the philosopher's distortion and the neuroscientist's neglect of the phenomena that interest him. But can he?

Like many other philosophers, Honderich thinks about the nature of consciousness by reflecting on his own experience and inviting others to share the way he finds things to be. He urges us over and over to just notice and accept that things are as he takes them to be. But why should this method produce good results when other philosophers, including many that Honderich discusses and disagrees with, do the same but come up with competing views having to do with having inner representations, or with the conscious experiences that have aboutness? It's safe to assume that no amount of insistence, even when based on what Honderich takes to be something he can simply read off his own experience will convince his opponents that, "Being conscious in perceiving isn't having representations of whatever sort of an existing thing out there—it's a thing existing out there" (2017, 130).

So what is *Actual Consciousness*? In attempting to say Honderich provides a number of pithy remarks that he hopes will convey to the reader what he's talking about for each of the three areas of consciousness he addresses: perceiving, thinking, and wanting. In the case of perceptual consciousness, what he offers again and again is an idea or image that to him crystallizes the doctrine. It is an image that works for him but which I confess to finding a little hard to get hold of, namely: "What is actual for me now with respect to my perceptual consciousness is only a room, a room out there in space" (2014, 191). Let me put this in my own terms, which I hope do justice to Honderich's key idea. My conscious perception at a given moment can be characterized by the region of the world in my immediate surroundings that I take in through acts of perceiving. As a consciously perceiving being I am immediately in touch with the ordinary things around me. When I awaken and come to consciousness a world is immediately made available to me containing a window, the bedside table with a lamp on it, a chair, and the wardrobe. All of that is immediately available to me as I open my eyes. I inhabit and belong to the world as experienced in these moments. This is what conscious perceiving does for us. And since each of us takes a unique spatio-temporal path through the world that no one else can occupy, we each have our own unique vantage point on the world from which we consciously perceive it. So even as someone beside me awakens and comes to consciousness, the world they take in will be a slightly different world—or the-world-as-they-experience-it will be slightly different because of their slightly different vantage point on it.

How the world as experienced by each perceiver is depends on the unique occupancy of the world by that perceiver and the individual cognitive, emotional, and sensory set-up of that perceiver. This is why the world brought to light by perceptual consciousness is, in Honderich's phrase, a *subjective physical world*, of which there are as many subjectively physical worlds as there are perceiving beings. It is a world that surrounds and fills out the conscious perceptual experience of the perceiver at that moment. The indicated uniqueness of *a* world or *a* room for each perceiver provides one gloss on what is subjective about the world of consciousness, namely individuality, but Honderich short changes us on a fuller account of what the subjectivity of consciousness perceiving consists in, and he leaves out crucial dependences of the conscious perception of the world at any moment on facts about the subject's body and perceptual mechanisms, which I will go on to explain.

But focus for now on Honderich's key image that conscious *is* a matter of a thing's existing out there so that in perceiving a room one is in, one's perceptual consciousness just *is* there being a room. This is a philosophical view and not something that we can simply read off how things are with us in perceptual consciousness. It goes beyond simple observation either because it is an interpretation of Honderich's experience of what is occupying his visual field, and so is not "untutored attention" to consciousness itself, although it is based on it. It leaves out certain crucial aspects of conscious perceptual experience, such as one's awareness of *seeing* that room, and awareness of one's own body and first-person perspective as part of the scene, including the predominantly selective vantage point of one's field of vision. These things are left out in order to establish the radical externalist thesis about consciousness that Honderich is keen to promote. However, to get at the subject matter, we need to acknowledge the first-person point of view: the vantage point from which to experience the world—the same world that others experience from their vantage points. We need to fashion an account that accommodates our inner view of an outer world, as I put it in a previous response to Honderich (Smith 2006).

The problem for Honderich's method, as already stated, is that acts of attending to, or thinking about, any particular conscious experience, while undergoing that experience, can either change the very shape and character of the experiential state, leave something out that is unattended, or supplying an answer that gets things wrong about that kind of experience it is. By contrast neuroscientists try to get underneath the surface by studying the mechanisms and processes that give conscious experiences their form and character. The usual criticism is that these investigations are either reductionist, or if not, they fail to capture the essential subjectivity of conscious states. But while the limitations of the second method of studying consciousness are well known and acknowledged by the best practitioners in this area, the limitations of the first method are often overlooked, and this should worry us more. It is less clear to philosophers of mind that their reflections on their conscious mental states may not give them complete and transparent access to those states.

How much of the detail of our experience can be accessed in the very moment that we are reflecting on that experience? Do we really get hold of each and every detail all at once, and do we even get the details right? It is far from clear that we do.

What does Honderich's take on his own conscious experience leave out? Remember, what Honderich yields in his "untutored attention" to his own conscious experience is meant to be a witness for anyone's conscious experience. We are reminded to confirm for ourselves that it is like this. Yet it tends to leave out—or leave out the possibility of—being aware of my own experience of perceiving in the very act of perceiving. As Mike Martin points out: "In being aware of the world, I am aware of my own awareness of it" (1988, 99). Honderich accepts the phenomenon but diagnoses it as a case of coming to think about that first awareness, denying that it can be part of perceiving (Honderich 2014, 196). That's because Honderich has a neat division of consciousness into three kinds: perceptual consciousness, cognitive consciousness, and affective consciousness. He tells us: "Your consciousness in general, consciousness in the primary ordinary sense, the core sense, the one in decent dictionaries, has those three different sides" (2014, 5). More particularly:

> There's perceptual consciousness *within* seeing and other perception—perceiving as a whole of course comes to more than consciousness, such as facts about eyes. And there's cognitive consciousness, which we can also label as thinking. And affective consciousness, which we can label as wanting and the like. (2014, 5)

But what makes Honderich so sure that there are these three separable sides to consciousness? Does experience tell him this, or does it seem this way to him when he reflects on his conscious experience? He is certainly to be congratulated for attempting finer divisions when discussing consciousness and not resorting to the usual philosopher's treatment of consciousness as a single, undifferentiable thing that we either have or lack at any moment. There are grades of consciousness and different types of conscious awareness and these can be usefully explored. But so far as the tripartite division Honderich settles for, we might ask whether these are theoretical ways of discussing and focusing on different aspects of our consciousness, or whether the phenomena of consciousness themselves separate out into these three kinds. At times Honderich warns us:

> Don't read into the tripartite division more than is intended. It isn't any of many old and elaborated claims about *faculties* or *powers* of the mind or consciousness, for a start. It's just three sides, parts or sets of elements of consciousness. (2014, 197)

But what are we to make of the tripartite division into perceiving, thinking, and wanting ("including feeling, desiring, inclination, valuing, intending, hoping, condescending, and more"). They can certainly overlap in many of our consciousness waking moments. But are they as easily extricable as Honderich's reply to Martin suggests. Honderich's take on Mike Martin's observation about awareness of the world goes in one direction; Martin and I go in another. Who is right and do the phenomena resolve this, whether we can know it or not?

Honderich acknowledges that you "can add other consciousness to perceptual consciousness … That doesn't matter. What is actual in our perceptual consciousness isn't more than rooms and the like" (2014, 197). This is boldly asserted because that's how Honderich takes them to be. But is that right? I don't doubt that's Honderich's take on his own experience, albeit one influenced by his tripartite division. But does his take on his own experiences get matters right?

I can be sitting by the sea on some rocks with my feet dangling in the water. I feel the coldness of the water, feel the warmth of the sun, and see the flecks of silver bouncing off the sea as the light reflects on the crests of the gentle waves. I notice the rocks and the sea while feeling the sensations of heat and coolness and take pleasure in these things, take pleasure in my experiencing them, in my noticing them. That appreciation of the scene is not just given by the scene but by my experiencing it. But I must not think too much about all of this or else that serene pleasure will be lost, will be replaced by a reflective awareness of what I'm undergoing that will distance me from simply and pleasurably undergoing it. And if I do slip out of that state of happy but attentive reverie at the shore, I will think about my thinking taking me away from it and eventually I will be too self-conscious to capture that intermediary state between simply taking in the scene and thinking about what it's like to enjoy it. That intermediate state includes my noticing the things I am perceiving, and it's my perceiving of them in that way that gives me pleasure. At that moment I don't want anything else than to continue being in that state, thrilled by being able to be conscious of it and glad of it. It's a state of simplicity, a conscious perceiving, but it's not just the shore, and it includes awareness of perceiving without thinking and reflecting on it.

Of course, all I am doing is narrating my own experience and hoping it resonates with something you have experienced, and to that extent it is doing nothing to convince you that this is how things really are. But I attempted to describe my experience as it was for me, not as a philosophical demonstration, and what can be added is the search for neuroimaging evidence that would tease apart these different levels I just reflected on. It may be difficult to get at these different states and their relations in an experimental set-up but some neuroscientists are trying, especially by looking at resting state and mind-wandering. How much are the sensory areas activated and how are the prefrontal areas involved? How much is ventromedial prefrontal cortex and how much is dorsolateral? Are some areas inhibited by more cognitive and evaluative tasks or judgements? Perhaps a combination of report, behavioural and neurological evidence can help us get more of a purchase on what is going on here.

Honderich is much less convinced than I am that empirical findings in cognitive neuroscience will cast light on the nature of consciousness, setting more store on what he can conclude by reflection on his mental states. This is, perhaps, because he thinks neuroscience will aim to provide on its own a reductive account of consciousness, and he thinks that is unlikely to succeed. But I don't think neuroscientists are obliged to see their task this way, and the best of them don't go in for reductionism but take seriously the participant's reports on what they experience: see or imagine, or recall. By studying the processes and mechanisms that give rise to various different sensory, perceptual, and affective phenomena, we learn more about them, and about what shapes our subjective experiences, learning sometimes about features of those experiences that went hitherto unnoticed in our take on our own experience. It doesn't take knowledge of neuroscience to recognize that what goes on at any moment in consciousness depends on what goes on outside consciousness, elsewhere and at other times. What breaks through into consciousness owes a great deal to the influences of mechanisms and processes at work below the level of consciousness, as well as to prior conscious memories and experiences that infuse the content of what now occurs in consciousness. We need to study the influence of both. In this way, neuroscientists and philosophers can make more progress by collaborating to bring to light insights about the form and character of conscious experience without fully accounting for what its nature is or having a definitive way to say how there can be such a thing in the first place. We need an account of how things strike us when seeing and hearing, or touching, tasting, and smelling and a way of relating that to what is going on in us and around us to produce those experiences. Working from both sides can provide us with a way to reconcile these very different perspectives, or, at any rate, refine our understanding of the form and character our experiences have, forcing us to ask why we may not always recognize this in having the experiences. Let's consider this in the case of conscious perception.

More than any other dimension of consciousness, what perceptual consciousness puts us directly in touch with is the world, by taking in the scene around us. But as far as accounts of perceptual consciousness go, quite reasonably we might want a little more than a reminder that perception does this for us. We want to know what puts us in the market to take in the details of the world around us, and as part of that, an account of just which details of the world our sensory apparatus equips us to perceive. As so often in the philosophy of perception, one encounters in Honderich's treatment of perceptual consciousness a certain visuo-centrism: what is actual with your perceptual consciousness now, say with your seeing, is indeed a stage or part of what we will get around to calling *a subjective physical world*. But what else is part of that subjective physical world? Does it have a smell, or make a noise? Do the items in your immediate vicinity have a feel? More could be said about how our sensory systems work together to make that world available to us, and to cast light on what they make available, and in what way. The account follows "what is called naive realism, that in perceiving we're in some kind of direct touch with what's out there—not with some image or other representation of it."

"What is actual is in fact not anything in your head. What is actual just *is* a room." But equally clearly it is not just a room. The world is not enough. The presence of some region of space does not require that there is someone perceiving it unless one is an idealist. There need to be some facts about how the perceiver is positioned with respect to that region and why they have the wherewithal to see a room without, say, suffering deficits in consciousness, like unilateral neglect, that would prevent them for seeing all of the room in front of them. What my consciousness encompasses at present is a train carriage. The carriage as seen, and felt through the gentle rocking, the dimly smelled seats, exists out there, but what makes it a *subjective* physical world also owes something to me. It exists just as it is when I fall asleep and switch off. It's being, *subjectively* physical, Honderich tells us, lawfully depends on the objective state of the world and neurally on my brain (presumably, on sensory systems, my prior states of memory and learning, etc.). This is meant to be a perceptually conscious state, and it is supposed to be independent of the other two parts of consciousness, actual thinking and wanting, which involve intentionality or aboutness:

> Your aboutnesses with thinking and wanting being actual also turn out to be their being *subjectively physical but differently so*, not only from the objective physical world but also from your subjective physical world with perceptual consciousness.

But how separate are these subjectively physical worlds? Cognitive effects on perception have to be taken into account, and affective states can have an impact on perception and cognition. Looking around the cabin of an aircraft, what I'd see would look quite different, or at any rate, be experienced differently, by someone who had never been in an aircraft cabin before, or someone who had a fear of flying. The parsing of our experience into the philosophically suggestive parts of perceiving, thinking, and wanting (or affect more generally) may not always be possible. Our conscious experience appears much more unified and indivisible than Honderich's tripartite division proposes, but why doesn't that count in accounting for *actual* consciousness?

Moreover, how things appear to us, even in perceptual consciousness, may not be quite as they seem, and an account of the underlying mechanisms responsible for our perceptual and affective states may help to bring their hidden details to light.

Honderich tells that "there's consciousness in perceiving by the five senses" and that "perceiving as a whole of course comes to more than consciousness, such as facts about eyes," and no doubt in *seeing* we take ourselves to be having a conscious experience created by the eyes—one of the organs of our five senses. But common sense, or the philosopher's gloss on it, can mislead us. We have far more senses than five. For a start, we have a sense of balance, and if it goes awry, lots of other sense experiences are altered and our vision and proprioception (another sense telling us where our limbs are) struggle to compensate. The senses also interact to create the conscious perceptions that we often take to be unisensory. When I am on board a plane and I look along the cabin while the plane is on the ground, I can see where everything is around me. Then I look again when I'm in the climb and now the front of the cabin looks higher than where I am. Of course, it is, but how can it *look* that way when I am in exactly the same optical relations to everything in the cabin? The answer is that what I am experiencing as a case of *seeing* is in fact not a product of the eyes alone but is a product of the visual system and the vestibular system—the system of ear canals that tells me which way is up and whether I'm moving forwards or backwards, up or down. It is because the fluid in my ears moves that I can tell I'm tilting backwards and this influences my vision leading to me "seeing" the front of the cabin as higher than I am. What we take to be a case of seeing is not just that.

And for the fearful passenger across the aisle beside me, each noise and vibration is intensified in signal and perceived as a sign of the aircraft being in danger. What's going on here is that the passenger's internal senses—her interoception that enables her to detect any changes in her internal bodily states such as changes in heart rhythm, or viscera—is ramping up the signal to what would be the appropriate and usual accompaniment when perceiving danger in the environment external. However, in this case, the external environment is not dangerous, but due to the internal state of the phobic flyer which is disrupting the usual matching between the inner and the outer senses, leading the passenger to perceive things in the environment—sounds, vibrations—as dangerous. Here, is a case where the affective state of the consciousness subject changes what Honderich calls the *subjective* physical world of the subject's perception. It can be like this for many of us, in non-phobic conditions, when how we perceive the world around us and ourselves as part of it can shift in balance more from inner to outer or vice versa. Sometimes I am more aware of the world around me; sometimes I am more aware of myself.

Affect and hedonic value can affect what we perceive and may even be a component part of it. Is pain the perception of part of one's body—a part that has undergone some tissue damage? It seems the most irreducible, simple example of a sensation, which is why philosophers often focus on it when talking about consciousness. It is not telling us something about the external world so much as telling us something about us. It is mere modification of consciousness, to use a phrase Willian Lycan once misused to talk about the experiencing of smelling an odour. So we might think of pain as a pure conscious experience. Would Honderich say that it is a perception? It's not the existence of something out there. But nor is it just thinking. It has affect, but it is not like the other states of wanting that Honderich talks about. It seems to be a composite of perception through feeling by touch, and affect or hedonic value; it's aversive. So how should we categorize it? And is it an indefinable, irreducible item of conscious experience, as pure as philosophers would hope to pick out when talking about what it's like. What it's like to feel excruciating pain in one's thigh is just a primitive, an existing item of conscious awareness. However, there is more to be said about that state as we know from work on chronic pain reduction through the technique of deep brain stimulation (DBS). Patients who suffer unrelieved pain that resists treatment by surgery or drugs can be offered DBS. A small hole is drilled in the skull and a wire is carefully inserts deep into the brain in a region called the periaqueductal grey. The wire is then threaded out of the skull under the skin to a battery placed under the skin on the chest. When the current is applied, the patients—who are conscious throughout the operation—will let out a cry of relief. When they are asked if they are still in pain, they will say no. But when asked if they still have the same sensation in the thigh, they will say yes. What we learn from this is that pain is a composite of a sensation or feeling and an aversive reaction to it. The DBS turns off the aversiveness of the pain but leaves the sensation. Cases like these help us see why our ordinary and philosophical ways of thinking about our own conscious experiences can sometimes mislead us and prevent us from making advances on what pain is and how it can be treated. The composite model allows us to understand better how we can empathize with another's pain. We don't feel the sensations others undergo but we can feel the aversiveness when we look at their injuries. (Though we also have some somatosensory activation in the areas corresponding in our body to the observed area on their body where the damage occurs, but without the intense feeling of that sensation.)

Smelling and tasting are cases where we may need to add the hedonic element to characterize the conscious perception correctly. In the case of smell, subjects can be presented under two conditions with the odour compound, isovaleric acid. When told it is a food, they will smell it as Parmesan cheese; when told it is an unpleasant odour, they will perceive it as vomit. The two ways of perceiving it are bound up with how people are thinking about it and the positive or negative hedonic value it has for them. It is not as simple as Honderich thinks to separate perception, cognition, and affect.

What of flashback memories, where the sounds, smells, and sights of a past experience come back to mind involuntarily and vividly. Are these memories just cognitions because they are not the existence of a world depending both on the subject neurally and the world around the subject currently? As conscious experiences, they certainly activate many of the perceptual areas, so while they have a cognitive element they also have a perceptual or quasi-perceptual. That's why theoretical neatness of Honderich's triparte division of consciousness breaks down when it comes to dealing with actual examples.

Finally, we are likely to get aspects of our own experience wrong unless we attend to the empirical details about the neural processes and mechanism that are responsible for those experiences. The case I know best from my own work is the multisensory perception of flavour, which philosophers and the folk routinely mischaracterize as a unisensory experience of tasting.

When people taste food and drink, they mostly believe that what they're experiencing is due to sensations on the tongue. It seems to them that they are relying on their sense of taste to pick up all the flavours they experience when eating and drinking. But this is not the case. In fact, the tongue provides us with very little. All it can provide is experience of the basic tastes due to sweet, salt, sour, bitter, savoury, and metallic receptors on the tongue. That's all we get from taste. Yet, we can "taste" banana, pineapple, peach, mint, mango, strawberry, cinnamon, melon, and raspberry. We don't have raspberry receptors on the tongue, or peach receptors, either. All these fruity flavours are due to smell, or rather, to the combined experience produced by the nose and the tongue.

By smell, here, I don't mean the inhaling of odours from the environment as most philosophers and the folk think of smell, but smell due to the odours rising from the mouth to the nose when we chew our food and swallow it. Swallowing pulses' odours to the receptors in the olfactory epithelium in the nose and together with the tastes from the tongue—salt, sweet, sour, bitter, and so on—that's when we get the integration of taste and smell we call flavour, and the folk call "taste." Gustation and olfaction are fused (or confused) to produce experiences of flavour that we wrongly think we're getting from the tongue. This location illusion is due to oral referral of olfactorily detected features to the tongue. But it's not just taste and (retronasal) olfaction that get combined. Touch plays a role in food flavours, making what we eat creamy or sticky, crunchy or smooth. And our conscious perception of the flavours of the foods and liquids we consume is due to the multisensory integration of these different sensory inputs, resulting in a single, unified experience of flavour.[1]

Vanilla ice cream has cream, eggs, milk, sugar, and vanilla. If asked to smell a vanilla pod, we will say it smells sweet, although sweet is a taste, not a smell, and the vanilla pod tastes bitter and has no sugar in it. Rather, it is the combination of vanilla aroma and sugar, and the creaminess of its texture, and the coldness of its temperature, that produce the flavour of vanilla ice cream.

When consulting their own experience of eating, people are inclined to say that they are having experiences they take to be tastes, and they fail to see that these experiences of flavour (not taste) are the result of a complex interaction effect involving touch, taste, and smell. The failure is in part due to the inability to do phenomenological decomposition of the tasting experience into its component parts. In particular, we cannot pull apart taste proper from the tongue and retronasal olfaction once they have been fused. Only by wearing a nose clip to eat the food without the contribution of smell can one distinguish what the tongue provides from the whole experience of a food's flavour. Though sometimes we can do it. Take a menthol lozenge. It's "taste" (flavour) comprises at least three things: a minty aroma, a slightly bitter taste, and a cool sensation in the mouth. Take any one of these away and it's not the "taste" (flavour) of menthol we're getting anymore.

What we are increasingly learning from cognitive neuroscience is that the multisensory integration of different sensory inputs is not the exception but the rule in explaining how our experiences come about. Our own reflections on our experiences do not tell us that at first and we have to be brought to look more closely at those experiences through understanding more about the processes that produce them.

The moral is that we cannot rely on just our intuitive take on our own experience to know what is going on there. What we seem to pick out, whether by misleading talk of "what it's like" or by "untutored attention," does not necessarily provide constraints on account of the nature of consciousness. Instead, we need philosophers, psychologists, and neuroscientists working together to elicit information from different sources in order to arrive at a collective view of how the different types of evidence and information fit together to produce the best explanation of the phenomena of consciousness we are interested. We have only recently begun that task but I think a large-scale, collaborative, and interdisciplinary project will, bit by bit, yield results, and will provide a useful corrective to the wrong turns we can take by assuming we have effortless, transparent, and accurate access to our own conscious experience.[2]

Notes

1. For an account of all the senses involved in the multisensory perception of flavour, see Smith (2015).
2. In writing this chapter I was hugely helped by talks with Tony Marcel and Sarah Garfinkel to whom I'm very grateful. Any weaknesses in the text are mine.

References

Dennett, Daniel C. 1991. *Consciousness explained*. New York: Little Brown.

Honderich, Ted. 1988. *A theory of determinism: The mind, neuroscience and life hopes*. Oxford: Oxford University Press.

———. 2014. *Actual consciousness*. Oxford: Oxford University Press.

———. 2017. *MIND: Your being conscious is what and where?* Chicago: Chicago University Press. [Cited page numbers are to the penultimate draft and not the published version.]

Marcel, A.J. 1993. Slippage in the unity of consciousness. In *Experimental and theoretical STUDIES of consciousness*, ed. G.R. Bock and J. Marsh, 168–179. Chichester: Wiley.

———. 2003. Introspective report: Trust, self-knowledge and science. *Journal of Consciousness Studies* 10: 167–186.

Rosenthal, David. 1986. Two concepts of consciousness. *Philosophical Studies* 49 (3): 329–359.

Smith, Barry C. 2006. Consciousness: An inner view of the outer world. *Journal of Consciousness Studies* 13 (7–8): 175–186.

———. 2015. The chemical senses. In *The Oxford handbook of philosophy of perception*, ed. Mohan Matthen, 314–352. New York: Oxford University Press.

7

Remarks on Consciousness Chapters

Ted Honderich

7.1 On Chomsky

The chapter by Noam Chomsky, of whom no reader of this book needs an introduction, is replete in uses of the science of linguistics as well as other propositions, conceptions, consonances—and flying buttresses from ancient philosophy. This little cathedral is a whole sequence of, by my count, 17 more particular and more general premises for his general conclusion against the possibility of what I contemplate my Actualism to be, an (or indeed the) adequate theory of consciousness. A theory in the sense of an explanation or understanding of what consciousness is, its nature. My response here, as in the case of other contributors, can only be remarks. These, which can do no more than touch on Chomsky's premises, will be more or less in the order of their first appearances.

After his good abstract, Chomsky immediately begins progress towards his general conclusion about Actualism in particular being no adequate theory of consciousness.

T. Honderich (✉)
University College London, London, UK

G. D. Caruso (ed.), *Ted Honderich on Consciousness, Determinism, and Humanity*, Philosophers in Depth, https://doi.org/10.1007/978-3-319-66754-6_7

He first reports that I have taken unconscious mentality to *be* only what has long been familiar to philosophers as *dispositional* as against *occurrent* belief. Say my ongoing dispositional belief that my legal name is Edgar a minute ago when in fact in an ordinary sense I was then thinking about only consciousness.

His mistake there is my fault. I somewhere mentioned dispositional belief as a large *example* of unconscious mentality, all of which I do conceive initially more or less as he does—as against consciousness in general. I did write about unconscious and conscious states in a careless use of a verb that it would be a fundamental mistake to *link* them—I meant to make them something like or on the way to identical in whole natures.

In fact in my Actualism, like Chomsky, at least in part, I have always taken it to be true that conscious and unconscious states *are* linked in the quite different sense of being lawfully connected. They are so most obviously in unconscious states being causally explanatory for at least most conscious states. Is it implied by Chomsky that unconscious states are also what you can bravely call related conceptually or maybe proto-conceptually to conscious states? Like Ouija boards, old adding machines, pocket calculators, and computers? All of which involve concepts but not in the sense of being themselves in any way conscious.

With respect to lawful connection in general, perhaps better understood in philosophy than science, it is not arcane. It is *whatever-else* connection. The understanding of that begins from but goes beyond entirely ordinary conditional or if-then statements. If it rained last night, the grass will be wet. But take the simplest case of lawful connection, an earlier complete *causal circumstance*, sometimes called a sufficient condition, for an effect. What the connection comes to is that whatever else is also the case, the circumstance's effect follows. Simultaneous lawful correlates, not causal, get basically the same sort of whatever-else analysis.

Of Chomsky's more general premises for Actualism being no adequate theory, the main and first premise, as I take it with some hesitation, is that elements of consciousness in general cannot be *extricated* without seriously misrepresenting mental life. My hesitation has to do with whether there being no extrication *is* itself the fact of the impossibility of a theory of consciousness. Anyway, conscious and unconscious states are related so closely in explanation of behaviour and thought that we cannot *free* the conscious ones from the unconscious ones and in particular come to an understanding of the conscious ones, given their nature. We cannot get to that goal of the philosophy of mind and whatever else.

Of Chomsky's more particular premises, the first one is that both our conscious and unconscious events and states are 99% of them uses of language—at least including talking to ourselves, inner speech. Thus, consciousness itself is immediately a matter of a defeating richness, indeed more than that, the defeating richness of language. Consciousness is, or includes, a myriad complexities found and struggled with in linguistics—the science rescued from behaviourism by Chomsky himself in the past.

This first more particular premise, the 99% one, is in my view false—whatever follows or does not follow from the falsehood. It is commonsensical that consciousness in general does indeed divide into perceptual, cognitive, and affective sides. That, by the way, is the fact in *all* philosophy and science of consciousness when it is not concerning itself with the entirely general question—and forgetting itself. The perceptual side, in a sentence, is the *actuality*, on analysis a certain physicality, of a subjective physical world, not representations of it or anything else, certainly not language.

The second more particular premise is that the science and other inquiry into consciousness will continue to encounter secrets of nature, inconceivabilities, the results of God's workings incomprehensible to us, ultimate absurdities, astonishing things, obscurities, proclaimed in the seventeenth century by the philosopher Locke with Newton's respect to Newton's gravity and other physical attractions and forces.

A question here in passing: Does Chomsky persist in his known previous judgement that since the rise of modern science, far beyond seventeenth-century particles, there has been no adequate conception of the physical? With the result that there is at least insufficient sense in the question of mind and brain, the mind-body problem? The problem which has in it and indeed depends absolutely on the problem of *what* consciousness is? I disagree, to say the least, about physicality being weak talk or worse, and here I may have the small satisfaction not only of worker consensus but of being one with the rest of mankind, almost all science and philosophy.

A third premise for no adequate theory of consciousness. Alan Turing of that well-known intelligence test is cited at least partly in support of the proposition that the subject of *thinking* is at least obscure. For me, and maybe you now or on one day to come, ordinary thinking and ordinary wanting consist in cognitive and affective consciousness—representations-with-attitudes. Representations are of course fundamentally different from the printed words on this page, different in being, in a clarified sense, *actual* and thus on further inquiry *subjectively physical.*

Then Chomsky's additional fourth premise, from the philosopher Wittgenstein, that we say not only of ourselves but also of dolls and spirits that they think. I excuse myself from work on this profundity by remembering that Wittgenstein was also the author of, among other things, the news that "no supposition seems more natural than that there is no process in the brain correlated with associating or thinking."

To come now to a premise not at all owed to a seer, there is Chomsky's notable and indeed promising fact of a shared conviction of ours. It is our saying to ourselves on occasion that a thing now said by us must before now have been in *the back of the mind.* A thought was forming without consciousness and furthermore inaccessible to consciousness. Yes, a great little indicator of the existence of unconsciousness, but much of a premise for the conclusion to come.

Now the related large problem about our consciousness, certainly about what is in consciousness, is raised by the ancient Greek. How is it that anyone can step into the same river twice—the general question of identity, of what makes anything the same thing again? It occurs to me to ask how it is that the identity problem, which presumably arises for anything whatever, makes consciousness especially difficult.

Then the premise for no theory that is the fact of the use of entirely ordinary concepts such as that of *a house*—of so much greater difficulty than allowed by Aristotle in taking it to be difficulty of matter and form, mind-dependence, and so on.

And also as far back as Aristotle great problems, solutions unknown, with what are called *mental universals* in unconscious mentality, say about word meanings. Here and elsewhere, there is the implication that the philosophy of mind needs linguistics—and maybe cannot get from it the help it needs.

To come to what are called representationalist doctrines, we are told they are a simplification, also false, of human thought and language. I repeat here the necessary reassurance that thanks to Actualism there is an immense difference between any thought or feeling of yours and just a printed representation on a page. And that any theory of consciousness that found *no* place for aboutness in consciousness could surely not demand attention? Nor should one, as you have already heard, that makes *all* consciousness into representation, including consciousness in just seeing a room.

Accept, I must, the next proposition, that human thought and language is not the lesser symbolic system of other animals, not as simple.

More generally, and beyond what was said earlier, there are proliferating real problems of language, such as ambiguities, the stuff of linguistics—and thought just *is* language. Just is that, I take it, despite the existence of mental imagery, on which there exists an excellent unmodish book. So, all the problems of language are problems of both consciousness and unconsciousness.

There is also the related fact that there is rule-following in unconscious mentality.

Again more generally, as you may indeed believe, have come to believe more, states of consciousness and unconsciousness interweave, and are interwoven, inextricably. There is intimate interplay, intermingling, interaction, between consciousness and unconsciousness in explanation of behaviour and thought. Fundamental to human nature it all is.

And there are indeed facts of unconscious mentality of which it is said, a little puzzlingly, that it will stay wholly inaccessible at *any* time to introspection. They issue in conscious events and states but are never in consciousness themselves.

There are in addition puzzling kinds of reasoning in unconscious mentality, one having to do with choices of theories, which choices are not at all just simple deductions but rather what is called abduction.

The neuroscientist Libet's results show that inaccessible unconscious processes intermingle with conscious processes. No doubt true, as you will have already come to believe. But it is hard for me to resist remembering that a scientist can begin by finding a fact of unconsciousness and then, conceivably, after seeing it as fatal to the free will he believes in, and finds some very different, science.

Finally, in this list of reasons for no understanding of consciousness, of what leads to voluntary motion, there are unconscious processes about which we do not know. Leading neuroscientists say "we are beginning to understand the puppet and the strings, but have no ideas about the puppeteer." So we're not yet out of sight of a soul moving a machine? I do indeed trust otherwise, but….

In all of that, from the 99% reason about language and consciousness, you have a fast recollection of what it is best to take as Chomsky's more particular and more general premises for his main thesis. That, as you have heard, is that our mental life, this being consciousness and unconsciousness, is such that no general theory of the nature of consciousness, including my Actualism theory, is possible. No adequate theory of unconsciousness either, I take it, although this is not mentioned, for the same reasons.

Is there a good reply?

All theories, whatever they are, I take it, are explanations of four kinds: Explanations *of* a thing, giving its nature, all of its own nature, saying what it is. Explanations of *why* a thing is as it is. These second explanations typically are of its causation—its being in other lawful connection with something else or a good deal else. There are also, thirdly, explanations by effects of a thing, saying what it does. And, fourthly, there are complete explanations: nature, causes, effects.

Does it follow from the pile of difficulties with consciousness, and with unconscious relations between them, that we can't give a general account of consciousness? That is the big question.

Before responding, I note that it is hard to resist the temptation of the idea that there is an inconsistency in Chomsky's position. He in effect says of two things at least for a start that they can't be separated. Then how did he understand them in order to do this? He's isn't just saying, is he, of two things, each of which he also says he knows not what they are, that they can't be freed in some way? He doesn't have just vague impressions of the two realms, does he? That would also stand in the way of knowing what the items are that turn up in the problems in the list, not to mention the general conclusion.

Does he, being a sensible fellow, in some such way as me, have something like Actualism's guiding idea of consciousness? A sensible but not perfectly consistent fellow? Maybe like me elsewhere.

To come closer to my conclusion, there is the pretty good fact that something's being made up of a multitude of stuff, and somehow dependent on a second multitude of stuff, simply does not entail that there is *no* general truth, no adequate summation of either the first or the second lot. That is the case even before doubts about some of the stuff.

My reply to Chomsky's seeming charge that I do not and that none of us can distinguish conscious mentality, consciousness, from unconscious mentality: I of course say flatly that I do distinguish them. I do so by (i) a reliance only on our holds on our consciousnesses as against unconscious mentality, these holds not being funny introspections but plain rememberings of what our particular consciousnesses a moment ago were like, (ii) adequately initially clarifying consciousness by way of a large and shared figurative database, (iii) the resulting general and still figurative characterization of consciousness as *something's being actual*, (iv) the literal and full specification of physicalities in general, (v) including the literal and fully specified different subjective physicalities with perceptual, cognitive, and affective consciousness.

Of course I take all that to distinguish conscious from unconscious mentality successfully. It includes, of course, an essential distinguishing of unconscious mentality.

I cannot resist something else relevant: a certain comparison. Armed as I am, if you will tolerate that verb 'armed', only by my boy's own science, I take it with certainty that the very greatest of theories, those of Darwin and Wallace, allow for at least perfectly adequate conceptions of two large things: *environmental change in general* and *variation of species in general.*

The theory is that some of the first is in the explanation of some of the second—explanation in a sense with which philosophy can help. And of course, as can be added, some of the second is in due course explanatory of the first—think in particular of our own species or prior species resulting in environmental change.

But now consider the wonderful richness and whatever falls under the first description 'environmental change in general', and the wonderful richness and many kinds of problems of whatever falls under the second description, 'variation of species in general'—and think in particular of our own species. Do these richnesses and problems destroy, disable, impede, or embarrass the theory of evolution? Patently they do not. Why should they?

So with much else in science, there is a counterpart fact with the lesser theory of Actualism. All I do allow is that I have never gone further than absolutely necessary in speaking of and inquiring into unconscious mentality. There was no real need for more.

I make more explicit something else. Actualism must and does allow of course for causal explanations of some facts of unconscious mentality partly by consciousness—and of course for more and different facts of consciousnesses being explained by unconscious mentality. Do the wonderful complexities of either body of facts stand in the way of these explanations? No more than complexity in Darwin and Wallace.

My conclusion is indeed that you certainly can't establish Chomsky's thesis if there is quite *other* and *independent* argument that does establish, confirm, or anyway tell strongly for the conclusion that there *is* what is denied to exist—a theory of what consciousness is.

You have heard that there is such an argument. It was sketched in the introduction to this book. It principally included a lot: (1) a database on ordinary consciousness, something different in kind from the run of arguments above, and then a good deal more; (2) a database on physicality and the difference of consciousness within it; (3) criteria got from failing theories of consciousness; (4) the general characterization of consciousness as something's being actual; (5) progress to literalness in place of figurativeness; (6) clarified accounts in terms of subjective physicalities; (7) various incidentals; and, finally, (8) table of physicality generally and the species under it.

A final question: Is Chomsky's line of reflection not a refutation of Actualism but something else—a reason for a good addition to the exposition of it? A making more explicit of something? Yes. His line of reflection is reason to give more attention to unconscious as against conscious mentality. We can do that right now right here by improving that table of physicalities. By adding a fourth column to the previous three. Yes, a column having to do with unconscious mentality—which of course as causal tells you of conscious mentality. Here is the new table of physicalities (Table 7.1).

So, my conclusion is that it simply does not follow from the many given premises about two categories of things that there can be no adequate general account of either. Noam's main thesis doesn't have premises as good as the premises of Actualism.

Table 7.1 Enlarged table of physicalities in general

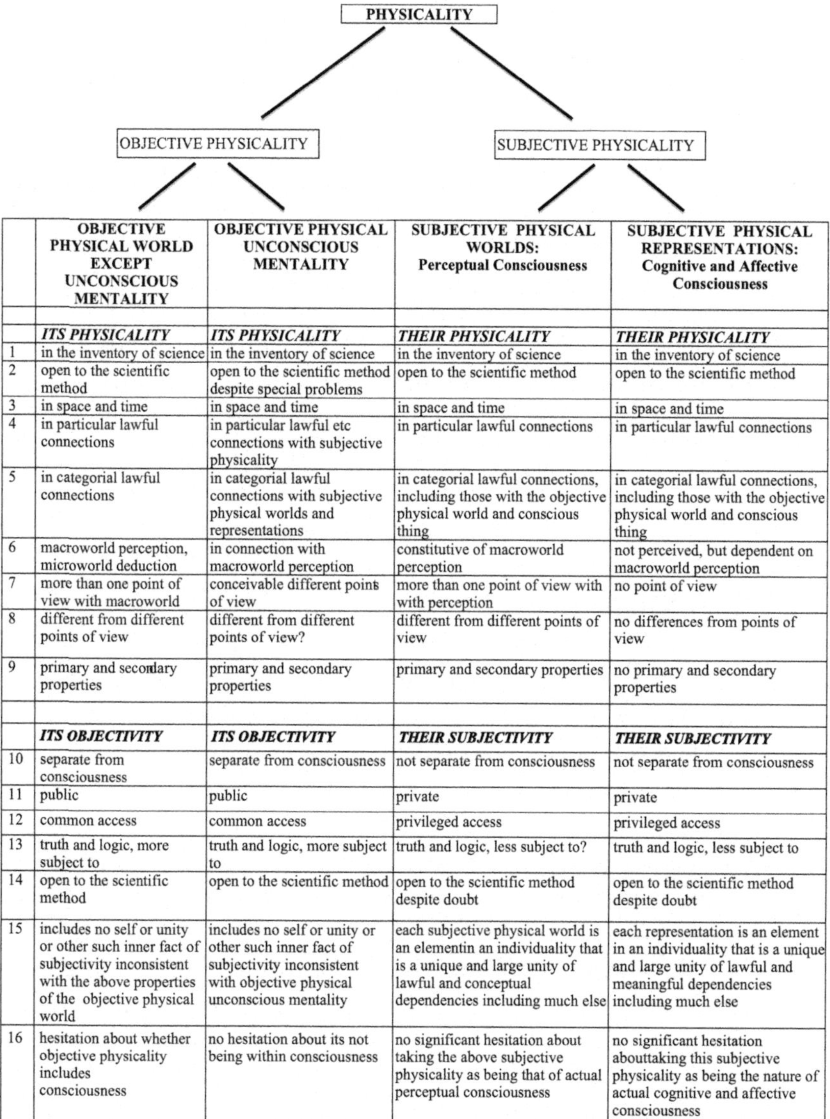

	OBJECTIVE PHYSICAL WORLD EXCEPT UNCONSCIOUS MENTALITY	**OBJECTIVE PHYSICAL UNCONSCIOUS MENTALITY**	**SUBJECTIVE PHYSICAL WORLDS: Perceptual Consciousness**	**SUBJECTIVE PHYSICAL REPRESENTATIONS: Cognitive and Affective Consciousness**
	ITS PHYSICALITY	***ITS PHYSICALITY***	***THEIR PHYSICALITY***	***THEIR PHYSICALITY***
1	in the inventory of science	in the inventory of science	in the inventory of science	in the inventory of science
2	open to the scientific method	open to the scientific method despite special problems	open to the scientific method	open to the scientific method
3	in space and time	in space and time	in space and time	in space and time
4	in particular lawful connections	in particular lawful etc connections with subjective physicality	in particular lawful connections	in particular lawful connections
5	in categorial lawful connections	in categorial lawful connections with subjective physical worlds and representations	in categorial lawful connections, including those with the objective physical world and conscious thing	in categorial lawful connections, including those with the objective physical world and conscious thing
6	macroworld perception, microworld deduction	in connection with macroworld perception	constitutive of macroworld perception	not perceived, but dependent on macroworld perception
7	more than one point of view with macroworld	conceivable different poins of view	more than one point of view with with perception	no point of view
8	different from different points of view	different from different points of view?	different from different points of view	no differences from points of view
9	primary and secondary properties	primary and secondary properties	primary and secondary properties	no primary and secondary properties
	ITS OBJECTIVITY	***ITS OBJECTIVITY***	***THEIR SUBJECTIVITY***	***THEIR SUBJECTIVITY***
10	separate from consciousness	separate from consciousness	not separate from consciousness	not separate from consciousness
11	public	public	private	private
12	common access	common access	privileged access	privileged access
13	truth and logic, more subject to	truth and logic, more subject to	truth and logic, less subject to?	truth and logic, less subject to
14	open to the scientific method	open to the scientific method	open to the scientific method despite doubt	open to the scientific method despite doubt
15	includes no self or unity or other such inner fact of subjectivity inconsistent with the above properties of the objective physical world	includes no self or unity or other such inner fact of subjectivity inconsistent with objective physical unconscious mentality	each subjective physical world is an elementin an individuality that is a unique and large unity of lawful and conceptual dependencies including much else	each representation is an element in an individuality that is a unique and large unity of lawful and meaningful dependencies including much else
16	hesitation about whether objective physicality includes consciousness	no hesitation about its not being within consciousness	no significant hesitation about taking the above subjective physicality as being that of actual perceptual consciousness	no significant hesitation abouttaking this subjective physicality as being the nature of actual cognitive and affective consciousness

I give in also to adding, since we are both claiming to be in touch with reality, or realities, that Actualism (9) makes clear sense of what has been the mystery of *subjectivity* with respect to consciousness—makes sense of it as individuality, personal identity. Subjectivity doesn't have to be a matter of just gesturing anymore. And (10) Actualism as a theory is at least a workplace. Fertile or productive for science including linguistics as well as for philosophy? And one more question—Is Actualism a *naturalism*? I say yes, aided by a certain decent definition.

Could it be that what has led to the divergence between Chomsky and me, a little embarrassingly, has as much to do with intellectual or anyway mental *inclinations* in inquiry, maybe *personalities* in inquiry, not pure inquiry itself? The way of science and the way of philosophy? Inclinations and personalities not much less real in science? Are we both keeping faith with a chosen respectable line of life?

But I could not be what I am, Chomsky's ally and in a way his follower in what is greatly more important, morals and politics, and not be true also to the extents of our difference about the lesser subject of consciousness.

* * *

7.2 On Snowdon

Paul Snowdon, as philosopher of Oxford and University College London, puts me in mind of the mild and seemingly tolerant prosecutor in a court of law who by knowing his line of life well and by orderly good sense still does not leave the accused overconfident. He provides a good piece of support for the idea that there is a likeness between philosophy and the practice of law, that they are both advocacies despite their differences. Still, the defendant can recover calm, return to a confidence, by way of the thought that in philosophy the final judgement is never today.

Paul, another sitter in the Grote chair at University College London, is like other contributors to this book, including lecturers on the day that prompted it, has more things to say than can even be remarked on in a couple of thousand words.

From the beginning he helps out his resolute project by what is not a ploy but certainly is a tactical insistence. He uses the term *physicalism* by itself in a certain way, for only *objective, scientific, standard,* or *devout physicalism*, what has traditionally been called *materialism*—and hence names me as an *anti-physicalist*. But I too *am* a physicalist: firstly, in the sense that I explicitly take consciousness to be within the genus *physicality in general*, and, secondly, in that I give full content to naming and explaining consciousness as subjectively physical. There are those 16 listed and very related characteristics of each of the species *objective physicality* and subjective physicality in my table of physicality in general.

As with most other chapters in this book, there is no possibility of defence against all the imputations against Actualism. Can I unsettle a jury generally by a selection of evidence?

Paul says about my beginning that no sane person would deny what I say, that when we are conscious, "something is actually going on." Agreed, but what I proposed was not that truism that there is some or other process or event happening. Rather, there is a process or event that has that character indicated in the database of figurative descriptions and summed up figuratively as the process of *something's being actual*—on which there was subsequently so much labour into literalness.

He considers my conviction that philosophers and others have at least often in effect had different things in mind in talking of consciousness, and that this has been an explanation of no agreement about what it is. He supposes my conviction was put forward only or mainly on a certain basis—what I called five recent leading ideas of consciousness—qualia, something it's like for a thing to be that thing, subjectivity, intentionality, and phenomenality. Paul objects that the ideas are or can be taken as being about the same basic phenomenon, and that the ideas are not incompatible.

I of course agree that in a sense they were talking about the same basic phenomenon—consciousness. That, of course, was assumed by me. And since they were doing that, and since each of them at least implied that he or she was giving the true or useful or best summary of consciousness, they were for that reason alone making incompatible claims. Of course the antecedent of that proposition is not simple, but how much philosophy would survive if it had to pass the implied test of being simple in that way?

Anyway, the idea that philosophers have been talking about different things wasn't based only on the five theories. It was as much based on a pile of other theories past and present—panpsychism, special contemporary physicalisms, naturalisms, and all the other controversy and mystery about consciousness.

And, to add a new thought as of this very day, consider the readiness of so many of us, philosophers, scientists, and the rest, to be undecided, in ongoing uncertainty, about whether consciousness is objectively physical or not. If you haven't got some confidence about that, *can* you have any first confidence about what consciousness is, what you're asking the question about?

But in fact we might scrap all that reflection of mine on the history and present of the philosophy of mind and the five leading ideas—and still think that the best way to proceed is to come to your own best clarification of consciousness, by way of the database, and proceed from there to a theory of its nature.

Paul of course is committed or more than inclined to objective physicalism about consciousness. He does not deal effectively, I say, with my depending in this issue partly on a fundamental criterion here for a good theory of consciousness—that consciousness is *different* from the rest of what there is. That is a source, of course, a main source, of my taking consciousness to be subjectively rather than objectively physical.

It is not fundamentally the same kind of stuff as the chair you're sitting on. I agree that talk of "stuff" is loose, by the way, and will try to do better.

He also objects that while we all take consciousness to be different in physicality from the chair, we don't all take it to be different in kind from a rather special kind of matter, certainly not the kind in the chairs. Rather, the kind in brains. He has in mind what I earlier spoke of as "wondrously complex but still only neural networks, networks of cells, in both cases fundamentally the kind of thing as the chair…."

Well, I stand by pretty much my judgement that the criterion includes that we do indeed take consciousness to be different from just neurons. Each of us has what has been called by me his or her *hold* on his or her conscious events and states. That is of course another of my premises. That is why abstract functionalists, to mention only them, but also various philosophers and scientists of consciousness, do not identify the consciousness with the neurons. It is why various objective physicalists try themselves about consciousness and the mind, say Dan Dennett for just a good start, to think up ingenious ideas that also somehow distinguish the consciousness from just neurons.

To come on to something else, it sure took me aback to hear from Paul that Actualism, since it distinguishes consciousness from objective physical states and events, is or resembles Property Dualism. That dualism takes mind and I guess consciousness in particular to consist in brain properties and also those other properties—properties with something of the character assigned to a funny self or subject or the like in Substance Dualism.

Your honour, I am a witness a world away from Property Dualism. See my table of physicalities, that culminating summary of Actualism—the columns in it about sides of consciousness. Whatever you think of Paul's superiorities to it, there's no lingering spiritualism in there at all. And in particular, with perceptual consciousness, Actualism gives it a partly externalist nature as distinct from any "in the head" stuff. Also, any brain-mind dualism is to the effect that something has both physical and *non-physical* properties. In Actualism *all* properties are generically physical.

Paul himself, by the way, *is* in danger of being told by a judge that he is an undeclared or closet property-dualist, anyway on the way to it. He says towards the end of his submission that as a philosopher he cannot decide on a relevant question of physicality. He has to wait for science.

But, not to linger on that point, should we all take his advice and go back to square one and start again and think not about consciousness but rather something else—*experience*? It surely is not the case, as he says, that what has struck philosophers as puzzling is experience rather than consciousness. Of course, Actualism contains an account of perceptual consciousness, which is much of what is called experience. I'd say consciousness contributes more to understanding of experience than experience contributes to understanding of consciousness.

Yes, my subject of course has been all of consciousness, consciousness in general, as well as each of the three sides of it. Is there idiosyncrasy in Snowdon's proposal? One or more of us may come to an opinion about that. But I do now remain calm in my choices of both consciousness as a subject matter and also three parts of it.

With respect to perceptual consciousness, he is shocked by my *two* rooms, the objective and the subjective ones. Two rooms? Two rooms! And out there! Yes, of course, it's a shock. Enough to make a philosopher on his pension say these aren't the good old days. But, I say, there can still be days of argument together with empiricisms rather than convention. Actualism about perceptual consciousness is a line of argument explicit and fully articulated, not stuff in mother's milk, not piety. Actualism, I bravely say, does give "solid support" to its shocking conclusion. Not something unknown in philosophy, or indeed in science.

Yes, we are instructed by conventionalists that we perceivers have no reason for taking a subjective physical world to have those spatial characteristics, to be out there—not in the head. Well, I seem to have the good reason for starters, even before we get to the line of argument, that that is my *hold* with respect to my perceptual consciousness. It lets me know. Very different indeed from my hold on my thinking and wanting.

I can, as a fact of my location in my subjective physical world, take measurements as to how far that wall is from me—the person, by the way, whose personal identity including a body, a clear personal identity being something else contributed to our philosophical well-being by Actualism. But I guess this is not the place for a listing of the theory's incidental contributions.

But there's something else. There's that amount of progress in argument from the database through other theories than Actualism, criteria for a good theory of consciousness, objective physicality, and the wholly unavoidable two questions "What is actual?" and "What is it for to be actual?"

Towards the end of his submission, as I've already remarked, he says that philosophers have to remain in doubt about whether consciousness is objectively physical. They haven't got the tools to answer the question yes or no. Well, I agree they haven't got the tools of science. And, I add, the practice of science doesn't have what is a pretty good old tool—the ordinary logic concentration of philosophy that is clarity, consistency and validity, generality, and completeness. Yes, of course, philosophy doesn't have the tools to go down into depth of detail with respect to brain and consciousness.

Does that stand in the way of its making a general case against objective physicalism about consciousness? No, Your Honour.

To come now to what affected me most in Paul's chapter, it was the middle sentence of its last paragraph.

"I suspect the same can be said of Ted Honderich as he sat in the chair in the room focused on a long-term battle with himself and others on this most complex of questions: the nature of consciousness. The room is actual and it is there, and it is still up there when he goes downstairs. But once the clutter of sense data, qualia, raw feels, and 'What it is like to be…' has been brushed aside, there is quite a lot more to unpack in actuality than just the chair and the room."

Does that second sentence mean that when I go downstairs and there is no one where there was an actual room, a subjective physical room, it itself is still there? It is one great nub of actualism that that is false. What there is, there is the objectively physical room. Yes, what was a subjective physical room has gone—better to say, maybe a stage of a subjectively physical room.

Whether or not Paul is thinking and maybe feeling it and responding to it by a denial owed to incredulity that is not Actualism. In the absence of a lawful dependency on me neurally, a necessary condition, when I am going downstairs, there is no such subjective room. Subjectively physical staircase, yes; such a room, no.

You may well recoil or recoil again from this nub and outrage of Actualism. You are not the first. And if I do in sense understand your recoil, I do not join you. Why?

Well, I rehearse the whole line of thinking that issues in the shock. (1) From a database we have it that being conscious is best clarified initially as the subject of something's being actual. (2) We cannot but think of some or other existence here. (3) There is prompted the possible response that the thing is physical in the ordinary sense, objectively physical, when that is surely rightly or anyway reasonably seen in terms of 16 characteristics it is evident that some of them stand in the way of an actual thing's being objectively physical. (4) As clearly, what is actual is what has partly identical but partly different characteristics.

There is, I take it, no possibility here for dispute. In which case, what is new, surprising and indeed shocking is true. To say otherwise of you in your all too human way, what is required of you is not exclamation marks. It is a disproof of the line of fact and argument leading to the shock. You may guess that I myself had more than one looks without success. I did not set out to be dramatic in philosophy.

There are too many more things of at least interest in Paul's submission for me to have dealt with them all here. What I have done is indicate at least some doubt with some things, I guess with the further intention of raising a little doubt about others. But a final brave piece of self-defence. The main line of argument in Actualism is strong enough to make weaknesses of detail temporary.

We have also exchanged prolonged friendly fire in the past. See the bibliography for an earlier book on *Radical Externalism*, the early sister of Actualism.

* * *

7.3 On Hannay

Alastair Hannay is the principal philosophical elucidator and translator in the English language of Soren Kierkegaard, the great Danish, personal, and religious existentialist. Hannay himself is a Scot, educated in philosophy first in Edinburgh, then at University College London. After higher instruction in the latter place of both of us, by A.J. Ayer and Bernard Williams et al., he took himself to Scandinavia. He became a professor at Oslo, and subsequently spent time as a research associate in the University of California at Berkely and as an academic visitor to the London School of Economics. To his work on Kierkegaard he added the books *Mental Images: A Defence* and *Human Consciousness*, while editing the principal philosophy journal *Inquiry*. Lately there have been forays in philosophical autobiography.

He begins his piece here with Naive Realism, so named by Ayer, to the effect that in seeing and other perception we are in direct touch with the objective physical world as traditionally understood, the world that is as there when it is unperceived. Seeing is not being in touch with representations or aboutnesses of any kind, seeing is not a kind of mental television. If Naive Realism is folk philosophy, which it is, to be put beside folk psychology, it also has its philosopher-defenders.

It is indeed to the effect that in seeing and other perception we are in something or other called direct touch with the objective physical world. Seeing and other perceiving is not a matter of sense data, images, qualia, content, or the like between us and the world. That is stuff that needs to be brushed aside. Seeing and other perceiving, as Alastair reports, delivers the world out there to us *clean*.

I agree that Actualism, if only insofar as it is about perceptual consciousness as against cognitive and affective consciousness, is *more* related to Naive Realism, also spoken of as Direct Realism, than to any other previous idea of or declaration on perceptual consciousness. Actualism inherits the vague strength of Naive Realism but goes far beyond it, certainly into the entire literalness. Also, it is at all like Naive Realism with respect only to perceptual consciousness. Neither the folk nor the philosophers inclined to Naive Realism so far as I know have got beyond essentially the expression of the view as just stated—indeed the mere words of it. The metaphorical relation of direct touch, I take it, has gone entirely unexplained.

In particular no Naive Realist, I think, has delayed long enough to get the objective world straight, say what it comes to, let alone find another one. There has been no ordered sequence of inquiry. None of an initial clarification of consciousness in a database, as something's being actual or anything else, or attention to the three sides of consciousness in treating of the whole of it, or criteria for a theory of consciousness better than existing theories, or relevant analyses of any physicality, or literal explanation of what is actual and what being actual is in each of the three sides, or resulting clarity on the mind-body or mind-brain relation.

Alastair and I are in agreement that there is less sense than common sense in the hopeless uninformativeness of Naive Realism. I take it we may also be in an agreement about the traditional stock-in-trade with respect to perceptual consciousness of the traditional adversaries of Naive Realism—that stock he speaks of, for himself rather than for me, I take it, as that rubbish and clutter of images, sense data, and the like.

Actualism might be thought to go further than any other developed theory in giving satisfaction to the inclination or conviction we have about subjectivity with consciousness. In terms of the order of exposition of it, there is the database, its issue in the clarification of consciousness as actuality, the seven expounded subjectivities recorded in the table that summarizes it, and the unity of the consciousness of each of us that is no matter of gesturing but is clear individuality and personal identity—in each of the three sides of consciousness that past complete or general theories of consciousness do not really distinguish.

There is no gesturing there, none of the elusiveness of intimations of *spirit*, none of the vagueness of ordinary philosophical talk of an inner entity that each of us is—no lack of the clarity and just existence that the really level-headed Hume could not espy when he tried to look inward and espy the traditional self urged on him. There is also the particular fact of subjective physical worlds and of course subjective physicality generally.

The burden of Alastair's chapter is that Actualism, despite all that, just fails really to register the facts of subjectivity or subjectivities of different kinds—that is, different facts of the likes of *you* for you in what we can hopefully call your most inner and most evocative use of that pronoun "I." Such a subject is taken as much involved, although presumably somewhat differently, in the consciousness of seeing and the rest of perceptual consciousness as in any other consciousness. Such a subject is at least part, in terms of Alastair's title, of what really needs to be unpacked in our understanding of ordinary consciousness.

There is no doubt that Alastair does not suppose that such subjects are adequately clarified—think of yourself here and elsewhere—as what I myself speak of as that *unity* with respect to your perceptual, cognitive, and affective consciousness. Such a unity, to be quick, is made such by connections between its elements in a corpus, causal, and other lawful connections and connections of meaning in a very wide sense, certainly connections of memory. What is sometimes called an organic unity? It is close enough to be true, then, that subjects and the fact of their subjectivity in the given sense amount to pretty much the same thing as something else that has been taken as at least problematic, personal identity. *Who* you are is the unity of consciousness you are, memories being important but not nearly all of the fact.

In his view, maybe, Actualism needs to be more replaced than supplemented by his other ideas. He, to repeat, takes perceptual consciousness as well as cognitive and affective consciousness to be best thought of and thought about, indeed understood, in terms of subjectivity where that is something or rather is several things taken having to do with a self, agent, ego, inner entity, or the like—a *subject* in common philosophical parlance. But, at least surprisingly, a self, such as the more or less level-headed French thinker Montaigne did not take to be just one thing.

Alastair speaks of a subject impressionistically in terms of a "subject pole" and an "object pole" in consciousness, of some world as a *life-place*, and of *the living of a life*, and of familiarity. And he says in an elucidatory email to me that for him "The objective physical world contains no chair as such, just the physical facts since the chair-ness of those facts is a subjective feature contained in the language and practices that we are brought up in. You may differ on this, but...." Well, I do want to differ from this demotion of objectively physical chairs, but....

In general, importantly since I trust that there is no dualism or spiritualism in all of his thinking, I do not deny the existence of his facts of what can certainly be called subjectivity. But they are things that Actualism can accommodate, aren't they? They can go into the elaboration of Actualism's basic and general account of subjectivity in terms of that unity of consciousness, an individual, a personal identity, a unity bound together by law and I guess meaning. What he offers is enrichment? Plantings in a fertile theory?

There is more to be said, however. For a start, I guess, I do not find his facts of subjectivity *in* the basic fact of perceptual consciousness. That is a certain existence of a world. The relevant short story here for me is that perceptual consciousness is often or very often or almost constantly accompanied or immediately followed by cognitive and affective consciousness. Or rather, more than that, perceptual consciousness is accompanied by cognitive and affective consciousness *with respect to* the perceptual consciousness. That does not make perceptual consciousness itself into more than the existence of a dependent subjective physical world.

It is as well for me to note for my readers that there is one of Hannay's sentences of quick summary that certainly went wrong—in my defensibly charitable view it could not originally have been intended to convey a particular thing. "The proposition can be summarized in two parts as the claim (1) that a room's being 'actual' means that it exists but when you are on hand, and (2) that while the room 'up here' is still there when you have gone downstairs, its being there is not the same as its being part of the 'objective physical world'."

The sentence in its end seems to assert that a room not in perceptual consciousness is not an objective physical room. On the contrary, whatever is added by someone about some thinking or other cognitive consciousness, Actualism is such that the room left behind *is* objectively physical. Without perception that is the only kind of thing it can be.

The mistake or anyway vagueness by an acute and freethinking philosopher unsettles me. I trust or hope that Actualism is not so far from common sense as to be incredible. I reassure myself by the truth that even acute common sense is not the only sense. There is the sense of beginning with a true premise and coming validly to a conclusion, however surprising.

In an email or two, he raises more questions about Actualism than I can think about here. I hope, in part uneasily, that he writes something more on our subject—more than his long review mentioned in the bibliography of the book *Actual Consciousness*.

To come to the end of these remarks, a suspicion or indeed an awareness of an extent of incredulity is not the happiest upshot of one's labour. Still, the history of philosophy has had a lot of incredulity in it. Some say the very temptation of philosophy has been that one of beginning with strong premises and proceeding to the new. Well, I leave it to you whether Actualism is a case in point. Take yourself back to the table of physicalities, plain facts, 17 lines of them. Truths there, I take it.

In these remarks, I say again I have not touched on much in the chapter, let alone unpacked it for closer examination. I have a sense, maybe more realistic than insecure, of the true and I guess deep difficulty of entering into what is not very usefully called another philosophical orientation to reality. No veiled superiority there for you to unveil. As said already, go to his *Human Consciousness*—start with the entry in the index on "first-person point of view, stance, vantage point." Go too to his long review of my *Actual Consciousness*.

* * *

7.4 On Montero

Barbara Montero, a stalwart of the Graduate Centre of the City University of New York, not much less firm in her philosophy of science and in particular her philosophy of physicality than she is in her feminism, mainly asks the question of whether the fact of being conscious is an *objective* physical fact. Is being conscious, as she very quickly clarifies to an extent, a fact that can be observed from different points of view, a fact that can be experienced by more than one person?

Her answer in the end, I take it, is at least that *yes* consciousness is within the category of objective physical facts. Physicalism, the theory or attitude that all things are somehow objectively physical, is not mistaken on account of consciousness being said to be, as just remarked, in a sense not a matter of different points of view and not a public fact.

Her chapter is to me puzzling but challenging, not easy to get into clear focus, no doubt in good part because of its home or of what it owes to the philosophy of science—whose progress has not been part of my life. That part of philosophy has had no attention from me despite my firm conviction about what used to be its basic problem. The conviction is that there is no problem of induction, what might have been that philosophy's central concern, the problem of holding why in certain ways the future will be like the past. That problem exists only if induction is looked at in a mistaken way, as being or being akin to *deduction*, premises entailing conclusions in the sense that assertion of the premises and denial of the conclusions is self-contradictory. The more or less inductive steps at the start of Actualism, from the database and from a clarification of the objectively physical, are not problematic.

Barbara's chapter being puzzling to me stands in the way of my objecting to it in brief, useful, and explicit ways—my saying anything here that can be trusted to be, or hoped to be, of some real use to you. So allow me mainly to follow a different course. That is quickly recalling something of my own response or sequence of responses to considerations or questions of consciousness and objectivity. And also now contemplating a sceptical reaction or two to that response or sequence of responses.

The large collection of common and evidently related figurative and sometimes metaphorical thinkings and feelings brought together in the database, I take it, were indeed at least usefully summed up in the figurative line that ordinary consciousness is *something's being actual.* Raising the two questions of literally what things or kinds of things, and what the being actual comes to.

There were next the consequential steps of taking external states of affairs to be *what* is actual with perceptual consciousness, and internal representations to be what is actual with cognitive and affective consciousness. And then, more relevantly to right now, the taking of actuality to have something to do with physicality, and then still more relevantly, starting with a full conception of objective physicality, the 16 characteristics.

Certainly the steps were novel. They were something different. That, you may know, for whatever little it matters, was what was asked for by noted philosophers and scientists of consciousness, if no motivation to me.

Yes, I did and do take the characterization of objective physicality to be superior to one based wholly on science. And of course, as Montero may agree, a characterization superior to one that is a matter of quick reference to the stuff of physics including quarks, leptons, bosons, and so forth.

This is indeed a consequence of the conception of philosophy as greater concentration on ordinary logic: clarity usually by analysis, consistency and validity, generalness, and completeness. Are the last two most important for my case? Anyway, science is not the handmaiden of philosophy, and philosophy is not the handmaiden of science. Both are useful to the other—even if science is more obviously useful to philosophy.

It was at least natural to face the question of to what extent consciousness, the actuality of characteristics, was a matter of the same or different characteristics as objective physicality. The upshot, of course, is summarized in the table given originally and the newly added-to table in this book. Consciousness has both the same and different characteristics. Subjective physicality. Stand by the mix I do.

But I take it from some reviews, lecture-audience reactions, and impulses in chapters, maybe an impulse in or under the very chapter we are considering, that the move from that to objective physicality and the move from that to the subjective physicalities were leaps. Not leaps in the dark, I say. Useful plodding. Go back and have a look.

But, by the way, do the steps put in question the general idea of philosophy as that greater concentration than that of science on clarity, consistency and validity, generalness, and completeness? Well, the first leap, if leap it was, was a matter of generalizing from the data, if in a way.

The second leap, to subjective physicalities, was natural enough, a response to an arising and indeed prompting question.

Can I say still another word for the steps? They have resulted in what is before you as decent answers to our main question—the different subjective physicalisms of perceptual, cognitive, and affective consciousness. Is it merely audacious to say a persuasive conclusion, a conclusion with the, or a, ring of truth, is not only something persuasive in itself, but also something persuasive with respect to the premises and process from which it comes? We got somewhere, which indicates we began somewhere OK. No doubt there is some philosophy of science somewhere on the matter.

Do you say, by any chance, that the novel process of steps puts into some question the general characterization of philosophy which you have heard from me? The greater concentration on clarity usually analysis, consistency and validity, completeness, and generalness? Well, I might struggle to put the steps into one or another or more of the four boxes there, but I leave this to you.

Something else comes to mind—in connection not only with Montero but with objective physicalists in general. Is Actualism unfit for the age of the computer, maybe even more unfit for an imaginable further age of the computer to come? When the question of computer consciousness has become just a little more asked? In fact, we can look forward now.

Actualism, in a nutshell, is that perceptual consciousness consists in external states of affairs dependent on a perceiver as well as on the objective physical world and that cognitive and affective consciousness consists in internal representations in different ways dependent on the thing that is conscious. Yes, the entities we know about are humans and other animals. Could something else in the future be conscious, be conscious according to Actualism? Well, why not? It is to me a recommendation of the theory both that it does not hurry one to speculations about computers, minds and consciousness, and that it is not a barrier to such future speculations and reflections.

Finally, last thoughts—three small and one larger.

1. Montero speaks of dependence of things on others in her own useful way or ways. My own talk of dependency relations, between objective and subjective physicality and also of course between facts of subjec-

tive physicality, is of the relations between causal connections or more generally all lawful connections. Dependency relations of the causal kind are understood at bottom in terms of causal circumstances or sufficient conditions and effects—the connection identified and stated by whatever-else conditional statements: If X and whatever else, then still Y. A service of philosophy to science.

2. I leave to you, too, further reflection on her various comments in the chapter that are in the direction, to be quick, of the table or chart of physicalities that summarizes Actual Consciousness.
3. And also the sad news about God. A pity she is a victim of useful and individual reflection on Actualism.
4. More generally, Montero's informed philosophy of science on physicality brings to mind something else defensive. It is that maybe a best summary of Actualism, or a summary as good as any, is in fact in terms of exactly physicality. The summary is that consciousness is both physical and different. Consciousness is physical, for a start, because it has physical effects. (That proposition, by the way, is in line with what is sometimes called the general principle of *causal closure*—physical events and states have wholly physical causes.) It is different, for a start, because of what you yourself have by way of your hold on yours right now. Actualism is the best summary of consciousness because it advances and articulates the proposition that consciousness is physical, but a different species from objective physicality.

Is that a too unfamiliar and too general and too radical a distinction? Radical in being more fundamental than philosophically familiar lesser distinctions made between consciousness and the rest of objective physicality? Sometimes distinctions in terms of the five leading ideas—qualia, something it's like to be a thing, subjectivity, aboutness, and phenomenality? Well, the history of philosophy is the history of unfamiliar and fundamental distinctions. Kant just for a start. Some last and some don't.

* * *

7.5 On Smith

Barry Smith, director of the Institute of Philosophy in the University of London and founder there of the Centre for the Study of the Senses, and visiting professor at Berkeley and at the Ecole Normale Superieure in Paris, is a general philosopher of mind and language and also a specialist philosopher of taste and smell, the editor of *Questions of Taste: The Philosophy of Wine.* Well prepared, then, to ask questions about actual consciousness—about something's being had, something being directly or immediately in touch, something being given, something's somehow existing or being real, something's being not deduced, inferred, posited, constructed, or otherwise got from something else, the experiencing of something, something being proximal rather than distal.

But it is much of his theme in his response that when we try to contemplate the general nature of consciousness, including its subjectivity, it eludes us, like his inner self eluded Hume. We only get a hold on something *in* consciousness, not consciousness itself. When we try to contemplate its nature, too much impinges on us in consciousness or infects its details. Questions arise. Are we conscious of all the things in our consciousness in the same way? How are we aware of them? Do we really know which conscious states we're in when we're in some conscious state or other? How does a first-person point of view fit into all this? If we answer the questions, does that tell us about the nature of consciousness?

There's a lot more in the chapter along these lines. When we approach consciousness, don't we distort it? Confuse the nature of consciousness with our thinking about it? Do we really have some immediate access to our consciousness itself? Or is it your thinking about it that leads to your theory? Are there consequential aspects of our consciousness that we momentarily overlook? Can't your being conscious be otherwise than you take it to be? Does it have something in it that you just overlook? A lot? Is there any simple or single source of information about your consciousness?

And he asks about that stuff in the database of Actualism, starting with being conscious is something's being *had*, and onward through about 35 items—isn't all that just "quirks" of mental life? There's an appearance-reality distinction in consciousness, isn't there? Consciousness isn't just something that "seems" to you, that "announces" itself. We don't know about our consciousness as it goes on—do we, say, know whether or what emotions suffuse our experience of tasting or smelling?

Still, despite all that, "no doubt there is some way 'the experience' (however it is to be demarcated) is, and this we can agree to, but…"?

Now to come on to Barry's consideration of my proposition that what is actual in perceptual consciousness is usually a room out there, well that is merely an "image," rather than what is set out in my pile of pages, including pages on kinds of physicality. Pages including, by the way, "crucial dependencies" are implied by Barry to be missing in my pages with respect to perceptual consciousness. And my giving space to attending or attention in our perceiving.

Also Barry's both complimenting me and, elsewhere at least, doubting the three sides of consciousness. And the reminder of the complexity of the rich experience of sitting by the seaside. And of the use of neuroscience—which, in fact, is written into Actualism, despite that theory's being presented by Barry as a kind of momentary revival of Naive Realism. And the facts of familiarity, and smelling, and pain, and the science of both familiarity and smelling, not to mention the wonderful complexity of vanilla ice cream.

My response to this affirmation of the mixed facts of consciousness is simple enough. As with the theory of evolution and any other general theory, certainly including general accounts of Quantum Theory, Actualism is just not put in question by very particular questions that arise. Not for a minute. Or, not to be too elevated, Actualism is like theories of road traffic management in London, or of relations of philosophy departments, or of the navigation of ducks on the ponds of Hampstead Heath, the latter already taken a little forward by me.

To end here with something implicit in what you've heard from me already, you know what my subject is right here and in those books—actual consciousness as clarified and then explained. I take it Barry's subject is something else. There is no doubt it includes what is not actual or anything like that—it includes more than in any of the related identifications of consciousness thought about by me. With Barry and me, do we have the most recent case of philosophers not asking the same question about consciousness?

Well, good luck to him in progress with all those philosophers, psychologists, and neuroscientists working together. The project of philosophy by itself is enough for me, of course including its limited relation to science. I propose keeping our eye on our ball—it's simpler than that case of the tennis champ Roger Federer, which I also take not to contribute much to Barry's obituary for Actualism.

As I say, all the questions and responses in his chapter strike me as overlooking or misunderstanding or somehow forgetting the first and fundamental basis of Actualism. This basis patently did not have to be one of making any such discriminations with respect to consciousness as any that Barry concerns himself with. No reader was asked to do anything, like decide anything tricky about tasting wine or the like. No one was asked to make any discriminations at all, to do anything of the kind.

We—not only me—were asked the general question of what it is for us to be conscious, what we take it to be—given our holds on our own consciousness. We made, typically in writing, the assortment of answers, the database, of which a few more items will bear mentioning. Being conscious is something's being apparent, for or to something else, open, something to which there is some privileged access, something presented, transparent in the sense of being clear straight-off, being right there.

That foundation phase was followed by my summation; of course, the generalization is that being conscious is *something's being actual*. There followed my phases, and I trust my readers advancing from the database through the further phases of coming towards and to literal answers to the equally general questions of what is actual with consciousness and what its being actual comes to, phases including consideration of physicalities, of the three sides of consciousness, of what is actual with respect to perceptual and with cognitive and affective consciousness. And on to subjective physical worlds and representations-with-attitude, some having to do with truth, some with forms and ways of goodness. Finally, the account of the being actual or rather the beings actual—the dependencies.

Whatever else is to be said of all that, I put it to Barry and to you that it raises none of the problems that he has in mind. We do not have to start on all that.

There is another large matter that needs more attention. What is the subject of his rumination? Well consciousness, but what does he take that to be. I am shocked to say that the answer, too plainly or combatively put, is that his consciousness partly is what is *unconscious*. The subject in terms of my and I hope your thinking is actual consciousness *and* something else. That makes everything harder in considering his objections. I don't know where I am, what I am supposed to be thinking about. We have here an illustration of the judgement that in the past and now the ongoing problem of consciousness has been and is owed to people talking about different things, having no agreed question.

Is his thinking deep or anyway deeper than that of Actualism—neither of those terms used with pejorative intent? I leave that to you. Maybe he is writing a book on fundamentally mixed states of consciousness. I'll sure have to read it.

At the end of Barry's chapter and those of Chomsky, Snowdon, Hannay, and Montero, do you remain agnostic about consciousness? Maybe a closet dualist-spiritualist? An abstract functionalist, which is to say a crypto-spiritualist? A devout objective spiritualist, maybe helped out by resistance to the detail of my down-to-earth table of physicalities? Were you caught young by Block, Chalmers, Dennett, Papineau, or Kim?

One last thing. Does Barry's line of argument against Actualism apply to *all* general theories or understandings of consciousness without exception? Yes. The lot. Are we all a little slow then? Well, my own faith in the philosophy of mind is still that line of propositions from database to objective physicality to criteria for a good theory of consciousness to the subjective physicality of worlds and representations, that literal existence. Dependent in ways on you neurally and the other thing out there, and with the plain and explicit subjectivity that goes with all that.

As somebody in a French lecture audience once said, maybe hoped, does Actualism look or glance back to Sartre, de Beauvoir et al.? Is it a very different indeed but still a belated English existentialism? Bloody far from it. So much plainer than that. Right down to earth. So much more philosophy as cognitive than affective consciousness. Anyway, despite objections, and its being a theory that is a workplace, I remain satisfied enough with it on account of my defences and other reasons given—the weight of all argument for and against.

Maybe you and I will think more about consciousness as a result of Barry's forceful chapter—and about what has been the spirited confrontation between a judgemental Scot and a defender of himself made more judgemental by his half-Scottish genes, and at 84 not going quiet into that good night.

It comes to mind to add here that there was in my life a close-enough predecessor of the theory of Actualism. This predecessor was named 'Radical Externalism'. It was the subject of, among other things, the book *Radical Externalism: Honderich's Theory of Consciousness Discussed* (Imprint Academic, 2006), edited by Anthony Freeman. The contributors to it were Harold Brown, Tim Crane, James Garvey, Stephen Law, E. J. Lowe, Derek Matravers, Paul Noordhof, and Ingmar Persson.

It also comes to mind to add here that if you want to go further into Actualism, and if you can't face the 214,000 words on it in Actual Consciousness (Oxford University Press, 2014), there is a summation of Actualism, a precis book, 40,000 words, *Mind: Your Consciousness Is What and Where?* (Reaktion Books, University of Chicago Press, 2017).

Part II

Determinism and Freedom

8

Honderich on Freedom, Determinism, and Meaning in Life

Derk Pereboom

Ted Honderich has made a very significant contribution to the debate about free will and determinism, in particular in his important book, *A Theory of Determinism* (Honderich 1988). I share his general perspective on this issue, which, like mine, is in the Spinozist camp (Spinoza 1677/1985), and I also agree with many of its specific features. His account of the aspects of our practice of holding moral responsibility that would have to be given up and which can be retained is nuanced and powerful. This is the part of the project that I have addressed in past works (Pereboom 2001, 2014). Here I will recount and expand on what I said there.

D. Pereboom (✉)
Sage School of Philosophy, Cornell University, Ithaca, NY, USA

G. D. Caruso (ed.), *Ted Honderich on Consciousness, Determinism, and Humanity*, Philosophers in Depth, https://doi.org/10.1007/978-3-319-66754-6_8

8.1 Honderich's Position on Free Will and Determinism

Honderich has an original way of framing the threat determinism poses to free will. I use the term "free will" as Al Mele (2006) does: to designate the strongest kind of control in free will action required for moral responsibility. "Moral responsibility" here stands for the specific aspect or sort that involves the notion of desert—that we deserve to be blamed or punished for the bad actions we knowingly perform, and to be praised or rewarded for the morally exemplary actions we knowingly perform. As I see it, the desert invoked in the notion of responsibility that's at issue in the free will debate is basic in that it is not grounded in further factors such as consequentialist or contractualist considerations (Pereboom 2001, 2014). By contrast, blaming and praising to form character, to promote strengthening of and reconciliation in relationships, and to deter bad actions and encourage good actions are not plausibly threatened by determinism.

In developing his account of the threat to our conception of moral responsibility and the attendant practice that determinism poses, Honderich sets out a sophisticated version of noncognitivism about moral judgments generally, with an emphasis on judgments that attribute moral responsibility. On his account, such judgments do not report moral facts, and do not have truth value, but instead express attitudes. But they nonetheless implicate factual and truth-evaluative propositional content in a distinctive way. For example, one might morally disapprove of a vicious politician for an immoral action he performs, where this disapproval involves a desire for retribution, that is, a desire for deserved recompense or retaliation. On Honderich's proposal, one will then, as a matter of the psychology of human nature, believe the action to be voluntary, that is, in accord with the will of the agent and thus not coerced or constrained, and originated, which involves being produced by agent without being causally determined by factors beyond her control. It is in this way that having a retributive attitude involves a commitment to propositional content (Honderich 1996, 856–859). In Honderich's view, it won't be *logically* inconsistent for one to have a retributive desire toward the politician and at the same time believe that he did not originate his action. Rather, given the psychology of human nature, having such a retributive desire will of necessity be accompanied by the belief that he originated the action. One might venture that it is a matter of psychological law that the two are linked.

Honderich then argues that giving up or losing the belief that an agent originated an action will result in the retributive attitude ceasing to persist. Or at least:

> it is agreed on all hands that *some* factual belief about an action's having been free is required by us for holding an agent responsible and of course for blaming or punishing her. If I lose the belief, I cannot persist in the attitude or the behavior. Currently, at any rate, that is a psychological impossibility. (Honderich 1996, 861)

In summary, on Honderich's account causal determinism is a threat to retributive desires, and more generally, to the reactive attitudes connected to the practice of holding people morally responsible, because belief in origination involves belief in the absence of causal determination, so believing in causal determinism results in giving up beliefs in origination, and our psychological nature is such that losing a belief in origination is of necessity paired with losing the attendant reactive attitudes. Honderich's detailed and careful empirical argument that causal determinism is in fact true thus yields motivation to reassess our commonly held retributive attitudes, and, more generally, the attitudes that are featured in our practice of holding morally responsible.

By contrast, with Honderich's noncognitivism, I have in the past endorsed the cognitivist position in which having such a reactive attitude essentially involves as a component a belief that its target basically deserves to be blamed for an action (Pereboom 2001, 2007; cf. Wallace 1994). On this conception, it would be doxastically irrational for a free will skeptic to have such an attitude, since she also believes that no agent basically deserves to be blamed for any action, and thus she would have conflicting beliefs. On Honderich's position, a free will skeptic's having a reactive attitude would result in doxastic irrationality because, given human psychology, it conflicts with a belief connected with the attitude. Austin Duggan and Justin Coates (in conversation) propose a noncognitivist position similar to Honderich's, but in which the tie to a belief of this conflicting sort is weaker, and on which it is psychologically possible to lose the belief that the agent is responsible in the sense at issue and still retain the attitude. On their view, if someone is generally opposed to justifications that invoke desert, she might be resentful or indignant and not have any desert-involving belief.

I continue to prefer the cognitivist option. On the view that seems most plausible to me, the attitudes of moral resentment and indignation include the following two components: anger targeted at an agent because of what he's done or failed to do, and a belief that the agent deserves to be the target of that very anger just because of what he has done or failed to do. An attitude does not count as resentment or indignation if it lacks these features. Animals and young children have attitudes similar to resentment and indignation that don't feature these cognitive components, but they don't count as resentment or indignation. Against Duggan and Coates, but in accord with Honderich, my sense is that whenever I am morally resentful or indignant, I have the desert-involving belief, despite my view that no agent ever basically deserves to be blamed. On these occasions I'm irrational insofar as I have conflicting beliefs.

I think the following compromise proposal is secure and would be acceptable to both Honderich and me. When a mature, normal human being makes some agent the target of an overt expression of resentment or indignation—both species of moral anger, it's at least close to psychologically impossible that she doesn't believe that the agent deserves to be blamed, and in fact overtly blamed (cf. McKenna 2012, 64–74).[1] We can leave it open that someone who rejects desert, say for theoretical reasons, be silently indignant with another without believing that he deserves to be blamed, but she is not overtly expressing her anger. Overt but feigned moral anger will typically not be accompanied by such a belief, but it wouldn't be an expression of genuine moral anger. Young children and animals might well overtly express attitudes phenomenologically similar in some respects to moral anger without having desert-involving beliefs, but they don't qualify as normal adult human beings. Given the credibility of this proposal, free will skepticism will challenge any practice of holding morally responsible that endorses as a core feature overt expressions of moral anger. As a result, the free will skeptic will be disposed to encourage ways of communicating in relationships that don't involve expressions of attitudes linked with beliefs involving attributions of desert.

A further feature of Honderich's view is that he rejects both compatibilism and incompatibilism. In his conception, incompatibilism fails to appreciate the importance of mere voluntariness, which is compatible with causal determinism, as opposed to voluntariness together with origination, while compatibilism mistakenly devalues the significance of origination. He argues that voluntariness can sustain significant features of human life that incompatibilists believe requires origination, including certain key components of morality and much of the aspiration we have for achievement and meaning in life. While I call myself an incompatibilist, Honderich does not, but I suspect that the disagreement is merely verbal. For me, incompatibilism is the position that the sort of free will required for basic-desert moral responsibility is incompatible with causal determination by factors beyond agents' control, and compatibilism is the position that it is compatible. There isn't a lot of daylight between the two views—but we can suppose that one might be agnostic about each, and in this way, given my definitions, one might be neither a compatibilist nor an incompatibilist. But Honderich's position isn't agnostic in this way. Moreover, I agree with Honderich that incompatibilists often overrate the importance of origination for what is significant in human life, but I think they are in these respects mistaken about what incompatiblism entails. As we shall now see, I also agree with his claim that voluntariness is significant for sustaining features of morality and aspiration for meaning. But my views on these issues also differ from his in certain respects.

8.2 Hard Incompatibilism and Life Projects: Sartre and Honderich

According to existentialist philosophy, the possibility of meaning in life is closely connected with our capacity for freedom of choice. Jean-Paul Sartre (1957) claims, famously, that it is up to each of us to freely determine purpose and meaning for one's life. We determine purpose and meaning for ourselves through free choice of our projects, our life-defining plans. Sartre argues in addition that we have free will as characterized by the incompatibilist, and that it is through the exercise of an indeterministic capacity in our choice of projects that meaning in life is achieved. If our choices weren't free in this way meaning in life could not be secured. In Honderich's terms, origination is required for the choices that result in a meaningful life.

Is Sartre's proposal credible? Discovering that one's choice of profession was determined by one's home environment to realize a parent's career fantasies might well threaten the possibility of fulfillment through that profession. Finding out that one's choice of spouse was determined by a tendency to persist in familiar but unhealthy patterns of interaction plausibly undermines the fulfillment that an intimate relationship might supply. But one might reply that causally determined choices for projects could as easily provide meaning for our lives. For example, suppose one discovered that one's career choice was determined by a deep interest, produced by the circumstances of one's upbringing, in finding solutions for some of the problems facing humanity. Or, imagine finding out that one's choice of spouse is explained by the healthy features of one's childhood environment, which one was causally determined to replicate because of the happiness it produced. Such discoveries wouldn't seem to detract from the sense of fulfillment provided by these choices and their attendant projects. More generally, one might reply that it could matter for meaning that the project one chooses be appropriate, that one chooses reasonably after reflection on salient options, and that one is not coerced in making one's choice. In Honderich's terms, choices that yield meaning in life must be voluntary. However, so far, we haven't seen a strong case for the requirement that they be originated.

Still, the advocate of Sartre's view might press on. Honderich contends that determinism generates both losses and gains for our sense of meaning in life. In his discussion, he focuses on what he calls *life-hopes*, that is, aspiration for what would make one's life fulfilled, happy, satisfactory, or worthwhile (Honderich 1988, 382). Life-hopes do not target what will happen to us, but rather our achievements. Life-hopes are for this reason dependent on our ability to initiate action, and this ability is essential to our conception of achievement. General causal determination by factors beyond one's control calls into question the extent to which we are capable of initiating our actions, and for this reason yields a potential challenge to our life-hopes.

Honderich proposes that when confronted with the prospect that our actions are causally determined, we have a pre-philosophical sense that our life-hopes are under threat. In his view, there is a pre-philosophical picture that explains our sense that causal determination yields this threat. This picture has two components. One is the belief that our futures are open, alterable, and unfixed. The other is the conviction that our futures are not produced by our dispositions, and that we can mold our futures by overcoming opposing dispositions (Honderich 1988, 385ff.). Pre-philosophically, we believe that we can overcome opposing dispositions by a "determinate center" that has the ability to initiate actions. This "center" is readily identified with a self that is distinct from its dispositions, and which has the ability to overcome them when they serve as obstacles to our aims, without being causally determined by those dispositions to fail in this endeavor. Thus, determinism's pre-philosophical threat to our life-hopes is that it jeopardizes the assumption that we are such selves, distinct from our dispositions, who can overcome the threat to our life-hopes that these dispositions might pose.

Honderich specifies three distinct responses to this determinist challenge. The first, which he calls *dismay*, is that our life-hopes are completely undercut by determinism. The second, *intransigence*, is that determinism makes no difference to our life-hopes (Honderich 1988, 391–400). The third response, *affirmation*, is that there is an aspect of our life-hopes that is undermined by determinism, but at the same time determinism does not eradicate them. Honderich endorses this last response. He argues that the feature of our life-hopes that does not survive determinism is the aspiration "for an unfixed future, a hope for a future in which we are not creatures of our environments and our dispositional natures" (Honderich 1988, 390). An important part of the pre-philosophical view is that no matter what dispositions to action or inaction one may have, and no matter what environment one finds oneself in, the self has a power for action-initiation that is not reducible to disposition and environment. If determinism is true, then this part of the pre-philosophical picture must be rejected. For this reason, the intransigent response is mistaken.

But Honderich also contends that a large part of the pre-philosophical perspective does survive the determinist challenge (Honderich 1988, 516–517). We have desires and intentions for the future that are potentially or actually opposed by features of the world such as natural impediments and people given to hostility and domination, or by psychological features of the agent, such as addictions and compulsions (Honderich 1988, 397). Life-hopes in this respect are hopes that my desires for achievement will not be frustrated by any such factors, and that I will therefore attain their satisfaction. By contrast with hopes that are undercut by causal determination, hopes of this kind do not involve "a hope for a future in which we are not creatures of our environments and our dispositional natures," and thus they can withstand determinism. The response of dismay, according to which no feature of our life-hopes survives the truth of determinism, is thus in Honderich's view also in error.

8.3 Honderich's Notion of Affirmation

Honderich, I think, is right to claim that the responses of dismay and intransigence are unjustified and mistaken. Given that the three responses he specifies are jointly exhaustive, affirmation is thus the only response left standing. I join him in declaring for affirmation, but with a few alterations.

In my own view, rejecting the response of dismay is justified for several reasons. Causal determination by factors beyond our control does not threaten the causal efficacy of the deliberation and decision by which we aspire to form our futures. This requires only compatibilist voluntariness (for my defense of this view, see Pereboom 2014, Chap. 5). Nor does it jeopardize the prospect of surmounting the kinds of external and internal impediments that Honderich discusses. For instance, such causal determination does not threaten the view that if others aim to make one's life miserable, one might achieve a happy life for oneself despite their efforts, nor the claim that if one has a proclivity to laziness that threatens to frustrate one's career aims, one might be able to overcome this tendency. For having dispositions that can serve to overcome such impediments is compatible with causal determination.

I suspect, however, that there is a difference between the philosophical determinist and the pre-philosophical perspectives on the prospect of overcoming these sorts of obstacles. In the determinist view, if one did not, as a matter of fact, overcome one's laziness, then there were factors beyond one's control—factors that one could not have altered or prevented—that produced this consequence. If one did in fact overcome one's laziness, then there were factors beyond one's control that produced this result. Someone who hopes to surmount his laziness will most often not know in advance which of these two epistemic possibilities will be realized. He will then be correct to acknowledge that it is epistemically possible that some aspect of the universe completely beyond his control may preclude him from overcoming his laziness.

Acknowledgments of this kind mark a difference from the pre-philosophical stance in how one views one's life-hopes. From the pre-philosophical point of view, it is most often true that if one envisions the possibility of failing to surmount one's laziness, one will also see oneself as yet being able to succeed by expending sufficient effort. For although one then envisions not actually expending enough effort, one also believes that one could expend enough by indeterministically self-caused efforts of will. Thus the pre-philosophical view would endorse the following reflection on the prospect of overcoming one's laziness: "Attaining fulfillment depends on overcoming my laziness. Whether I succeed is wholly within my power. If I fail, it will be because I did not expend effort that I could have expended. And so, whether I achieve my life-hope is up to me." The philosophical determinist's reflection differs in a significant regard: "Attaining fulfillment in life depends on my overcoming my laziness. It might be that there are factors beyond my control that will produce this failure. So, whether I succeed, in an important respect, is not up to me." In the determinist's perspective, if one is to overcome one's laziness, one's efforts to do so will typically be causally efficacious in bringing it about. Still, achieving one's life-hopes is in an important respect outside of one's control, a respect in which it is not outside one's control on the pre-philosophical conception.

As we've seen, in Honderich's account, the intransigent response is also in error, for important aspects of our life-hopes in fact undermined by determinism. The aspect he singles out is the dependence of our life-hopes on a conception of a self with an indeterministic causal power. He contends that if the notion of such a self is rejected, we are left with a view in which our actions are caused solely by our dispositions and environments, and "a hope for a future in which we are not creatures of our environments and our dispositional natures" must be rejected. Here I disagree with Honderich. He argues, correctly I believe, that an aspect of our ordinary self-conception is that we are selves distinct from our mental states and dispositions to act, and that these selves have causal powers. On one such conception, we are selves of this sort and they have indeterministic causal powers. But such agent-causal selves might also be components of a deterministic system (Markosian 1999; Nelkin 2011; Pereboom 2015). The Stoics, for example, maintained that we are selves that are distinct from our dispositions, capable of withstanding opposition from them, but that determinism is true (Inwood 1985; Pereboom 1994).

I believe that the thesis that such a self can initiate action independently of dispositions and environment fares as well in the determinist as it does in the indeterminist picture. Suppose, for example, that a person had a life-hope that she would behave morally despite all her dispositions and her environment, and that she would do so by the causal power of a self-motivated solely by moral principles she had adopted independently of the influence of her dispositions. This life-hope is amenable to either a determinist or an indeterminist view. It does not fit with a determinist view according to which all of our actions are causally determined by our dispositions, but one might hold, with the Stoics, that selves and their power to act independently of dispositions are an additional causal factor in the production of action. Determinism per se does not rule out the view that a self can select principles of action, and initiate action on their basis independently of the influence of her dispositions and environment.

Thus, in one respect the intransigent response may fare better than Honderich maintains. The determinist must reject the notion of a self that has the power to overcome its dispositions and the effects of its environment indeterministically, but she need not deny that we are determined selves with the power to overcome these factors. This is an important concession to the intransigent response. One can be a determinist and deny that we are creatures of our dispositions and environment in the way that Honderich envisions. But nevertheless, the pre-philosophical position does include the assumption that factors beyond our control do not generate our futures, because we are selves whose choices are not produced by factors beyond our control. Perhaps this assumption is tied to the belief that there is an intrinsic value to shaping aspects of our lives that were not determined prior to our decisions, and that there are such aspects of our lives.[2] The determinist is forced to give up these assumptions, and this respect the intransigent response is mistaken.

However, the degree to which we have found the intransigent response deficient so far is not as substantial as one might have feared. On the determinist view, given that we lack knowledge of how our futures will turn out, we can still reasonably hope for success in achieving what we want most even if our prospects will in fact be hindered by our dispositions or our environments. Indeed, such hopes will often be reasonable even if we are fully creatures of our environments and our dispositions. The reason is that we almost never have adequate knowledge of what our environments and dispositions are or will be. Accordingly, it is often true for any disposition or difficulty in an agent's environment that stands to oppose the realization of a life-hope that it is epistemically possible that she also has a disposition that will allow her to overcome it. For example, someone might think that her laziness might frustrate her aim to become a successful brain surgeon, while at the same time it is epistemically possible for her that she has a disposition that will facilitate overcoming this laziness. As a result, she might reasonably hope that she will overcome her laziness and succeed in her aspiration. In the determinist view, if she does overcome her laziness, it won't be by an indeterminist causal power of the self, and for this reason it won't be an achievement in as robust a way as she might have believed. But it will be the agent's achievement is a significant sense nonetheless.

It might be argued that the intransigent response is more deeply mistaken than has so far been suggested. Life-hopes, one might venture, involve an aspiration for praiseworthiness, which causal determination undercuts. Because life-hopes are aspirations for achievement, and it is not possible to have any achievements for which one is not also praiseworthy, giving up praiseworthiness dispenses with life-hopes altogether. Responding to this sort of objection, Honderich proposes that the significance for life-hopes of relinquishing praiseworthiness is moderated by the fact that actions may still have the "credit of rational action, or action in accordance with desires that serve my fundamental end ... or the credit of strong character, or sensitivity, or judgment, or decency, or of rising over mere conventionality" (Honderich 1988, 513).

An objection to this response is that if it's agreed that determinism rules out praiseworthiness, then it also rules out desert of any sort, including creditworthiness for moral and rational actions. However, achievement and life-hopes may not be tied to praiseworthiness in the strong way assumed by the objection. If one hopes for a certain result and succeeds in attaining it, it can qualify as one's achievement, albeit in a diminished sense, even if one is not praiseworthy for it. For instance, if someone hopes that her efforts as a parent will result in flourishing children, and it does in fact have this consequence, there is a clear sense in which she achieved what she hoped for, even if due to causal determination by factors beyond her control she does not deserve praise for her efforts.

But how significant, all told, is the aspect of our life-hopes that we must give up supposing causal determination? Saul Smilansky in effect disagrees with Honderich and me when he argues that although our view leaves some room for a sense of self-worth that results from achievement or virtue, it can nevertheless "be extremely damaging to our view of ourselves, to our sense of achievement, worth, and self-respect." He claims, first of all, that "if any virtue that one has exhibited, if all that one has achieved, was 'in the cards,' just an unfolding of what one has been made out to be, one's view of oneself (or important others) cannot stay the same" (Smilansky 1997, 94; cf., Smilansky 2000). He then contends that the foundation for self-respect provided by a sense of moral accomplishment would be under serious threat:

> Even after admitting the compatibilist claim that on one level we have, say, reason to be morally proud of ourselves because we are honest (after all, we chose to be), when we reflect on life as a whole, it matters when we realize that we lack libertarian free will. We begin to see ourselves in a new light: what we choose ... is the unfolding of what we are, the choices result from that which is not under our control (and ultimately is luck). We are honest,

> and we are honest despite the fact that (compatibilistically) we were able not to be. We chose to be honest because we are moral. But that we are this person (who chose freely as she did because she was moral) is not our doing. We deserve respect as morally worthy (not just useful) people, but not ultimately for being such people. (Smilansky 1997, 92–93)

Smilansky does allow that losing the ground for incompatibilist moral worth may be valuable in some respects. Hard determinism facilitates pursuit of moral goals purified of the concern for this kind of moral worth. Hard determinism yields the beneficial thought that in a sense we are all ultimately equal; "this realization presents the anti-luck 'here but for the grace of God' thought overwhelmingly" (Smilansky 1997, 95). However, Smilansky contends that the potential damage to self-respect would be so severe that as a defense it would be best to retain the illusion of free will (Smilansky 1997, 96–98; Smilansky 2000).

I agree with Smilansky that there is a kind of self-respect that has incompatibilist presuppositions, the ground for which would be undercut if causal determinism were true. I do have an issue with him, however, on how damaging it would be for us to be forced to give up this kind of self-respect, and thus whether the radical move to illusion is warranted; and here I think Honderich would agree. First, we should not underestimate the extent to which our sense of self-worth, our sense that we are valuable and that our lives are worth living, is due to factors that are not even produced by voluntary endeavor, let alone indeterministically originated. Smilansky quotes an especially pithy expression of this insight from George Santayana:

> Even now, who of us in his heart would not be a rake rather than a hunchback, a villain rather than a fool? In spite of all the moralizing, we cannot admire desert or merit as much as the gifts of nature and fortune. There is nothing of which we are so proud as of a good family, a handsome face, a strong body, a ready wit—all of those things indeed, for which we are not responsible. (Santayana 1885; quoted in Smilansky 1997, 87)

Without going so far as to endorse Santayana's thoughts in their entirety, it is evident that we place substantial value on good looks, athletic ability, and native intelligence, none of which is produced voluntarily. Let me add that many sorts of creative achievement fit this category as well. When one alights on a new philosophical idea or a solution to a mathematical problem, one does not will the idea or solution into existence. Phenomenologically, insights of this sort happen to the agent and are not produced by her; this is perhaps why the metaphor of inspiration by the Muses seems so apt. But we also place great value on voluntary efforts and their results—on hard work and the achievements it yields, on moral resolve and the character it produces. Still, how much does it matter to us that these voluntary efforts also be indeterministically originated? Less than Smilansky supposes, I think.

Consider first his example of moral character. The belief that morally impressive character is a product of upbringing is widespread in our society. Parents think of themselves as having failed if their children turn out to have bad character, and many take great care to raise their children well in order to prevent such an outcome. In accord with perspective, the following realization is not at all uncommon: "I turned out well due to how I was brought up—because of the love my parents had for me and the skill with which they raised me." Of the many people who have this thought, I suspect that very few would be overcome with a sense of dismay if they came to believe that moral character is to a large extent not their own doing. Those who come to this conclusion tend to feel fortunate and thankful for the upbringing they received, and not to have any sense of loss at all. Moreover, we don't typically react with dismay when we come to understand the degree to which achievement in a career, or financial success, depends on the opportunities that society provides, the assistance of colleagues, and good luck. These thoughts typically produce a sense of thankfulness and of being fortunate, and seldom dismay. Why then should we believe that people will generally be overcome with dismay when they come to hold that because determinism is true, we do not originate our character and our achievements, and that thus we do not for this reason deserve respect?

There might well be some who would react with dismay upon having such thoughts. For them, would it be advisable to maintain the illusion that they do deserve respect for originating their moral character and achievements? I suspect that most people would be capable of facing the truth, at least eventually, without much loss overall, and that those for whom it is painful will typically have the psychological resources to pull through. Smilansky, I think, overreacts when he contends that such thoughts can be extremely damaging to our view of ourselves. I believe that the intransigent response to his claims is almost exactly right, and here I think that Honderich and I agree.

Notes

1. This proposal emerged from a discussion with Austin Duggan.
2. Carl Ginet makes a similar suggestion (in correspondence).

References

Honderich, Ted. 1988. *A theory of determinism*. Oxford: Oxford University Press.

———. 1996. Compatibilism, incompatibilism, and the smart aleck. *Philosophy and Phenomenological Research* 56: 855–862.

Inwood, Brad. 1985. *Ethics and human action in early stoicism*. Oxford: Oxford University Press.

Markosian, Ned. 1999. A compatibilist view of the theory of agent causation. *Pacific Philosophical Quarterly* 80: 257–277.

McKenna, Michael. 2012. *Conversation and responsibility*. New York: Oxford University Press.

Mele, Alfred. 2006. *Free will and luck*. New York: Oxford University Press.

Nelkin, Dana. 2011. *Making sense of freedom and responsibility*. Oxford: Oxford University Press.

Pereboom, Derk. 1994. Stoic psychotherapy in Descartes and Spinoza. *Faith and Philosophy* 11: 592–625.

———. 2001. *Living without free will*. Cambridge, MA: Cambridge University Press.

———. 2007. Hard incompatibilism. In *Four views on free will*, ed. Robert Kane, John Martin Fischer, Derk Pereboom, and Manuel Vargas, 85–125–191–203. Oxford: Blackwell.

———. 2014. *Free Will, Agency, and Meaning in Life*. Oxford: Oxford University Press.

———. 2015. The phenomenology of agency and deterministic agent causation. In *Horizons of authenticity in phenomenology, existentialism, and moral psychology: Essays in honor of Charles Guignon*, ed. Megan Altman and Hans Gruenig, 277–294. New York: Springer.

Santayana, George. 1885. A junior forensic. *The Daily Crimson* 7 (Supp 15): 3.

Sartre, Jean-Paul. 1957. The humanism of existentialism. *Existentialism and the human emotions*. Trans. Bernard Frechtman. New York: Philosophical Library.

Smilansky, Saul. 1997. Can a determinist help herself? In *Freedom and moral responsibility: General and Jewish perspectives*, ed. C.H. Manekin and M. Kellner, 85–98. College Park: University of Maryland Press.

———. 2000. *Free will and illusion*. Oxford: Oxford University Press.

Spinoza, Baruch. 1677/1985. Ethics. In *The collected works of Spinoza*, Vol. I., ed. and Trans. Edwin Curley. Princeton, NJ: Princeton University Press.

Wallace, R. Jay. 1994. *Responsibility and the moral sentiments*. Cambridge, MA: Harvard University Press.

9

Free Will and Affirmation: Assessing Honderich's Third Way

Paul Russell

In the third and final part of his *A Theory of Determinism* (1988), Ted Honderich addresses the fundamental question concerning "the consequences of determinism" (1988, II, 4).[1] That is, what follows if determinism is true? This question is, of course, intimately bound up with the problem of free will and, in particular, with the question of whether or not the truth of determinism is compatible or incompatible with the sort of freedom that is supposed to be required for moral responsibility. It is Honderich's aim to provide a solution to "the problem of the consequences of determinism," and a key element of this is his attempt to collapse the familiar compatibilist/incompatibilist dichotomy. More specifically, Honderich offers us a third way—the response of "Affirmation" (2002, 125–126). Although his account of Affirmation has application and relevance to issues and features beyond

P. Russell (✉)
University of British Columbia, Vancouver, BC, Canada
and University of Gothenburg, Gothenburg, Sweden

G. D. Caruso (ed.), *Ted Honderich on Consciousness, Determinism, and Humanity*,
Philosophers in Depth, https://doi.org/10.1007/978-3-319-66754-6_9

freedom and responsibility, my primary concern in this chapter will be to examine Honderich's theory of "Affirmation" as it concerns the free will problem as it is generally understood.

9.1

The first part of Honderich's overall position in *A Theory of Determinism* is concerned with "the question of whether there does exist a conceptually satisfactory determinist theory of our lives" (1988, 4). The second part addresses the question of whether the theory as articulated in the first part is well supported and argues that it is true. The core of this theory, as Honderich interprets it, is expressed in these terms:

> …determinism is only a view of our own nature—in essence, the view that ordinary causation is true of us and our own lives, that in our choosing and deciding we are subject to causal laws. In this use of the word, determinism comes to no more than a yes answer to the question of whether we are in one fundamental way like plants or machines. Determinism in this sense does not include or imply an answer to the question of whether we are free or not. That question, maybe surprisingly, is left pretty well untouched. (2002, 3)

The account of the theory of determinism is developed by Honderich largely in terms of a theory of causation and laws, along with an accompanying theory of mind and action. The theory of causation is one that holds that causes necessitate their effects, such that, given the occurrence of the former, whatever else happens, the latter will also occur (2002, 14–15). Causal relations and natural laws are understood as in terms of "regularities or as nomic connections" (2002, 15–16). Given this general account of causation, the question arises of whether or not "our lives are a matter of effects … events that really have to happen because of earlier causal circumstances" (2002, 21). To answer this question, as it concerns our choices and actions, Honderich advances his theory of mind and action.

There are three basic elements to Honderich's account of mind and action. The first is what he calls Mind-Brain Determinism. This concerns the suggestion that each mental or conscious event, including choosing and deciding, is nomically related to neural events in such a way that the "neural event by itself or together with some other non-mental thing necessitated the mental one" (2002, 63). The second component is "Initiation Determinism," which maintains that nomically related neural and mental events have their causal origins in bodily (and environmental) events that involve no mental events. The third, and last, component in this general account of mind and action is "Action Determinism," which claims that each and every action is the effect of an "active intention," what is sometimes referred to as a volition or act of willing (2002, 59–60). The details of these three elements of Honderich's theory of mind and action involve, of course, a number of controversial issues but for our present purposes what matters is that they serve as the background set of proposals and assumptions that serve to articulate the general theory of determinism and bring us directly to the problem of the "consequences" (so interpreted). It is worth noting that Honderich does not assert simply "that determinism is true." What he claims is that it is "strongly supported, and that certainly it *has not been shown to be false*" (2002, 90 [original emphasis]). Honderich also allows that there may be some "micro-indeterminism" at the level of small particles but it is "not amplified into indeterminism at the macro-level" (2002, 74–76). Even if micro-determinism is true, we are still left with strong support for the truth of a "macro-determinism" or "near-determinism" (2002, 90).

Throughout his account of a deterministic theory of mind and action, Honderich makes clear that there is an opposing view—namely, what he calls the "philosophy of Free Will," which presupposes the truth of indeterminism (2002, 2, 4, 35, 41–42, 49, 69, 76). What philosophers of Free Will require is that responsible agents are originators of their actions. If we are genuinely free, each of us must have "a kind of personal power to *originate* choices and decisions and their actions" (2002, 2). It will not suffice for us to be mere "initiators" of our actions in a manner that is consistent with these events to be (necessitated) effects via a causal chain or process (2002, 3). The guiding aim behind the idea of Free Will, Honderich argues, is that we need to understand responsibility *in a certain way.* What this requires, above all, is that we are "able now to choose differently from how we do, given the present and ourselves exactly as they are and the past exactly as it was" (2002, 41–42; and cp. 98, 109, 117). This form of absolute responsibility not only requires the falsity of determinism it also requires some sort of "ongoing entity" that possesses the "active power" required to produce or not produce a given action (2002, 42, 49). If we accept the truth of (near) determinism, then we must reject the idea of Free Will, so understood.

What is the significance of having to abandon or discard the idea of Free Will? Honderich analyses this issue within wider fabric of what he refers to as a set of "life-hopes." Life-hopes involve our attitudes to a range of features of the world that we care about, particularly as this concerns how our future activities may affect or influence how our lives unfold. In respect of these matters, we may be fortunate or unfortunate and, depending on this, we will *feel* a general attitude of a positive or negative kind. An attitude is an "evaluative thought" about something that we either approve or disapprove of. The question that presents itself in relation to determinism is, therefore, whether our life-hopes are in some relevant way threatened or damaged if the thesis of determinism is true.

It is with respect to this matter that the loss of Free Will is of some concern. The idea of Free Will, as we noted, involves a conception of ourselves as agents that are true originators of our actions. There is, Honderich maintains, a set of life-hopes that rests on this stronger conception of free agency (2002, 93, 111–112). We want to be able not just to achieve success but to *earn* it and we want our achievements, whatever they are, to be more than just a causal product of our inherent nature and environment. While this is of importance to us if determinism is true, we do not have it (2002, 104). This situation will license an attitude of dismay about our predicament and circumstances so understood. It is for this reason, Honderich suggests, "that many people have found determinism to be a black thing" (2002, 95; and cp. 104).

Life-hopes are not, however, the only things that rest on the concept of freedom understood in terms of origination. Among other things that depend on this notion of initiated action as originated are certain attitudes or personal feelings to other people on the basis of their conduct toward us (e.g. resentment and gratitude). These personal feelings and reactions are closely bound up with our *moral* feelings and responses—an issue that has been the primary focus of attention in the free will debate. What is crucial here is that the concept of freedom as originated action is essential to moral responsibility. The moral standing of an individual, on this account, rests on the assumption that they have not just acted voluntarily but possess the power to originate their actions and could have acted otherwise in the same circumstances. If these metaphysical foundations of agency are threatened, the whole fabric of morality will collapse, including our understanding of retributive justice and (deserved) punishment (2002, 101). Our sense of dismay, in face of the apparent truth of determinism, is felt most strongly in relation to this issue.

It is at this juncture that the split between compatibilism and incompatibilism becomes relevant. The analysis provided so far is one that turns on a concept of freedom (i.e. origination) that the incompatibilist embraces and endorses as the only true or genuine account of freedom that is relevant to these modes of concern. From the perspective of compatibilism, however, this entire analysis is mistaken. It is mistaken because what we really mean by freedom is a matter of voluntariness—not origination (2002, 96, 98). Free actions have a certain kind of causal history and are, as such, effects of a particular kind (2002, 96). When we secure a proper grasp of the concept of freedom, in terms of voluntariness, we can draw all the relevant distinctions we need concerning moral responsibility (2002, 98–99). There is, therefore, according to the compatibilist no conflict between freedom and responsibility and the truth of determinism. Even if determinism is true, nothing changes and nothing we have reason to care about is threatened. Instead of dismay, the attitude of the compatibilist is one of "satisfied intransigence" (2002, 97).

It is Honderich's central claim that neither of these approaches offers a satisfactory response to the likely truth of determinism. The oppositions we encounter between these two sides leave us in an unsatisfactory and unstable situation that demands a new response to determinism.

> We need to get into a different way of feeling about determinism. We need to come to a response that takes into account not only its truth, and the two sets of attitudes, but also the two responses we have in the first instance, dismay and intransigence. So the final upshot, if we are to be successful, will partly be a response to the two initial responses. (2002, 122–123)

Honderich's response to compatibilism and incompatibilism is that they are *both mistaken.* Both, moreover, are mistaken over several overlapping claims that they are agreed about. The first of these is that we possess some single, ordinary idea of freedom and that the alternative conception is either inadequate or incoherent (or both). The truth about our situation, Honderich maintains, is that we plainly have two distinct ideas of free choice and action and that both compatibilists and incompatibilists are wrong to dismiss the alternative view as irrelevant to our appreciation of the consequences of determinism. Any proposed solution along these lines will inevitably be one-sided and incomplete and will fail to identify properly the (inescapable) split we experience in our dual responses and attitudes (i.e. *both* dismay *and* intransigence).

Honderich argues that both parties in this debate mistakenly suppose "that the problem of the consequences can be settled by logical, intellectual, philosophical or linguistic means as traditionally conceived" (2002, 114) This approach, he suggests, over-intellectualizes the whole problem. The real problem is that we have two sets of attitudes, rooted in two sets of desires, and they issue in the divergent responses we have considered—dismay and intransigence. Neither response, taken by itself, is entirely satisfactory. Compatibilist intransigence comes across as mere "bluff" and requires us to suppress and ignore the other side of the equation. On the other hand, simple dismay also ignores essential and inescapable features of ordinary life and our social experience. The relevant problem is how this "Attitudinarian instability and discomfort can be overcome and the two parties reconciled" (2002, 125–126).

Honderich's solution to this problem takes the form of what he calls "Affirmation" (2002, 126). What this requires is that, assuming the truth of determinism, we must

> try to give up whatever depends on thoughts inconsistent with it. Above all we have to try to accept the defeat of certain desires. This is bound up with *trying to be happier about, or more reconciled to, the desires in which we can persist,* the ones consistent with determinism. (2002, 125)

This means in the first place, in accepting that "our attitudes involving voluntariness cannot really allow us to be intransigent." If determinism is true, we cannot claim that "nothing changes" and that this "leaves things just as they are" (2002, 97, 99, 125). At the same time, making these concessions "need not give rise to dismay, taking everything as wrecked" (2002, 125). By this route we achieve some balance between dismay and intransigence, whereby we recognize and accept that some things important to us are discredited or lost, to the extent that they are based on assumptions about origination, but that there is also a great deal that we care about and that which matters to us remains untouched and survives.

Honderich summarizes his account of Affirmation as follows:

> To put the proposal in a nutshell, our new response should be this: trying *by various strategies to accommodate ourselves to the situation we find ourselves in—accommodate ourselves to just what we can really possess if determinism is true, accommodate ourselves to the part of our lives that does not rest on the illusion of Free Will.* We can reflect on what is perhaps the limited worth of what we have to give up, consider the possible compensations of a belief in determinism, take care not to underestimate what we can have, and consider a certain prospect having to do with genuine and settled belief in determinism. (2002, 126 [emphasis in original])

To embrace this response of "Affirrmation" is, Honderich suggests, to adopt "a philosophy of life," one which consists in feelings that provide us with some support and as much satisfaction as the truth will allow. Although Affirmation rejects all forms or reliance on illusions of any kind, it nevertheless rejects any (pessimistic) suggestion that determinism leaves us "defeated" or without any substantial and significant sources of consolation. This is not just a matter of "putting a good face on things" but of recognizing gains as well as losses that come with the belief in determinism (2002, 131). Among the gains is that we are in a position to withdraw from retributive sentiments and practices that are grounded in our illusory belief in Free Will. This is all achievable without the world going "cold," or leaving no scope for personal emotions and feelings, or losing all sense of achievement and meaning (see Pereboom 2001, 2013, 2014). The upshot of all this is that the response of Affirmation is one that rejects undiluted "dismay" or "intransigence" but offers, instead, a *blend* or *mix* that avoids the one-sided, monochromatic alternatives that have generally been advanced.

9.2

Having reviewed the essential features of Honderich's theory of "Affirmation," we can now ask if this is indeed, as Honderich claims, the solution we have been seeking for "the problem of the consequences of determinism" (2002, 133). The short answer to this—as with the theory itself—is in some ways "Yes" and, in other ways, "No." Let us begin with what seems to be right and illuminating about "Affirmation." The best way to appreciate the significance of Affirmation is by locating it within the matrix of other available positions on offer. Affirmation is one of several positions on this subject that involve significant modifications and amendments to the more familiar classical accounts. (As Honderich points out, neither the compatibilist or incompatibilist tradition is "absolutely uniform" (2002, 110).) Although several of these theories contain overlapping or common elements, each takes a different turn on some key issues—and Affirmation needs to be distinguished from them in respect of these elements.

Affirmation is most obviously opposed to the idea of Free Will, understood in terms of the form of origination that libertarians seek to secure. In this respect, determinism and Affirmation plainly imply skepticism about the metaphysics of libertarian agency—which is, according to Affirmation, a persisting source of dismay. However, although Affirmation is skeptical about free will and origination, it rejects *complete*, global skepticism about freedom and responsibility. The reason for this is that it rejects the suggestion that origination is our (sole) true idea of freedom. According to Affirmation, voluntariness serves as one kind of freedom and provides a basis for surviving credible forms of responsibility based upon it. It follows from this that any *unqualified* form of dismay or pessimism cannot be supported or sustained, simply because origination is incompatible with the truth of determinism. Affirmation, therefore, rejects "incompatibilist" arguments about freedom and responsibility, and any unqualified pessimism that it may be taken to license on the ground that they fail to accommodate the dual nature of our concepts of freedom and responsibility (see, e.g. Strawson 1994).

Not all skeptics about freedom and moral responsibility take themselves to be committed to dismay or pessimism as a metaphysical attitude that flows from the truth of determinism. An important recent development in the free will debate has been an effort, by Derk Pereboom, Gregg Caruso and others, to defend "Hard Incompatibilism" or "Optimistic Skepticism," which holds that the only form of freedom that grounds desert-based theories of responsibility is origination and that, although this is impossible, no deep or unqualified pessimism flows from this. On the contrary, there are, they claim, significant *benefits* to this skeptical outlook (see, e.g. Pereboom 2001; Waller 2011; Caruso, forthcoming; Pereboom and Caruso 2018). There are certainly some important affinities between Honderich's Affirmation and "Hard Incompatibilism," but, as Honderich shows, there remain important points of divergence (2002, 143). One aspect of this is that Affirmation remains firmly committed to the stance of dismay (or pessimism)—rooted in skepticism about the idea of Free Will—which is a stance that Hard Incompatibilism aims to discredit or minimize. The crucial point here is that Affirmation refuses to deny the source of dismay that determinism generates, as grounded in skepticism about the (incompatibilist) idea of free will or origination.

One further theory that we should consider in this context is "Illusion," as advanced and defended by Saul Smilansky (2000, 36–38). As with Hard Incompatibilism, Smilansky's "Illusionism" bears some family resemblance to Affirmation. One important feature they share is a "dualist" view about the nature of freedom and responsibility, which denies that we have just one conception which renders either compatibilism or incompatibilism true or false. Where they diverge, however, is that "Illusionism" takes the importance of origination to be so deep and pervasive in our ethical lives that for practical reasons we should encourage and promote *belief* in origination—even if we have some theoretical reason for doubting it (e.g. evidence of the truth of determinism). For Illusionism, the truth of determinism and abandoning the idea of free will would be so catastrophic and disastrous for our ethical and social lives that we must reject any option or theory that would encourage skepticism about the idea of Free Will. This is a view that Honderich, explicitly rejects. The philosophy of life that Affirmation embraces insists that the path of Illusion is neither necessary nor desirable and that Affirmation secures all that is needed to sustain and support a worthwhile life and a viable ethical community (2002, 126, 131–132).

Where does this taxonomy of Affirmation in relation to other alternative views leave us? In my view, Affirmation not only presents a distinctive stance and position on this issue, on all the points and issues that separate it from its alternatives mentioned above, it generally takes the right view. Affirmation is correct, for example, to reject "Monism" about the concept of freedom as it concerns moral responsibility. Related to this, it is right to reject any unqualified skepticism about freedom and responsibility, along with any unqualified pessimism or dismay that may be based on it. Finally, I would also agree that Affirmation is right to repudiate "Illusionism" as a way of dealing with the "probable" truth of determinism, insist instead on being truthful about our human predicament. In several respects Affirmation shares some of the key merits and strengths in P.F. Strawson's influential contribution to this topic in his paper "Freedom and Resentment."[2] Along with Strawson, Affirmation places emphasis on moral sentiments or reactive attitudes in accounting for moral responsibility. Both aim to "reconcile" the main parties in this dispute by means of accepting some of their claims and not others and present a position that gives us a recognizable picture of human agents as part of the natural world. However, what does separate Affirmation from Strawson's theory is that it does not claim to "leave things just as they are" (2002, 99). Affirmation insists on recognizing the real losses, as well as the gains, that come with this philosophy of life (2002, 126, 131). In all these respects, so it seems to me, Affirmation is firmly on the right track and highly illuminating.

Having indicated what makes Affirmation distinctive, illuminating, and credible, let me now consider some other important matters in respect of which it is less convincing. In order to do this, I want to compare Affirmation with another perspective on the free will problem—a view I will call Free Will Pessimism (Russell 2017a). The label Free Will Pessimism does not involve a metaphysical attitude that is based on some form of free will skepticism. On the contrary, whereas free will skepticism is the view that our vulnerability to conditions of fate and luck serve to discredit our view of ourselves as full and responsible agents (e.g. as implied by the truth of determinism), Free Will Pessimism *rejects* free will skepticism. The basis of its pessimism rests with the assumption that we *are* free and responsible agents who are, nevertheless, subject to fate and luck. According to Free Will Pessimism, all the major parties and positions in free will debate (both compatibilists and incompatibilists) are committed to modes of evasion and distortion regarding our human predicament in respect of agency and moral life. The question that arises, therefore, is whether or not the "dualism" involved in Affirmation, in respect of both its understanding of two concepts of freedom and the associated split in our metaphysical attitudes, effectively identifies and overcomes these modes of evasion?

In order to describe the alternative picture that Free Will Pessimism presents of the free will problem as it relates to the consequences of determinism, we need to consider, first, the core incompatibilist argument against all compatibilist strategies and proposals. Let us call this incompatibilist argument the Basic Exclusion Argument (BEA):

1. There is a set of conditions φ (under some contested interpretation) such that an agent is free and responsible for an action or set of actions when these conditions are satisfied.
2. There is another set of conditions β (under some contested interpretation) such that an agent's action or set of actions are subject to fate and luck when those conditions are satisfied.
3. Any action (or set of actions) that satisfy φ cannot be such that it also satisfies β. That is to say, if an action X satisfies φ it cannot also be subject to β. < *Exclusion Premise (EP)* >.
4. Any and all compatibilist interpretations of φ are such that they may be satisfied and still be subject to β (i.e. compatibilist conditions φ^* do not support or satisfy EP/ #3 above).

---

5. It follows that we must reject any and all compatibilist interpretations φ^*, as they are inadequate as judged by a standard that compatibilists do not and cannot reject (EP).

Libertarians believe that their own interpretation of conditions φ can satisfy EP and avoid the skeptical conclusion, although this requires the falsity of determinism. Skeptics maintain that there is no avoidable set of conditions φ that serve to satisfy EP and, hence, the skeptical conclusion goes through either way—whether determinism is true or false.

Proponents of BEA are entirely justified in claiming that compatibilists have consistently adhered to EP and aimed to satisfy it. What compatibilists have denied is premise #4, the claim that compatibilism fails to satisfy the standard set by EP (premise #3). Let us consider, then, the classical compatibilist argument that is launched against premise #4, an argument aiming to show that agents who satisfy suitably interpreted compatibilist conditions (φ^*) are not subject to fate and luck (i.e. conditions β). The core feature of this argument is that the incompatibilist claim (premise #4) relies on a basic confusion between fatalism and determinism. More specifically, if we properly interpret conditions β (i.e. as conditions β^*), then premise #4 is groundless. Fatalism is the doctrine that all our deliberations and actions are *causally ineffective* and make no difference but nothing about the thesis of determinism implies that this is the universal condition (see, e.g. Ayer 1954, 22–23; and especially Dennett 1984, 104–105, 129).

This line of response, aimed at refuting premise #4, may be found doubly unconvincing. First, appealing to this distinction between determinism and fatalism is a shallow and evasive understanding of incompatibilist concerns. The relevant issue is not about the causal influence *of* the agent but rather the causal influence *on* the agent. On the assumption of determinism, however complex the mechanisms or capacities involved, the ultimate source or origin of conduct and character is external to the agent and not within the agent's control or influence. For this reason, we need to distinguish "contributory fatalism," which concerns the universal causal impotence of agents, from "origination fatalism," which concerns the causal source or origins of an agent's conduct and character and the limits of control over this. Whereas determinism does not imply universal contributory fatalism, it does imply universal origination fatalism—and it is this that is found particularly troubling (Russell 2000, 2017a).[3]

The second objection flows from the first. Given the issue of origination fatalism and the limits of control over conduct and character, as generated on compatibilist models, we run directly into worries about moral luck. The general worry here is about agents being subject to moral evaluation (i.e. reactive attitudes etc.) in ways that are sensitive to factors they do not control (Nagel 1976). Granted that it is intuitively unjust to hold agents responsible for aspects of their conduct and character that they do not control (as per EP, premise #3), conditions of freedom and responsibility cannot be sustained in these circumstances where an agent is subject to fate and luck along the lines described. The familiar compatibilist line of response to this, consistent with much contemporary compatibilist thinking, is that human agents are "not just lucky," we are "skilled self-controllers" (Dennett 1984, 94). Once again, however, this general line of reply seems not to engage with the real force or basis of incompatibilist concern. Incompatibilists recognize, of course, that compatibilist accounts of self-control and reason-responsiveness do not leave us "merely lucky" or unskilled, unable to enhance our abilities and talents. The point is, rather, that the specific capacities we have, the way we actually exercise them, and the occasions we are provided for employing them, all depend, given deterministic assumptions, on external factors and conditions no agent ultimately has control over.

On this account, the free will problem, as generally understood, turns on the assumption that EP is correct and that the most effective compatibilist strategy depends on refuting premise #4. Incompatibilists claim that this cannot be done and that determinism implies skepticism about freedom and responsibility. There is, however, an alternative strategy we may call "Critical Compatibilism." Critical Compatibilism *accepts* premise #4 and agrees with incompatibilists that orthodox compatibilist attempts to refute are shallow and evasive and, as such, fail. At the same time, critical compatibilists reject the skeptical conclusion because they reject EP/ premise #3. According to Critical Compatibilism, *any plausible* form of compatibilism must recognize and acknowledge the influence of fate and luck on the manner and context in which our capacities of rational self-control operate. In taking this view, Critical Compatibilism maintains that any plausible form of compatibilism must accept Free Will Pessimism, which allows that free and responsible agents may still be subject to significant forms of fate and luck (contrary to the requirements of EP).

An important feature of Critical Compatibilism is the particular set of metaphysical attitudes that this stance naturally licenses or occasions. In circumstances where EP is not satisfied, we have (deep) reasons for being "troubled" or "disconcerted" by our predicament as this relates to human ethical life and moral agency. Even if we are "fortunate" in the particular ethical trajectory our lives may take, there is no basis—as incompatibilists rightly insist—for an easy optimism when fate and luck intrude into our ethical lives and the way we may exercise our moral agency. The crucial point, in relation to Critical Compatibilism, is that a pessimism (or sense of "dismay") of this nature is not rooted or grounded in skepticism about free will and moral responsibility. On the contrary, it presupposes that we *reject* any skepticism of this kind, since the form of pessimism that is occasioned depends on viewing ourselves and others as agents who are free and responsible but, nevertheless, subject to fate and luck in the exercise and operation of our moral capacities.

With this understanding of the central features of Free Will Pessimism in place, we may now turn back to Affirmation and ask where it stands in relation to Free Will Pessimism? We can begin by asking, more specifically, where Affirmation stands on the issue of whether to accept or reject EP (premise #3 of BEA)? Clearly, Affirmation may go in one or other of two directions. Affirmation may be interpreted—and, on the face of it, is most plausibly interpreted—as offering a "dualist" response to EP which holds that it is *both* satisfied and not satisfied, depending from which side of the compatibilist/incompatibilist fence we are viewing it. Given the truth of determinism and the consequent impossibility of origination or free will, Affirmation will agree with Incompatibilists that EP cannot be satisfied in *terms of this concept*—and this will license our sense of dismay based on skepticism about freedom and moral responsibility (as suggested by BEA). This is, however, only one side of the mixed dualism of Affirmation. Since we have another concept of freedom, understood in terms of voluntarism, which allows for a different set of implications relative to freedom and responsibility, EP may be satisfied by the relevant set of compatibilist standards. This is the case, if we accept the orthodox compatibilist project, which turns on a refutation of premise #4 (and an acceptance of EP).

If Affirmation is interpreted in the manner described above, then neither of its dualist components involves rejecting or discrediting EP and embracing any form of Free Will Pessimism. The incompatibilist side holds that EP cannot be satisfied but must be respected (hence the skeptical conclusion follows). The compatibilist side holds that EP can be satisfied, as long as we do not conflate modes of freedom and responsibility secured by voluntariness with those that are based on origination or free will. According to Affirmation, both these views can be held together, without contradiction. The two views, along with their accompanying set of attitudes, can be simultaneously held and are insulated from each other because both rest on ideas and concepts that are equally firmly rooted in ordinary life. For this reason, given the truth of determinism, our reflections about EP will generate a measure of both dismay and intransigence—such that the truth of determinism neither leaves our lives in ruins nor leaves everything unchanged and where it was. The crucial point remains, however, that although dismay attaches to the loss of origination, it does not generate any form of Free Will Pessimism, since, on both sides, Affirmation remains committed to *respecting* EP (if not satisfying it). Affirmation, so interpreted, denies the very possibility of Free Will Pessimism (i.e. it accepts EP as it appears in BEA). Another way of putting this point is that, along with the orthodox compatibilist, Affirmation holds that compatibilists should hold onto EP and reject premise number #4, which claims that compatibilist conditions may be satisfied while agents are still subject to fate and luck. The compatibilist element of Affirmation is, on this account, orthodox and not Critical Compatibilist in content. Like other views in the free will debate, Affirmation does not take the step taken by Critical Compatibilists and Free Will Pessimism, which involves discarding the entire ambition of satisfying EP or to find a "solution" conceived in these terms.

Although Affirmation may be interpreted in these terms, it is unsettled and open-ended enough, in relation to these matters, that another interpretation is available to it. Affirmation may accept, with Critical Compatibilism, that any plausible and credible form of compatibilism must accept and embrace Free Will Pessimism. That is to say, the Compatibilist component of Affirmation would not only reject simple intransigence because determinism implies skepticism about origination and the idea of free will, but also because compatibilism, understood in terms of freedom and moral responsibility based on voluntarist views, has its own independent sources of pessimism. This distinct and independent source of pessimism is the claim that free and responsible agents (in compatibilist terms) are still subject to significant modes of fate and luck. All orthodox compatibilist efforts to dismiss this (via refutations of premise #4) are rejected as themselves evasive and shallow responses to a more truthful account of the human predicament. On this interpretation, therefore, there is nothing about Affirmation that *precludes* it from endorsing Free Will Pessimism. The difficulty with Affirmation, as presented, is that despite its other insights, it fails to provide a clear assessment of these issues relating to EP and Free Will Pessimism, leaving its compatibilist component *indeterminate* with respect to these important matters.

One reason why these matters are of such importance is that the sort of "solution" we are looking for here depends on how we understand the problem of determinism in relation to the free will problem. Honderich presents Affirmation as a solution to the problem of determinism based on its dual "Attitudinarian" components (2002, 104, 120–121, 122, 126, 133). He presents Affirmation as restoring a kind of balance and stability in our divergent and contrary responses to the truth of determinism and as providing us with a "philosophy of life" that allows us to recognize and accept certain losses while retaining sufficient resources to carry on with some comfort and confidence. The difficulty we are faced with, however, is to identify carefully and precisely the relevant persisting sources of dismay or pessimism and how exactly they relate to the compatibilist side of Affirmation. As presented, Honderich's account seems to locate all relevant sources of dismay with the loss of origination. If the Critical Compatibilist is correct, this is a mistaken and inadequate analysis of the problem. It is not just that we cannot satisfy the aim and aspirations of EP in Incompatibilist terms but that we need to discard EP *altogether* as a standard for an acceptable solution to the free will problem (a matter which even the skeptic is mistaken about). The *cost* of rejecting or discarding EP as a basic assumption for assessing proposed "solutions" to the free will problem is that we must allow that free, responsible agents are still subject to fate and luck—and this is something that is independently disturbing and troubling and plainly cannot be based on any general skepticism about freedom and responsibility. If Affirmation embraces Free Will Pessimism, then it must abandon any suggestion that it is a "solution" to the free will problem conceived in terms of the ambition to *satisfy* EP on some relevant interpretation. The Free Will Pessimist claims that what we have here is not a (puzzling) problem to be solved, but a *troubling predicament* to be acknowledged. All the major parties in the free will debate—including orthodox compatibilists—are resistant to the suggestion that free, responsible agents may still be subject to significant modes of fate and luck. What still needs to be clarified, however, is where Affirmation stands on this matter.

The foregoing problem is indicative of weaknesses in Affirmation's commitment to the two concepts/two attitudes formula at the heart of its analysis. The split between compatibilism and incompatibilism that serves as the framework of its analysis conceals what all the traditional parties share—namely, a commitment to standards of freedom and responsibility that satisfy EP. As we have noted, even the skeptic shares this standard, taking the view that EP must be respected, even if it cannot be satisfied. It is this *more fundamental conception* that is the real obstacle, not just for understanding the consequences of the truth of determinism, but for understanding the truth about the human predicament with respect to agency, whether (near) determinism is true or not. The question we need to ask, at this juncture, is why have *compatibilists* been so reluctant to embrace Critical Compatibilism and Free Will Pessimism? I have provided a more extended answer to this question elsewhere, but for now a brief summary will suffice (Russell 2017a). What is it about EP that orthodox compatibilists find so difficult to abandon? There are, I suggest, two considerations that run deep in orthodox compatibilist thinking that account for this resistance to jettisoning EP. The first concerns the relationship between the exclusion premise and "the morality system" and the second, related to the first, concerns the question of optimism.

With respect to the first point, the exclusion premise may be understood as an essential feature of what Bernard Williams calls "the morality system" (1985a, Ch. 10). Among the various distinguishing features of "the morality system" is its insistence that moral responsibility, rightly understood, must somehow be capable of "transcending luck," providing a purity that only genuine "rational" agency of some kind makes possible (Williams 1985, 217; see also Nagel 1976). Although orthodox compatibilists resist the aspirations of libertarians to secure some form of absolute or ultimate agency (qua origination), they remain committed to the particular conception of responsibility encouraged by the morality system and believe that it can be satisfied *within compatibilist constraints* (see, e.g. Wallace 1994, 39, 64–66). It is these aims and aspirations that Critical Compatibilism rejects. The trouble with Affirmation, from this point of view, is that, on the face of it, it simply absorbs or incorporates the orthodox compatibilist aims and assumptions of the morality system into its own proposed "solution" to the problem. If this is the case, then both components or dimensions of Affirmation theory retain the problematic baggage of "the morality system" and its peculiar aims and assumptions.

The second point is intimately concerned with the first. A further feature of "the morality system" is its aspiration to secure *optimism of a certain kind*—a comforting and consoling picture about our ethical lives and predicament. This feature of "the morality system" is deeply resistant to any account that suggests that the exercise and operation of our moral and rational capacities depends on large measure on factors that are not controlled or governed by those same capacities and powers. All the parties in the free will debate—libertarians, compatibilists, and skeptics alike—hold onto EP and the particular form of optimism that it insists on. This form of optimism denies the very *possibility* of Free Will Pessimism, much less accepts it as the *truth* about our human predicament.

We may, in light of the above, ask to what extent Affirmation remains committed to this form of optimism as secured by an adherence and commitment to EP? It is certainly evident that, unlike orthodox compatabilism or libertarianism, Affirmation dispenses with any pure or simple optimism. It insists, more specifically, on the need to accommodate "dismay" as having a secure foothold, given the truth of determinism. However, as has also been explained, this form of dismay is grounded entirely in skepticism and the origination of free will. Retaining this form of dismay is consistent with remaining committed to an optimism that rejects the very possibility of Free Will Pessimism (e.g. the skeptic may be pessimistic because EP cannot be satisfied but will not allow that EP should be discarded or abandoned altogether). As things stand, it is not clear whether Affirmation is able or willing to accommodate forms of dismay or pessimism based on rejecting EP and the associated aims and aspirations of the morality system.

Let me conclude by describing an analogy that may help us to appreciate both the strengths and weaknesses of Affirmation. There is an aspect of Affirmation that we may think of in terms of the Duck/Rabbit Gestalt switch. It is a basic feature of Honderich's overall argument that a single image is not the whole truth on this topic. To insist on one side or the other as having the whole truth, and the other as being mistaken, is an error that both compatibilists and incompatibilists share. We can and should, it is argued, accommodate and reconcile the partial truth contained in each perspective or position. We can, as it were, reconcile the view of the Incompatibilist Duck with that of the compatibilist Rabbit, as long as we do not insist on the sole truth of either. Despite its attractions, however, this reconciliation project has its own vulnerabilities. More specifically, if Free Will Pessimism is right, both the compatibilist and incompatibilist components that are absorbed by Affirmation share a deeper and more problematic set of assumptions about the nature and conditions of freedom and moral responsibility. The aims and assumptions in question are those that are encouraged and endorsed by "the morality system." It may be that Affirmation can distance itself from these shared aims and assumptions but, as presented, it does not do this and, to this extent, it fails to identify the deeper difficulties that present themselves with respect to the consequences of determinism and its relevance to the freewill problem as generally understood.[4]

Notes

1. My discussion in this chapter focuses largely on Honderich (2002), which, although it "follows the same path" as the earlier work, is intended to be more than a mere précis of it. As Honderich points out, *How Free Are You?* is not only shorter and more recent, it advances some new lines of argument and interest (2002, 6–7). For all these reasons, it seems the best work to focus my attention on for the purpose of this chapter—but readers

should also consult Honderich's first and larger work for more detailed arguments and discussions relating to his views.

2. There are several overlapping features of Honderich's approach here that run parallel to P.F. Strawson's famous contribution in "Freedom and Resentment" (1962). This includes the importance of not "over-intellectualizing" this issue and, related to this, an understanding of this debate in terms of broadly optimistic and pessimistic metaphysical attitudes.
3. Whether we attach the label "fate" to this concern is merely a verbal matter—the substantial concern or issue remains with us.
4. It may be argued that Honderich's commitment to a dualist picture of our conceptual commitment and metaphysical attitudes requires a richer genealogical approach—one that is more sensitive to how we (modern, Westerners) have acquired the aims and assumptions of "the morality system" and its specific views about moral freedom and ethical life. This is certainly one feature that divides Honderich's (ahistorical) approach from William's more self-conscious genealogical account. See, in particular, Williams (1993).

References

Ayer, A. J. 1954. Freedom and necessity. Reprinted in *Free will*, ed. Gary Watson, 15–23. Oxford: Oxford University Press.

Caruso, Gregg D. forthcoming. Free will skepticism and its implications: An argument for optimism. In *Free will skepticism in law and society*, ed. Elizabeth Shaw, Derk Pereboom, and Gregg D. Caruso. Cambridge, MA: Cambridge University Press.

Dennett, Daniel. 1984. *Elbow room: The varieties of free will worth wanting*. Oxford: Clarendon Press.

Honderich, Ted. 1988. *A theory of determinism: The mind, neuroscience and life hopes*. Oxford: Oxford University Press.

———. 2002. *How free are you?* Oxford: Oxford University Press.

Nagel, Thomas. 1976. Moral luck. Reprinted in *The philosophy of free will: Essential readings from the contemporary debates*, eds. Paul Russell and Oisin Deery, 31–42. New York: Oxford University Press.

Pereboom, Derk. 2001. *Living without free will*. Cambridge, MA: Cambridge University Press.

———. 2013. Optimistic skepticism about free will. In *The philosophy of free will: Essential readings from the contemporary debates*, ed. Paul Russell and Oisin Deery, 421–449. New York: Oxford University Press.

———. 2014. *Free will, agency, and meaning in life*. Oxford: Oxford University Press.
Pereboom, Derk, and Gregg D. Caruso. 2018. Hard-incompatibilist existentialism: Neuroscience, punishment, and meaning in life. In *Neuroexistentialism: Meaning, morals, and purpose in the age of neuroscience*, ed. Gregg D. Caruso and Owen Flanagan. New York: Oxford University Press.
Russell, Paul. 2000. Compatibilist fatalism. Reprinted in *The philosophy of free will: Essential readings from the contemporary debates*, eds. Paul Russell and Oisin Deery, 450–468. New York: Oxford University Press.
———. 2002. Pessimists, pollyannas and the new compatibilism. In *The Oxford handbook of free will*, ed. Robert Kane, 229–256. New York: Oxford University Press.
———. 2017a. Free will pessimism. In *Oxford studies in agency and responsibility*, vol. 4, ed. David Shoemaker. Oxford: Oxford University Press. Reprinted in Russell (2017b).
———. 2017b. *The limits of free will: Selected essays*. New York: Oxford University Press.
Russell, Paul, and Oisin Deery, eds. 2013. *The philosophy of free will: Essential readings from the contemporary debates*. New York: Oxford University Press.
Smilansky, Saul. 2000. *Free will and illusion*. Oxford: Oxford University Press.
Strawson, Peter F. 1962. Freedom and resentment. Reprinted in *The Philosophy of free will: Essential readings from the contemporary debates*, eds. Paul Russell and Oisin Deery, 63–83. New York: Oxford University Press.
Strawson, Galen. 1994. The impossibility of ultimate moral responsibility. Reprinted in *The philosophy of free will: Essential readings from the contemporary debates*, eds. Paul Russell and Oisin Deery, 363–378. New York: Oxford University Press.
Wallace, R. Jay. 1994. *Responsibility and the moral sentiments*. Cambridge, MA: Harvard University Press.
Waller, Bruce. 2011. *Against moral responsibility*. Cambridge, MA: MIT Press.
Watson, Gary, ed. 1982. *Free will*. Oxford: Oxford University Press.
Williams, Bernard. 1985a. *Ethics and the limits of philosophy*. With a commentary by A.W. Moore and a foreword by Jonathan Lear. Routledge: London and New York: Routledge Classics (edition 2011).
———. 1985b. How free does the will need to be?. Reprinted *Making sense of humanity*, ed. B. Williams, 3–21. Cambridge: Cambridge University Press (1995).
———. 1993. *Shame and necessity*. Berkeley: University of California Press.

10

Attitudinism, the Compatibility Question, and Ballung Concepts

Kevin Timpe

In earlier work, I argued that Ted Honderich's attempt to give us an account of free will that is neither compatibilist nor incompatibilist fails. In the present chapter, I revisit my earlier argument. Drawing on work regarding the social constructionism of Ballung concepts, I now think there's a better way of understanding Honderich's Attitudinism that may avoid my earlier criticism.

10.1 Honderich's View[1]

While there are many issues in the voluminous contemporary free will literature, one of the central questions is what Robert Kane calls 'the Compatibility Question': "Is free will compatible or incompatible with determinism?" (2002, 9). Those who answer this question with 'compatible' are referred to as, not surprisingly, 'compatibilists'; and those who answer with 'incompatible' are, again not surprisingly, 'incompatibilists'.

K. Timpe (✉)
Calvin College, Grand Rapids, MI, USA

G. D. Caruso (ed.), *Ted Honderich on Consciousness, Determinism, and Humanity*, Philosophers in Depth, https://doi.org/10.1007/978-3-319-66754-6_10

While this distinction is at the heart of much of the contemporary free will literature, a number of philosophers have suggested that the distinction between compatibilism and incompatibilism is unhelpful, and perhaps even misguided.

Among them is Ted Honderich. Honderich not only thinks that the Compatibility Question is not the most important question regarding the nature of free will, but also that it falsely suggests that one must be either a compatibilist or an incompatibilist. Consider here the title of one of Honderich's articles on the subject: "Determinism as True, Both Compatibilism and Incompatibilism as False, and the Real Problem" (2002a).[2] This is certainly a provocative title. And while Honderich doesn't shy away from philosophical provocation, it's important to see exactly what he means here.

Neither Compatibilism Nor Incompatibilism

Honderich is careful to distinguish the thesis of causal determinism, as it traditionally figures in the debates about free will and moral responsibility, from the thesis of near-determinism. Causal determinism is typically taken to be the thesis that the course of the future is entirely determined by the conjunction of the non-relational past and the laws of nature.[3] In contrast, 'near determinism,' or 'determinism-where-it-matters,'

> allows that there is or may be some indeterminism but only at what is called the micro-level of our existence, the level of the small particles of our bodies, particles of the kind studied by physics. At the ordinary level of choices and actions, and even ordinary electrochemical activity in our brains, [deterministic] causal laws govern what happens. (Honderich 2002b, 5)

In the present context, what Honderich means by determinism is the following:

> Let us understand by determinism the family of doctrines that human choices and actions are effects of certain causal sequences or chains—sequences such as to raise the further and separate question, as traditionally expressed, of whether the choices and actions are free .... Determinism so conceived is a matter only of macro events. (2002a, 464f)

In other words, in claiming that "determinism is true," Honderich is not embracing the thesis of causal determinism as it is typically understood; he is instead making a weaker claim that all macroscopic events, including all human actions and choices, are effects of causal chains that necessitate their occurrence. But the truth of determinism by itself doesn't settle the question of whether those choices and actions are free or not. That question depends on how one answers the Compatibility Question.

Here, it is important to note that Honderich makes a distinction between 'free will' and 'Free Will.' When Honderich uses the term 'Free Will' (i.e., the capitalized form of the term), he has in mind a conception of free will in which our choices are not causally determined:

> According to this idea [of Free Will], each of us has a kind of personal power to *originate* choices and decisions and thus actions. Their coming-about or initiation definitely wasn't just a matter of [deterministic] cause and effect. Thus on a given occasion, with the past just as it was and the present and ourselves just as they are, we can choose or decide the opposite of what we actually do choose or decide. (2002b, 2)

The last part of this quotation makes clear that Honderich understands Free Will as incompatible with the truth of causal determinism and involving both the ability to do otherwise and origination (or sourcehood).[4] But he does not think free will—what he calls "free will in the ordinary sense" (2002b, 3)—is undermined by the truth of determinism.

Honderich then claims that various aspects of human attitudes—he discusses life-hopes, personal feelings, attitudes about knowledge, and various moral feelings—are not uniform. Given the close connection between free will and moral responsibility in the contemporary literature (including Honderich's writing), I'll focus primarily on what he says about moral feelings; but what he says there parallels what he says about the other kinds of attitudes. Honderich agrees with compatibilists and incompatibilists that free will and responsibility are inseparable: "any ascription of responsibility that there is … contains a conception of freedom …. So if you ascribe responsibility, you have an idea of freedom that goes with this, and vice versa" (2011, 452). But insofar as free will and Free Will are not identical, we'll also have two sets of the related attitudes mentioned above. Here Honderich writes:

> Consider moral responsibility. The subject-matter is sometimes left or made obscure, but it comes to holding people (including ourselves) morally responsible for something bad, and crediting people (including ourselves) with moral responsibility for something good .... These attitudes fall into two kinds, and each of us has both .... If a man injures my daughter in the street, or defrauds her in a financial transaction, or concocts evidence against her in a court, I can focus on his action as voluntary but also originated. I hold him responsible where that involves my seeing his action in a certain way. It came out of his desires and the person he is, *and* it was such that he could have stopped himself from doing it given things as they were. (2002b, 101)

These feelings, Honderich grants, would be unjustified if determinism were true—for if determinism were true, then there is neither Free Will nor the origination which undergirds this set of feelings. "What these reflections show is that holding someone responsible can be something that is inconsistent with determinism. To think of this way of holding people responsible, and to contemplate that determinism is true, is to face dismay" (Honderich 2002b, 102).

But this isn't the whole of the story for Honderich, since there is another set of feelings which are also involved:

> There is no doubt that I can in another way hold the injurer of my daughter responsible. I can focus just on the fact that the injury he did to her was voluntary. It was really owed to him and to his own desires. I can enlarge on this fact to myself in various ways. I can without doubt have strong feelings about him, and speak of his voluntariness as the reason. They will include feelings of repugnance for this person who was able to do the thing in question, and desires for the prevention of such injuries. There is the same possibility in the different case where I morally approve of someone. (2002b, 102)

Honderich doesn't, to my knowledge, give us a worked out theory of the nature of moral responsibility. That's fine, since I don't have one either. However, it is clear from the above comments that he thinks we can be intransigent about one set of attitudes involved in moral responsibility even if we became convinced, as he is, of the truth of determinism. As for the other set of attitudes, we'd have to give them up, leading to dismay for it is true that "determinism *does* threaten something important to us" (2002b, 104). Honderich calls this view—the view that we have these two kinds of attitudes—'Attitudinism.'

Attitudinism as Compatibilism

Attitudinism requires that we realize that when voluntariness (free will) and origination (Free Will) come apart, our reaction to the truth of determinism would also be twofold, including both dismay and intransigence. Dismay is "the sad response to determinism ... of thinking that something ... [is] destroyed or must be entirely given up because determinism is true, of that this is the likely prospect because determinism is likely to be true" (2002b, 155). What must be given up? Our belief in Free Will and the moral responsibility that it is required for. In contrast, intransigence is "the tough response to determinism" in which we realize that things involving free will "are untouched by it" (2002b, 157).

For Honderich, the problem with being convinced of the truth of determinism is not found in either set of reactions considered in isolation, but in our need to see that we have (and should have) them both:

> What all this leads to is the real problem of the consequences of determinism—which is not the problem of proving something to be our one idea of freedom, or our only self-respecting one, or what you will along these lines. The real problem of the consequences of determinism is that of dealing with the situation in which we have both the idea of voluntariness and also the idea of voluntariness plus origination, and these two ideas run, shape, or at least color our lives, and the second conflicts with determinism. We may attempt to bluff and carry on intransigently in the pretence of what matters is only the first idea and what it enters into, our family of attitudes. This is the response of intransigence. On the other hand we may respond with dismay to the prospect of giving up the second idea and what it enters into, the other family of attitudes. (2002a, 473f)

Honderich calls this needed realization of both sets of attitudes 'affirmation':

> What we have to do is try to give up whatever depends on thoughts inconsistent with [the truth of determinism]. Above all we have to try to accept the defeat of certain desires .... What we need to see first is that our attitudes involving voluntariness cannot really allow us to be intransigent, to go on as if determinism changes nothing. We can't successfully barricade ourselves in them. And secondly, our attitudes involving both voluntariness and origination need not give rise to dismay, taking everything as wrecked. That is to forget that in part or in a way these attitudes can persist. They can persist in so far as they involve voluntariness. (2002b, 125)

Honderich thinks we can try to accommodate ourselves and our beliefs to what we can possess if determinism is true—to *affirm* them—while also realizing that there are other beliefs and attitudes we are no longer justified in holding.

To see why in earlier work I argued that Attitudinism should be understood as a form of compatibilism, consider what I've referred to as the 'central compatibilist claim' (CCC) about free will and causal determinism:

CCC: free will is compatible with the truth of determinism.[5]

What makes an account of free will a compatibilist account is simply its endorsement of CCC. According to incompatibilists, CCC is false and the truth of determinism is sufficient to show that there is no free will. Applying bivalence to CCC, we get as a matter of logical necessity either compatibilism or incompatibilism is true.[6] And insofar as he thinks that there is a kind of free will and responsibility which can exist even if it turns out that determinism were true, he too affirms CCC. Honderich, to his credit, anticipates such a response:

> You may want to reply quickly that logically or necessarily it either has to be true that our ordinary conception of freedom is compatible with determinism or that it is not. Just as it either has to be true that you're over six feet tall or that you're not. One or the other has to be true. You may say there is a law of logic about that. But the either-or statement states, or anyway presupposes, something else—that *there is one thing in question with respect to what is called our ordinary idea of freedom*. If there isn't one

> thing, then saying that our ordinary idea of freedom either is or is not compatible with determinism may be perfectly pointless and in fact as good as false. (2002b, 110f)

Insofar as there are numerous different concepts that are picked out by the term 'free will,' and if more than one of these concepts falls under 'the ordinary idea of freedom,' then there is a sense in which Honderich is right. (More about this in the next section.) I've suggested in a number of places that free will should be understood as the control condition on moral responsibility.[7] And there is, as we've seen, a kind of moral responsibility which Honderich thinks is compatible with the truth of causal determinism. Of course, he also thinks that the truth of determinism would not leave moral responsibility untouched, insofar as he thinks there are two aspects to moral responsibility, only one of which is compatible with determinism.

Unlike other compatibilists, Honderich thinks that some aspects of moral responsibility would have to be abandoned if we were to come to discover that determinism were true. But he is quite clear that another aspect of responsibility would remain untouched. Thus, in his view there is a kind of moral responsibility (and thus a kind of free will) which is possible even if determinism were true, and his comments above do not prevent Attitudinism from properly being labeled compatibilism.

In a similar dialectic context, Vargas raises the worry that "we have paid entirely too much attention to the labels of traditional philosophical categories" (2005, 420), such as compatibilism and incompatibilism. And this is a sentiment which I think Honderich would endorse as well. I'm willing to grant that there are important differences between Attitudinism and other extant compatibilist theories. But the term 'compatibilism' (as with the term 'incompatibilism') isn't meant to capture *every* important (or even *the most important*) feature of free will. It may well be that a cluster of theories sharing certain key features cuts across the compatibilism/incompatibilism divide.[8] Nevertheless, Attitudinism (like Vargas's revisionism) shares a key feature with other compatibilist theories: it holds that agents could be free and morally responsible even if causal determinism were true. And while there are important differences between Attitudinism and other leading varieties of compatibilism, this doesn't mean that it does not share a common commitment to CCC.

10.2 Free Will as a Ballung Concept

I appreciate that Honderich wants us to be aware of ways that our actual attitudes and practices are justified, given that he thinks we lack Free Will, and that Attitudinism might help us accomplish this goal. That is why, despite my earlier argument that Attitudinism is a form of compatibilism, I want to consider a reply that might at least mitigate some of my earlier criticism. One element of Attitudinism, the importance of which I think I didn't properly understand in my earlier work, is Honderich's claim that we have more than one idea of free will. And while these ideas often overlap, they're not coextensive—as the distinction between free will and Free Will helps make clear.

Honderich claims that the presumption, which he thinks is shared by both sides of the compatibility debate, that there is *just one* kind of freedom is problematic. Furthermore, it has led astray both compatibilists and incompatibilists:

> They [both compatibilists and incompatibilists] share some single settled idea of what has to be true of a choice if it counts as free, and hence of what has to be true of an action if it counts as free .... The sides differ, as just remarked, about what we are supposed to take a free choice to be .... Both sides agree in assigning to all of us a certain belief, which they take to be a plain truth .... Might it not be that both sides are wrong? ... Might they be wrong in believing that one side or the other in their battle has got to be right? ... It's easy to be inclined to agree with that belief of theirs. You will want to say either that determinism is consistent with freedom or that it isn't. One of those *has* to be true. Just as it *has* to be true that either you're over six feet tall or you're not. (2002b, 6 and 110)[9]

But as the title of his "Both Compatibilism and Incompatibilism as False" article mentioned above indicates, Honderich thinks this approach is mistaken.

Central to Attitudinism is the idea that we do not have a single settled idea of what it means to say that a choice is free, just as we do not have a single settled idea of what it means to be morally responsible. The mistake in the traditional approach to the Compatibility Question is the presupposition that there is a single idea of freedom which undergirds the plethora of our emotions and practices. "We don't have *any* definition of a free choice if a definition is supposed to be the one and only correct description of a thing" (2002b, 112). As a result, we need not be led to feel simply intransigence (as compatibilists think) or simply dismay (as incompatibilists think) if determinism is true. Both of these responses are unsatisfactory.

To better understand Honderich's view, I think it would be useful to draw here on the philosophy of social science literature regarding measurement. Nancy Cartwright and Rosa Runhardt describe measurement as involving three interconnected tasks:

> You may most immediately associate measurement with assigning a number to a specific unit (think, for instance, of measuring someone's height). But deciding to put an individual unit in a specific category is as much as measurement as assigning to them a number or value for some quantity like height or income .... Measurement, though, isn't just assigning values or numbers or putting things into categories; it is doing so in a systematic and grounded way. This involves three different kinds of activities: *characterization*—laying out clearly and explicitly what the quantity or category is, including any features of it that we intend to make use of in assigning a number category to a unit; *representation*—providing a way to represent the quantity or category in our scientific work; and *procedures*—describing just what must be done to carry out the measurement successfully. (2015, 267)

Our interest here will just be with the first of these three tasks, that of characterization. "Before we can measure a quality or specific procedures for deciding if an individual fits into a category, we need to be clear what that quantity or category is" (Cartwright and Runhardt 2015, 267).

Categorization in the social sciences, Cartwright and Runhardt argue, often involves Ballung concepts: "concepts that are characterized by family resemblance between individuals rather than by a definite proper. *Ballung* is a German word for a concentrated cluster" (2015, 268). Furthermore, they argue that, "there is no right or wrong characterization of these Ballung, socially constructed concepts" (2015, 278). The claim that our concepts are socially constructed is developed at greater length by scholars such as Ron Mallon and Ian Hacking. Mallon, for instance, argues that our concepts are socially constructed rather than natural 'givens'; they are not 'discovered' but rather arise out of social practices of a community (Mallon 2015, 2). Different communities and social practices could then construct concepts in slightly different ways; in fact, a Ballung concept could be constructed by different practices within the same community, given the plurality of social practices there. (Think, for instance, of the role that 'disability' plays in legal, educational, medical, and philosophical contexts within contemporary Western culture. We have, it seems to me, a Ballung concept of disability shaped by the plurality of these contexts rather than a single concept.) Furthermore, the selection of a particular concept from this cluster for a particular use is not theory neutral: "ideas do not exist in a vacuum. They inhabit a social setting" (Hacking 1999, 10). The selection of a particular concept from a cluster of interrelated concepts is connected with the use that we want to put that (selected) concept to. Suppose there is a cluster of seven concepts that are logically distinct but related by family resemblance. Which of those we appeal to or seek to utilize in a particular context will depend on what use one intends to put it to. Our concepts are tools "fit for a purpose," and our selection of a particular tool (here, a particular concept from a cluster) can lead us astray if we think that they are universal and fit for all purposes rather than purpose-specific.

I've suggested in passing above, and have argued at greater length elsewhere, that we have at least two fundamentally different conceptions of what free will is in the contemporary literature:

> There seem to be at least two different fundamental notions of what free will is in the contemporary literature. The first of these, which seems to have garnered the most attention in the last century, works under the assumption that for a person to rightly be said to have free will, she must have the ability to do otherwise than what she does, in fact, do. Under this view, I could be said to have freely chosen to drive to work only if I also could have freely chosen, for example, to bike to work or to skip work altogether. This approach to free will is referred to as a 'leeway-based approach' or an 'alternative-possibilities approach.'
>
> In contrast, a smaller percentage of the extant literature focuses primarily on the issues of 'source,' 'ultimacy,' and 'origination.' This second approach doesn't focus immediately on the presence or absence of alternative possibilities. On this approach, I freely choose to drive to work only if

> I am the source of my choice and there is nothing outside of me from which the choice is ultimately derived. In what follows, we refer to the first of these conceptions—the conception that free will is primarily a matter of having alternative possibilities—as the 'leeway-based' conception. Similarly, we will refer to the second of these conceptions—that free will is primarily a matter of our being the source of our choices in a particular way—as the 'sourcehood' conception. (Timpe 2017, 213f)

Now, in addition to these different conceptions of free will (which I have argued are orthogonal to the compatibilism/incompatibilism debate), it may be that the concept of free will is itself a Ballung concept.[10] Our free will concept (or perhaps better, concepts) arises from phenomenology, concerns about responsibility and fairness, the law, moral development, and religious doctrine.[11] I find it implausible that we have a single concept from all of these sources, and that that concept is doing the same theoretical and practical work in all of these contexts.

Suppose that this is right; that is, suppose that 'free will' might be such a constructed concept, one that is actually constructed out of many similar but overlapping concepts that we deploy for different ends. This approach might provide a way of understanding Honderich's claim, quoted at greater length above, that the "real problem of the consequences of determinism" is in the thinking that we all share "some single settled idea of what free will is." As Honderich writes, "we don't have *any* definition of a free choice if a definition is supposed to be the one and only correct description of a thing" (2002b, 112). In my own philosophical work on free will, I've focused especially on the roles our various 'free will' concepts play in underwriting claims about moral responsibility. But even here, given that Honderich also thinks we don't have a single unified idea of moral responsibility, simply limiting our interests to moral responsibility doesn't guarantee a single unified concept.

10.3 Conclusion

As a result, I'm now less certain of my criticisms of Honderich's Attitudinism than I was in the past. I think that before turning to the Compatibility Question, which presupposes that we have a single concept of a set of capacities that either is or isn't compatible with the truth of determinism (or near-determinism), we need to explore the nature of concepts and the ways that their intended employment in our philosophical theorizing might shape our understanding or construction of those concepts. Philosophizing, particularly about issues that interest with so many different social practices, is difficult. And the assumption that the concepts that we use are given and uncontestable is an assumption that, in part because of Honderich's work, that I've come to be skeptical of.

Notes

1. This section is largely drawn from Chap. 3 of Timpe (2013).
2. Insofar as libertarianism is typically understood to be "the conjunction of incompatibilism [the thesis that free will is incompatible with the truth of determinism] and the thesis that we have free will" (van Inwagen 1983, 13f; see also Kane 2002, 17; Pereboom 2006, xiv). I confess that I'm perplexed by those views that go by the name 'libertarian compatibilism' (see Vihvelin 2000 and Arvan 2013) as on the standard use of the terms involved, the name appears to involve a contradiction. For a brief discussion, see Timpe (2017, 213).
3. In his "How to Think about the Problem of Free Will," Peter van Inwagen suggests that everyone ought to define determinism as follows: "Determinism is the thesis that the past and the laws of nature together determine, at every moment, a unique future" (van Inwagen 2008, 330).
4. For a discussion of the relationship between these two ways of understanding the nature of free will, see Timpe (2017).
5. Timpe (2013, 44).
6. Furthermore, both compatibilism and incompatibilism are typically taken to be necessarily true if true at all; thus, it is either the case that compatibilism is necessarily true and incompatibilism is necessarily false or that incompatibilism is necessarily true and compatibilism is necessary false. However, this further point need not concern us here.
7. Timpe (2013) and Timpe and Jacobs (2015). For a contrary view of how free will should be understood, see van Inwagen (2008). For why I reject his advice, see Timpe (2013, 11).

8. As an example, in some ways Ned Markosian's agent-causal compatibilist view shares more in common with Timothy O'Connor's libertarian agent-causalism than it does with Harry Frankfurt's hierarchical compatibilism. Compare Markosian (1999), O'Connor (2002), and Frankfurt (1971).
9. For a similar discussion, see also Honderich (2011, 448ff), where he suggests that there is empirical data supporting the view that we have two conceptions of free will. A similar view can be found in Vargas (2013). In Timpe (2013), I argued that Honderich's view is, like Vargas' view, a form of 'revisionism.' At the heart of revisionist accounts is the belief that we need to revise our view of free will.
10. Experimental philosophy could presumably give us evidence in favor of this claim. In fact, I think that much of the existing experimental work on free will supports this reading, though I will not canvas the relevant literature here.
11. This list is not intended to be exhaustive.

References

Arvan, Marcus. 2013. A new theory of free will. *Philosophical Forum* 44: 1–48.

Cartwright, Nancy, and Rosa Runhardt. 2015. Measurement. In *Philosophy of social science: A new introduction*, ed. Nancy Cartwright and Eleanora Montuschi, 265–287. Oxford: Oxford University Press.

Frankfurt, Harry. 1971. Freedom of the will and the concept of a person. *Journal of Philosophy* 68 (1): 5–20.

Hacking, Ian. 1999. *The social construction of what?* Cambridge, MA: Harvard University Press.

Honderich, Ted. 2002a. Determinism as true, both compatibilism and incompatibilism as false, and the real problem. In *The Oxford handbook of free will*, ed. Robert Kane, 461–476. New York: Oxford University Press.

———. 2002b. *How free are you? The determinism problem*. 2nd ed. New York: Oxford University Press.

———. 2011. Effects, determinism, neither compatibilism nor incompatibilism, consciousness. In *The Oxford handbook of free will*, ed. Robert Kane, 2nd ed., 442–456. New York: Oxford University Press.

Kane, Robert. 2002. Introduction: The contours of contemporary free will debates. In *The Oxford handbook of free will*, ed. Robert Kane, 3–41. New York: Oxford University Press.

Mallon, Ron. 2015. *The construction of human kinds*. New York: Oxford University Press.
Markosian, Ned. 1999. A compatibilist version of the theory of agent causation. *Pacific Philosophical Quarterly* 80: 257–277.
O'Connor, Timothy. 2002. *Persons as causes: The metaphysics of free will*. Oxford: Oxford University Press.
Pereboom, Derk. 2006. *Living without free will*. Cambridge, MA: Cambridge University Press.
Timpe, Kevin. 2013. *Free will and its alternatives*. 2nd ed. London: Bloomsbury.
———. 2017. Leeway vs. sourcehood conceptions of free will. In *Routledge companion to free will*, ed. Kevin Timpe, Meghan Griffith, and Neil Levy, 213–224. New York: Routledge.
Timpe, Kevin, and Jonathan D. Jacobs. 2015. Free will and naturalism: How to be a libertarian and a naturalist too. In *The Blackwell companion to naturalism*, ed. Kelly Jame Clark, 319–335. Malden, MA: Blackwell.
van Inwagen, Peter. 1983. *An essay on free will*. Oxford: Clarendon Press.
———. 2008. How to think about the problem of free will. *Journal of Ethics* 12: 327–341.
Vargas, Manuel. 2005. The revisionist's guide to responsibility. *Philosophical Studies* 125: 399–429.
———. 2013. *Building better beings: A theory of moral responsibility*. New York: Oxford University Press.
Vihvelin, Kadri. 2000. Freedom, foreknowledge, and the principle of alternative possibilities. *Canadian Journal of Philosophy* 30: 1–24.

11

Origination, Moral Responsibility, and Life-Hopes: Ted Honderich on Determinism and Freedom

Gregg D. Caruso

Perhaps no one has written more extensively, more deeply, and more insightfully about determinism and freedom than Ted Honderich (1988, 2002a, 2002b, 2004, 2013). His influence and legacy with regard to the problem of free will—or *the determinism problem*, as he prefers to frame it—loom large. In these comments I would like to focus on two main aspects of Honderich's work: (1) his defense of determinism and its consequences for *origination* and *moral responsibility*; and (2) his concern that the truth of determinism threatens and restricts, but does not eliminate, our *life-hopes*. In many ways, I see my own defense of *free will skepticism* as the natural successor to Honderich's work (see Caruso 2012, 2013, 2016, 2017a, forthcoming). There are, however, some small differences between us. My goal in this chapter is to clarify our areas of agreement and disagreement and to acknowledge my enormous debt to Ted. If I can also move him toward my own more optimistic brand of free will skepticism, then that would be great too.

G. D. Caruso (✉)
Corning Community College, Corning, NY, USA

G. D. Caruso (ed.), *Ted Honderich on Consciousness, Determinism, and Humanity*, Philosophers in Depth, https://doi.org/10.1007/978-3-319-66754-6_11

11.1 Determinism and Its Consequences

Since Honderich's views on determinism and freedom are by now well known, I will provide only a brief summary of them here. To begin, Honderich defends the thesis of determinism, which maintains that ordinary causation is true of all events and that in our choosing and deciding we are subject to causal laws. This amounts to the claim that all our mental events, including choices, decisions, and actions, are effects of causal sequences or chains and therefore have to happen (or are necessitated) and cannot be owed to *origination* (see Honderich 1988, 2002a). More recently, Honderich has preferred to state the thesis of determinism in terms of explanation—saying that determinism is better called *causalism* or *explanationism*, "which names convey that every event has a causal explanation but does not imply something darker than that" (2017). Understood this way, all events or happenings, without exception, are effects or lawful correlates such that each has a fundamental explanation.

If we are good empiricists, as Honderich contends we should be, then we should accept determinism as true since all experience counts in its favor. In fact, "no general proposition of interest has greater inductive and empirical support than that all events whatever, including the choices or decisions and the like, have explanations" (2002b, p. 462). Honderich has further argued that quantum mechanics has not falsified determinism. Not only has there been "*no direct and univocal experimental evidence* of the existence of quantum event" (2002b, p. 463), he argues that the standard interpretation of quantum mechanics is a "logical mess" and contains "contradiction" in it (see 1988, 2002a, 2002b, 2004, 2013).

Throughout his corpus, Honderich has also explored the consequences of determinism for our lives and for free will. He has argued that both compatibilist and incompatibilist approaches fail to adequately deal with the problem of determinism because they both share the mistaken assumption that there is only one conception of free will. Honderich instead argues that there are actually two conceptions of free will—free will as *voluntariness* and as *origination*. While the former is compatible with determinism, the latter is not. Honderich acknowledges, however, that the truth of determinism and the loss of origination create concerns for our "standing" as human beings and for our "life-hopes." In an attempt to preserve some of what is lost when we give up the idea of origination and the responsibility attached to it, Honderich has introduced his "grand hope" for humanity, which involves abandoning the "politics of desert" and embracing the *Principle of Humanity* (see Honderich 2013), which aims at getting and keeping people out of bad lives.

Before exploring the consequences of determinism for our *life-hopes* in the following section, let me first say something about Honderich's views on origination and moral responsibility and how they line up with my own position of free will skepticism. *Free will skepticism*, as I conceive it, maintains that what we do, and the way we are, is ultimately the result of factors beyond our control and because of this we are never morally responsible for our actions in the *basic desert* sense (Pereboom 2001, 2014; Strawson 1986; Caruso and Morris 2017)—the sense that would make us *truly deserving* of praise and blame. In the past, the standard argument for free will skepticism was *hard determinism*: the view that determinism is true, and incompatible with free will and basic desert moral responsibility—either because it precludes the *ability to do otherwise* (leeway incompatibilism) or because it is inconsistent with one's being the "ultimate source" of action (source incompatibilism). For hard determinists, libertarian free will is an impossibility because human actions are part of a fully deterministic world and compatibilism is operating in bad faith.

While hard determinism had its classic statement in the time when Newtonian physics reigned, it has very few defenders today—largely because the standard interpretation of quantum mechanics (despite Honderich's best efforts) has been taken by many to undermine, or at least throw into doubt, the thesis of universal determinism. This is not to say, of course, that determinism has been refuted or falsified by modern physics, because it has not. Honderich is a testament to the fact that determinism still has its modern defenders. We also need to acknowledge that the final interpretation of physics is not yet in. Furthermore, it is important to keep in mind that even if we allow some indeterminacy to exist at the microlevel of our existence—the level studied by quantum mechanics—it's still likely that there remains what Honderich calls *near-determinism* or *determinism-where-it-matters* (2002a, p. 5).

That is: "At the ordinary level of choices and actions, and even ordinary electrochemical activity in our brains, causal laws govern what happens. It's all cause and effect in what you might call real life" (2002a, p. 5).

My own reasons for accepting free will skepticism, however, are best described as a version of *hard-incompatibilism* (see Pereboom 2001, 2014; Pereboom and Caruso 2018). Hard incompatibilism amounts to a rejection of both compatibilism and libertarianism. It maintains that the sort of free will required for basic desert moral responsibility is incompatible with causal determination by factors beyond the agent's control and *also* with the kind of indeterminacy in action required by the most plausible versions of libertarianism. Against the view that free will is compatible with the causal determination of our actions by natural factors beyond our control, I contend that there is no relevant difference between this prospect and our actions being causally determined by manipulators (see Pereboom 2001, 2014). I further argue that it is incompatible with an agent's *ability to do otherwise*, a necessary condition for free will. Against event causal libertarianism, I object that on such accounts agents are left unable to *settle* whether a decision occurs and hence cannot have the control required for moral responsibility (Caruso 2012, 2015; see also Pereboom 2001, 2014). The same problem, I contend, arises for non-causal libertarian accounts, which also fail to provide agents with the control in action required for basic desert moral responsibility. While agent-causal libertarianism could, in theory, supply this sort of control, I argue that it cannot be reconciled with our best physical theories and faces additional problems accounting for mental causation (Caruso 2012). Since this exhausts the options for views on which we have the sort of free will at issue, I conclude that free will skepticism is the only remaining position.

While I generally accept Honderich's conception of determinism with regard to human choices, decisions, and actions—and agree strongly with *near-determinism*, or what I have elsewhere called *hard-enough determinism* (Caruso 2012)—my primary reason for accepting free will skepticism is hard-incompatibilism. That is, I am officially agnostic about the kind of indeterminism posited by the traditional interpretation of quantum mechanics. While my view is similar to Honderich's, then, it is not identical. I also imagine that Honderich would resist my univocal treatment of *free will* and my label of *free will skepticism* since he shuns the traditional categories of the debate. I would, however, like to push on this latter point a bit to see if can get Honderich to at least agree that his view is a *form* of free will skepticism—in fact, the form *most relevant* to the traditional debate.

In the historical debate, the variety of free will that is of central philosophical and practical importance is the sort required for moral responsibility in a particular but pervasive sense. This sense of moral responsibility is set apart by the notion of *basic desert* (Pereboom 2001, 2014; Strawson 1986; Caruso and Morris 2017) and is purely backward-looking and non-consequentialist. I follow Derk Pereboom in defining basic desert moral responsibility as follows:

> For an agent to be morally responsible for an action in this sense is for it to be hers in such a way that she would deserve to be blamed if she understood that it was morally wrong, and she would deserve to be praised if she understood that it was morally exemplary. The desert at issue here is *basic* in the sense that the agent would deserve to be blamed or praised just because she has performed the action, given an understanding of its moral status, and not, for example, merely by virtue of consequentialist or contractualist considerations. (2014, p. 2)

I have elsewhere argued that we can also understand basic desert moral responsibility in terms of whether it would ever be appropriate for a divine all-knowing judge (who didn't necessarily create the agents in question) to administer differing kinds of treatment (i.e., greater or lesser rewards or punishments) to human agents on the basis of actions that these agents performed during their lifetime. The purpose of invoking the notion of a divine judge in the afterlife is to instill the idea that any rewards or punishments issued after death will have no further utility—be it positive or negative. Any differences in treatment to agents (however slight) would therefore seem warranted only from a *basic desert* sense, and not a consequentialist perspective (see Caruso and Morris 2017).

Understood this way, free will is a kind of power or ability an agent must possess in order to justify certain kinds of desert-based judgments, attitudes, or treatments in response to decisions or actions that the agent performed or failed to perform. These desert-based judgments, attitudes, and treatments would be justified on purely backward-looking grounds and would not appeal to consequentialist or contractualist considerations. It is this kind of free will and moral responsibility that is being denied by free will skeptics like myself, Derk Pereboom (2001, 2014), Galen Strawson (1986), and Neil Levy (2011). And I would argue that it is also the kind of free will rejected by Honderich since his position maintains that determinism is incompatible with origination and the kind of moral responsibility attached to it.

According to Honderich, "[t]he theory of determinism we are putting together, and more particularly the fundamental part that can be called Initiation Determinism, takes a choice to be a real effect, like the neural event associated with it" (2002a, p. 37). *Initiation Determinism* maintains that all choices and other conscious events are effects of heredity and environment. The importance of this with regard to the traditional free will debate is that such determinism is incompatible with what Honderich calls *origination*—that is, the idea that an action is owed to a choice or decision that is uncaused and yet within the control of the actor (2013, p. 57). According to Honderich, the conception of free will as origination is "the primary ordinary sense, the sense that matters" (2013, p. 57). Furthermore, our being free in the origination sense, "and hence our being held responsible and credited with responsibility for our actions, not to mention our prospect of heaven, is our being free in a way logically incompatible with determinism" (2013, p. 57). Lastly, according to Honderich: "[I]t is likely that a Free Will theory really cannot get rid of the embarrassment of an originator. It has to have *something* that is going to be responsible. A past decision itself, whether it was probable or self-causing or teleological or anything else, isn't what we hold responsible for actions or give a kind of moral credit to for actions" (2002a, p. 54). Given such comments, I maintain that it is legitimate to label Honderich a free will skeptic since the kind of free will he denies is precisely the kind free will skeptics deny. While *voluntariness* is an important concept, neither Honderich nor I believe it is enough to ground basic desert moral responsibility. And since basic desert moral responsibility is, I contend, what is of central philosophical and practical importance in the historical debate, I think Honderich should embrace a more full-throated free will skepticism.

Now, I imagine that Honderich may disagree with my last point (about what is of central philosophical and practical importance) but I have elsewhere argued that there are several distinct advantages to defining free will in terms of the control in action required for basic desert moral responsibility: (1) it provides a neutral definition that virtually all parties can agree to—that is, it doesn't exclude from the outset various conceptions of free will that are available for compatibilists, libertarians, and free will skeptics to adopt; (2) it captures the practical importance of the debate; (3) it fits with the commonsense (i.e., folk) understanding of these concepts; and, perhaps most importantly, (4) rejecting this understanding of free will makes it difficult to understand the nature of the substantive disputes that are driving the free will debate (see Caruso and Morris 2017 for a detailed defense of (1)–(4)). If I am correct that basic desert moral responsibility is what is of central philosophical and practical importance in the free will debate, then the following argument can be given for labeling Honderich a free will skeptic:

1. According to Honderich, only *origination*—the idea that an action is owed to a choice or decision that is uncaused and yet within the control of the actor—can preserve the kind of free will needed for basic desert moral responsibility. [*Voluntariness* is not enough to ground basic desert moral responsibility—i.e., "our being held responsible and credited with responsibility for our actions, not to mention our prospect of heaven, is our being free in way logically incompatible with determinism" (Honderich 2013, p. 57).]
2. Origination is incompatible with determinism (and near-determinism).
3. Determinism (or near-determinism) is true.
4. Hence, we lack the kind of free will needed for basic desert moral responsibility—that is, we are never truly deserving of praise and blame in the backward-looking, non-consequentialist sense. [This is the thesis of free will skepticism.]

Honderich should accept this conclusion since it is entailed by his own arguments and commitments. I therefore encourage Honderich to self-identify as a free will skeptic and drop his pluralistic approach to the traditional debate. By rejecting the traditional compatibilist/incompatibilist distinction and embracing two different conceptions of free will, Honderich gives the *mistaken* impression that he takes voluntariness to mean the same thing that compatibilists do. This, however, is not the case since most compatibilists take voluntariness (appropriately defined and qualified) to be *sufficient* for basic desert moral responsibility—something Honderich clearly rejects. Honderich is therefore a traditional incompatibilist when it comes to the core question: Is determinism compatible with the kind of free will required for basic desert moral responsibility?

To avoid confusion moving forward, however, I will adopt the terms *origination skepticism* and *moral responsibility skepticism* for the more specific positions Honderich embraces and restrict *free will skepticism* for my own broader set of assumptions.

11.2 Life-Hopes

We have just seen that according to Honderich, the truth of determinism requires that we give up the concept of "origination" and with it the promise of an open future. While we might have been the author of own actions and thus held accountable and morally responsible in a way more acceptable to common sense, determinism (and hard-incompatibilism) rules out this possibility. While most *origination skeptics* and *moral responsibility skeptics* appear to welcome the practical implications of such a view, Honderich expresses a genuine sense of real loss. Unlike the *optimistic skepticisms* of Derk Pereboom, Bruce Waller (2011, 2015), and myself, Honderich is authentically "dismayed" by the consequences of determinism since he thinks it threatens and restricts our *life-hopes.*

According to Honderich, life-hopes give an individual's life a good deal of its meaning and they tend to have two kinds of content. The first kind of content has to do with a state of affairs that we hope for—say becoming a successful philosopher, being a good father, or simply having a decent life. Here a *hope* is defined as "a desire for something, involving an approving valuation of it, bound up with feeling, and such that it is not certain that the thing will come about" (2002a, pp. 92–93). The narrow state of affairs that make up the content of our hopes is important, but less important than something else: "The other kind of content of a hope has to do with our future actions, maybe a long campaign of them" (2002a, p. 92). For Honderich, life-hopes are about more than just wanting things—they are about our *future actions*. This is because it is through our own actions that we will get what we want. "We are not fatalists of a certain ancient kind," he writes, "who feel that what will happen in their future will have nothing to do with their own actions." Instead, we think of our futures in terms of our coming actions—that is, "we think in terms of what can be called *initiating* our actions" (2002a, p. 92).

The problem, we are told, is that we have a kind of life-hope that is incompatible with a belief in determinism. This kind of life-hope involves thinking of our future as open or unfixed or alterable. As Honderich writes: "If I have a hope of this kind, I take it that questions about my future are not yet answered—it is not that the answers are already settled and stored up, but that they do not yet exist. I've got a chance. It's up to me. Maybe I can succeed" (2002a, p. 93). This kind of life-hope can be said to involve thinking that our futures are not just products or automatic upshots of our characters, past experiences, situational circumstances, or natures. Life-hopes, understood this way, require free will and origination since they require that the future is open and my nature and environment is overcomable.

For Honderich, the fact that determinism is incompatible with such life-hopes is dismaying:

> Suppose you become convinced of the truth of our theory of determinism. Becoming really convinced will not be easy, for several reasons. But try not to imagine a day when you do come to believe determinism fully. Also imagine bringing your new belief together with a life-hope of the kind we have been considering, this natural way of contemplating your future. What would the upshot be? It would almost certainly be *dismay*. Your response to determinism in connection with the hope would be dismay. If you really were persuaded of determinism, the hope would collapse … This is because such a hope has a necessary part or condition on which the rest of it depends. That is the image of origination. There can be no such hope if all the future is just effects of effects. It for this reason, I think, that many people have found determinism to be a black thing. John Stuart Mill felt it as an incubus, and, to speak for myself, it has certainly got me down in the past. (2002a, pp. 94–95)

It seems, then, that while Honderich is the foremost champion of determinism, he does not find its consequences completely welcoming—at least not with regard to our life-hopes. While he acknowledges that there is another kind of life-hopes which is *not* threatened by determinism—hopes that have in them the picture of future actions done out of *embraced desires* (2002a, p. 95)—he nonetheless feels that dismay is a legitimate reaction with regard to life-hopes of the first kind (the kind that requires origination and not just voluntariness). While I do not completely disagree with Honderich's assessment of life-hopes, especially if one includes in it his discussion of rejecting dismay and achieving a kind of "satisfied intransigence" (2002a, Chap. 8) or better yet adopting an attitude of *affirmation*, I tend to be more optimistic in my reaction to determinism and origination skepticism than he is (but he can correct me if I am wrong about this).

I consider myself an *optimistic skeptic*. As such, I maintain that life without free will (of the origination variety) and basic desert moral responsibility would not be as destructive as many people believe. I have elsewhere argued, for instance, that prospects of finding meaning in life or of sustaining good interpersonal relationships would not be threatened (see Pereboom and Caruso 2018). And although retributivism and severe punishment, such as the death penalty, would be ruled out, incapacitation and rehabilitation programs would still be justified (see Caruso 2016, 2017b; Pereboom and Caruso 2018). I have also extended my optimism about the practical implications of free will skepticism to the question of creativity (Caruso 2017a). Since creativity resembles in many ways Honderich's life-hopes—in that both manifest a desire for creative agency through which we strive for and hopefully achieve our creative, artistic, and life goals—I would like to offer a solution to Honderich's dismay which builds on my response to the *question of creativity*.

One aspect of the traditional free will debate that is often overlooked is the *question of creativity*—that is, whether free will (and origination) is required for genuine creativity and whether agents justly deserve to be praised and blamed for their artistic and creative achievements. The question of creativity, I have argued, is relevant to the problem of free will because it raises important questions about human agency, ability and effort, origination, assessment and evaluation, just deserts, and reward and punishment (see Caruso 2017a). Artistic activities, for instance, involve factors intrinsic to the agent such as *developing* their talents or *taking advantage* of their abilities (e.g., being good at the piano is not a matter of *pure luck*—unlike, say, being born with beautiful green eyes) (Russell 2008, p. 309). While we may acknowledge the role luck plays in terms of innate gifts, opportunities, and artistic achievements (e.g., awards and recognitions), we nonetheless believe that agents are capable of exercising *effort* and working hard to *develop* their artistic skills and abilities. The fact that Wolfgang Amadeus Mozart was born into a musical family with a father who was a professional musician, does not change the fact that he needed to *take advantage* of this opportunity and work hard to *develop* his musical talent.

Additionally, from the perspective of the spectator, artistic activities also invite us to take up what Paul Russell calls the "evaluative stance" toward the agent as well as the performance, creation, or product (2008, p. 310). Human beings not only evaluate the moral actions of their fellows, but also evaluate their artistic activities. We may say of a work of art or performance that it was done well or poorly and we may administer rewards and punishments in response to it. It should also be noted that such praise and criticism are not limited to the artistic performance or creation but go down deeper to the qualities of the *agent* considered as the *source* of the performance. As Russell notes: "Great performances and achievements secure rewards and prizes, criticism and condemnation, for the *person* who produced them. It is the *agent* who receives whatever retributive response is called forth by her activities or performance" (Russell 2008, p. 310). What I'm calling the *question of creativity* should therefore be understood as the question of what conditions are required for genuine creativity and whether agents justly deserve to be praised and blamed for their creative and artistic activities.

Without going into too much detail here, the position I have defended maintains that while people do not deserve praise or blame in the basic desert sense, there are replacement reactive attitudes that could serve similar functions. I contend that forward-looking accounts of moral responsibility (e.g., Pereboom 2014), which are perfectly consistent with free will skepticism, can justify calling agents to account for immoral behavior as well as providing encouragement for creative activities since these are important for future formation and development. I further argue that relinquishing belief in free will and basic desert would not mean the death of creativity or our sense of achievement since important and realistic conceptions of both remain in place. Let me briefly explain (see Caruso 2017a for more details).

This year we celebrate the centenary of Albert Einstein's discovery of a new theory of gravity—general relativity. It is easy to find in the media statements like the following: "Einstein's achievement required perseverance and enormous creativity, as he struggled over a rough and winding road for eight years to formulate the theory" (Smeenk 2015). Some defenders of origination fear that if determinism or free will skepticism were true, we would be unable to legitimately attribute "perseverance" and "enormous creativity" to Einstein. There is no reason to think, however, that this would be so. If these traits were constitutive of Einstein's character, if they were reflective of who he was, then we are warranted in attributing them to Einstein the person. The denial of free will and basic desert moral responsibility does not prohibit us from making such attributions, nor does it prohibit us from acknowledging the important role character plays in determining outcomes. The free will skeptic can recognize that the virtues of Einstein's character were responsible for his great success, including his perseverance and enormous creativity, without also thinking that he was responsible for creating his own character.

In fact, Einstein himself was a determinist and free will skeptic who believed that his "enormous creativity" was not of his own making. In a 1929 interview in *The Saturday Evening Post*, he states: "I am a determinist. As such, I do not believe in free will … I believe with Schopenhauer: We can do what we wish, but we can only wish what we must" (1929, p. 114). He goes on to add: "My own career was undoubtedly determined, not by my own will but by various factors over which I have no control" (1929, p. 114). He concludes by rejecting the idea that he deserves praise or credit for his creative achievements: "I claim credit for nothing. Everything is determined, the beginning as well as the end, by forces over which we have no control. It is determined for the insect as well as for the star. Human beings, vegetables or cosmic dust, we all dance to a mysterious tune, intoned in the distance by an invisible player" (1929, p. 117).

Honderich and I both agree with Einstein that he does not deserve credit or praise in the basic desert sense for his "enormous creativity" or for achieving one of his major life-hopes. Saying this, however, does not prevent us from legitimately ascribing creativity to Einstein. Since desert claims are about *accountability* and ascriptions of creativity are about *attributability*, there is no inconsistency in free will skeptics attributing "creativity" to agents (see Caruso 2017a). As long as the actions and attitudes we attribute to agents are reflective of their evaluative judgments or commitments, the requirements for attributability are satisfied. In Einstein's case, he had a long-standing desire to satisfy his own curiosity about the nature of gravity; he exhibited patience and perseverance in the face of obstacles during his long journey toward the final formulation of general relativity; he played the piano and violin to clear his mind and stimulate his creativity; and so on. All of these character traits are reflective of his evaluative judgments and commitments and hence can be legitimately attributed to him. I therefore contend that we can, without inconsistency, say that Einstein was enormously creative and attributability-responsible for his creative achievements, *without also saying* that he was responsible in the accountability sense.

At this point, critics of my view may be willing to concede that attributability is consistent with free will skepticism but nonetheless object that something important is still missing from such an account. If free will skepticism were true, they fear, we would lack the sort of control over our creativity that would allow us to derive fulfillment from our creative projects and pursuits. Furthermore, there would be no "true desert for one's achievements" (Kane 1996, p. 82) and no sense of accomplishment. While I understand these fears, I believe they are overblown. I acknowledge that adopting the skeptical perspective would mean that agents are never morally responsible in the backward-looking, basic desert sense. I also acknowledge that some loss may be experienced in relinquishing our pre-theoretical beliefs about free will and origination. There is a growing body of empirical evidence, for instance, that indicates people are folk psychological indeterminists—that is, they think that their choices aren't determined (see Nichols and Knobe 2007; Sarkissian et al. 2010; Deery et al. 2013). It is not just that they don't have the belief that their choices are determined. Rather, they positively think that their choices are not determined. Giving up the belief in indeterminist free will may be difficult for some, but it would by no means undermine the fulfillment in life that our creative projects and life-hopes can provide.

For instance, it is not obvious that *achievement* is tied to praiseworthiness in the strong way assumed by critics. As Derk Pereboom has argued: "If one hopes for a certain outcome, then if one succeeds in acquiring what one hoped for, intuitively this outcome can be one's achievement, albeit in a diminished sense, even if one is not praiseworthy for it" (2001, p. 194). Einstein, for example, hoped that his efforts would result in a new theory of gravity. Given that they did, he would have an accurate perception of having achieved what he hoped for, even if he does not deserve praise for his efforts. Achievement, I contend, is best understood in terms of effortful fulfillment of one's goals, desires, and hopes. One can do this, however, without also being praiseworthy in the basic desert sense. Since free will skepticism is consistent with agents exerting effort and working toward their various goals, there is no need to reject the notion of achievement. To say that praiseworthiness is required for *true achievement* would be question begging without additional argumentation.

I imagine one could argue that there *is* a necessary link between praiseworthiness and achievement since the concept of achievement entails that when an agent achieves a goal they become legitimate targets of praise. I see no reason, however, for thinking this is true. First, while we often associate praiseworthiness with achievement, there is no necessary connection between the two. If we reject the notion of praiseworthiness, as free will skeptics do, a perfectly meaningful conception of achievement remains in place—that is, one that defines achievement in terms of effort and fulfilling one's goals, hopes, and desires. Second, without praiseworthiness there would still remain sound forward-looking reasons for encouraging creativity and pursuing one's life-hopes. Lastly, we do not believe agents are praiseworthy or blameworthy for creative omissions—for example, Einstein failing to have the creative insight that led him to formulate general relativity. This throws into doubt, I believe, the supposed necessary connection between praiseworthiness and achievement. The fact that Einstein hoped that his efforts would result in a new theory of gravity, and they did, means he achieved his goal. But the fact that he *could have just as easily failed* to achieve his goal by failing to have a creative breakthrough, and this failure would have had nothing to do with a lack of effort on his part, suggests to me that the conditions for praiseworthiness are independent of, and likely more demanding than, the conditions for achievement.

Now, some philosophers, including Honderich perhaps, fear that without a conception of ourselves as credit- or praiseworthy for achieving what makes our lives fulfilled, happy, satisfactory, or worthwhile—that is, for realizing our life-hopes—we will become dismayed. Here I follow Pereboom in arguing that while there is an aspect of these life-hopes that may be undercut by skepticism, the skeptical perspective nevertheless leaves them largely intact. Free will skepticism need not instill in us an attitude of resignation to whatever our behavioral dispositions together with environmental conditions hold in store. Suppose, for example, that someone reasonably believes that he has a particular disposition that might well be a hindrance to realizing a life-hope. Let's say that he wants to become a professional concert pianist but is afraid that his stage fright will prevent him from achieving his goal. Because he does not know "whether this disposition will in fact have this effect, it remains open for him—that is, epistemically possible for him—that another disposition of his will allow him to transcend this impediment" (Pereboom 2014, p. 194; see also Chap. 8 this volume). As a result, he might reasonably hope that he will overcome his disposition and achieve his goal. For the free will skeptic, if he in fact does overcome his stage fright and succeed at his life's-hope, this will count as an achievement—perhaps not the kind of achievement libertarians had in mind, but an achievement in a substantial sense nonetheless.

I further contend that our sense of self-worth is to a non-trivial extent due to features not produced by our volitions, let alone by free will. As Pereboom correctly points out, people "place great value on natural beauty, native athletic ability, and intelligence, none of which have their source in our volition" (2014, p. 194). Of course, we also value voluntary efforts, but it does not matter much to us that these voluntary efforts are also freely willed. Consider how good character comes to be:

> It is plausibly formed to a significant degree by upbringing, and the belief that this is so is widespread. Parents regard themselves as having failed in raising their children if they turn out with immoral dispositions, and they typically take great care to bring their children up to prevent such an outcome. Accordingly, people often come to believe that they have the good moral character they do largely because they were raised with love and skill. But those who believe this about themselves seldom experience dismay because of it. We tend not to become dispirited upon coming to understand that good moral character is not our own doing, and that we do not deserve a great deal of praise or credit for it. By contrast, we often feel fortunate and thankful. (Pereboom 2014, p. 195)

The same is true for creativity and our life-hopes. When one realizes the extent to which creative and artistic success, or achievement in one's professional career, is dependent on upbringing, the opportunities that society presents, the support of parents and teachers, and plain luck, one does not typically react with dismay. Rather these thoughts frequently engender thankfulness and a sense of being fortunate. This seems to be how Einstein reacted when he realized: "My own career was undoubtedly determined, not by my own will but by various factors over which I have no control" (1929, p. 114). Given that this is a common reaction, and at least one open to skeptics to embrace, I maintain that there is no reason to think meaning in life, our senses of achievement, and our life-hopes, would be threatened by free will skepticism.

Now, Honderich seems to acknowledge that this is a legitimate reaction when he discusses the second kind of life-hopes, the kind that *is* compatible with determinism. These life-hopes have to do with actions that flow from our embraced desires, that is, voluntary actions. According to Honderich, when this second kind of life-hope is brought together with determinism, we see that "determinism can be true without affecting these hopes at all" (2002a, p. 96). That is: "There is nothing in them that is inconsistent with [determinism]. There is nothing about embracing desires and situations that conflicts with determinism" (2002a, p. 96). Honderich is therefore willing to acknowledge that determinism (and free will skepticism more broadly) leave the second kind of life-hopes "untouched and untroubled." In fact, he goes so far as to say that our response to determinism may involve thoughts about the first kind of life-hopes (the incompatible kind) and our disregarding them as unimportant: "We may feel we don't have to think about them. This response as a whole involves rejecting dismay. This way with determinism is a kind of satisfied intransigence" (2002a, p. 97).

Honderich also argues that we can choose the attitude of *affirmation* rather than intransigence or dismay (2002a, Chap. 10). Having two different sets of attitudes is unsatisfactory, so what we need to try to do is to take into account all of it, and find or make a new response to determinism. Honderich's proposed solution is to try to give up whatever depends on thoughts inconsistent with the truth of determinism or near-determinism. Affirmation, then, is:

> trying *by various strategies* to *accommodate ourselves* to *the situation we find ourselves in—accommodate ourselves to just what we can really possess if determinism is true, accommodate ourselves to the part of our lives that does not rest on the illusion of Free Will.* We can reflect on what is perhaps the limited worth of what we have to give up, consider possible compensations of a belief in determinism, take care not to underestimate what we can have, and consider a certain prospect having to do with genuine and settled belief in determinism. (2002a, p. 126)

While Honderich appears to be embracing some form of optimism here, as undoubtedly he is, our views differ to the extent that he *continues to experience dismay* at the loss of origination. Personally, I experience very little loss or dismay and am in fact quite bullish about the prospects of life without belief in free will (or origination) and basic desert moral responsibility. My view is that these beliefs do more harm than good since they tend to stifle personal development, encourage punitive access in criminal justice, and perpetuate social and economic inequalities (see, e.g., Caruso forthcoming).

From Honderich's perspective, however, both reactions to determinism are legitimate—that is, the reaction of dismay and intransigence. He maintains that, "Neither kind of attitude to the future, considered in itself, can be regarded as any kind of mistake. There is no room for the idea of mistake" (2002a, p. 97). While I agree with Honderich that people are *capable* of experiencing both types of reactions, and even perhaps that they are *natural*, I challenge the claim that they are both *legitimate* reactions and stand on equal footing. In fact, I contend that the conception of life-hopes born of belief in origination and open futures involves doxastic irrationality and is pernicious in nature since it gives credence to the notion of just deserts and leads to increased punitiveness. Rather than being dismayed at its loss, I think we should set out to destroy it, drive a stake in its heart, and bury it at the crossroads (to borrow a phrase from Bruce Waller).

Consider briefly the reactive attitudes (P.F. Strawson 1962) of resentment, indignation, blame, and moral anger. Since these reactive attitudes can cause harm, they would seem to be appropriate only if it is fair that the agent be subject to them in the sense that she *deserves* them. We can say, then, that an agent is *accountable* for her action when she deserves, in the basic desert sense, to be praised or blamed for what she did—that is, she deserves certain kinds of desert-based judgments, attitudes, or treatments in response to decisions or actions she performed or failed to perform, and these judgments, attitudes, or treatments are justified on purely backward-looking grounds and do not appeal to consequentialist or forward-looking considerations, such as future protection, future reconciliation, or future moral formation.

The version of free will skepticism I defend maintains that agents are never morally responsible in the basic desert sense, and hence expression of resentment, indignation, and moral anger involves doxastic irrationality (at least to the extent it is accompanied by the belief that its target *deserves* to be its recipient). Now I imagine one could, and most compatibilists would, raise the following Strawsonian question: Can we ever *really* relinquish these reactive attitudes? In response, I would first say that it is important to distinguish two different questions here: (1) Would it be desirable? and (2) Is it possible? With regard to the first question, I maintain that the moral anger associated with the reactive attitudes of resentment and indignation is often corrosive to our interpersonal relationships and to our social policies. As Pereboom (2001, 2014) has argued, the expressions of these reactive attitudes are suboptimal as modes of communication in relationships relative to alternative attitudes available to us—for example, feeling hurt, or shocked, or disappointed.

My response to the second question—that is, "Is it possible to relinquish these reactive attitudes?"—begins by distinguishing between *narrow-profile* emotional responses and *wide-profile* responses (Nichols and Knobe 2007; Pereboom 2014). Narrow-profile emotional responses are local or immediate emotional reactions to a situation. Wide-profile responses are not immediate and can involve rational reflection. I believe it is perfectly consistent for a free will skeptic to maintain that expression of resentment and indignation is irrational *and still acknowledge* that there may be certain types and degrees of resentment and indignation that are beyond our power to affect. That is, free will skeptics can expect that we will not keep ourselves from some degree of narrow-profile, immediate resentment when we are seriously wronged in our most intimate personal relationships. Nevertheless, in wide-profile cases, I contend that we do have the ability to diminish or even eliminate resentment and indignation, or at least disavow it in the sense of rejecting any force it might be thought to have in *justifying* harmful reactions and policies.

To what extent Honderich disagrees with anything I just said is not entirely clear—especially given his concept of *affirmation*. Perhaps there is not much daylight between us. Of course, I would be extremely pleased to hear that Honderich is more optimistic about the consequences of origination skepticism than he sometimes appears. Perhaps it is even the case that since Honderich has paved the way for origination skepticism, he has made it possible for *me* to experience less dismay. Nietzsche felt he had come too early for the message he carried, and perhaps Honderich has also had to endure more dismay as a pioneer than those who followed. Either way, I look forward to hearing Ted's reply, and I am truly thankful for his work in this area.

11.3 Conclusion

Here, I have discussed two main aspects of Honderich's work: first, his defense of determinism and its consequences for *origination* and *moral responsibility*; second, his concern that the truth of determinism threatens and restricts, but does not eliminate, our life-hopes. I have also compared my own views to Honderich's in an attempt to seek clarification on two main fronts. First, I have maintained that what is of central philosophical and practical importance in the free will debate is the kind of free will needed for basic desert moral responsibility. Honderich, however, prefers to talk, not of a single historical debate but of *two* conceptions of free will—one that goes back to Kant (origination) and the other to Hume (voluntariness). The problem with this, however, is that the tradition following Hume has taken voluntariness (appropriately qualified and detailed) to be *sufficient for basic desert moral responsibility*. Honderich, however, like other free will skeptics and deniers, seems to agree that voluntariness is not sufficient for basic desert. To the extent then that Honderich denies the existence of the *only* kind of free will that can preserve basic desert—that is, origination—I recommend that he relinquish his conceptual dualism and become a full-fledged member of the free will skeptic club—either as a traditional hard determinist or as a hard-incompatibilist. Second, I have argued that there is no reason to experience dismay at all even if we lack origination and the kind of free will needed for basic desert moral responsibility, since life-hopes, achievement, and meaning in life can all survive.

References

Caruso, Gregg D. 2012. *Free will and consciousness: A determinist account of the illusion of free will*. Lanham, MD: Lexington Books.

———., ed. 2013. *Exploring the illusion of free will and moral responsibility*. Lanham, MD: Lexington Books.

———. 2015. Kane is not able: A reply to Vicens' "self-forming actions and conflicts of intention.". *Southwestern Philosophy Review* 7–8: 7–15.

———. 2016. Free will skepticism and criminal behavior: A public health-quarantine model. *Southwest Philosophy Review* 32 (1): 25–48.

———. 2017a. Free will skepticism and the question of creativity: Creativity, desert, and self-creation. *Ergo* 3 (23): 591–607.

———. 2017b. *Public health and safety: The social determinants of health and criminal behavior*. London: Research Links Books.

———. forthcoming. Free will skepticism and its implications: An argument for optimism. In *Free will skepticism in law and society*, ed. Elizabeth Shaw, Derk Pereboom, and Gregg D. Caruso. Cambridge: Cambridge University Press.

Caruso, Gregg D., and Stephen G. Morris. 2017. Compatibilism and retributive desert moral responsibility: On what is of central philosophical and practical importance. *ERKENNTNIS*. https://doi.org/10.1007/s10670-016-9846-2.

Deery, Oisin., Matt Bedke, and Shaun Nichols. 2013. Phenomenal abilities: Incompatibilism and the experience of agency. In Oxford studies in agency and responsibility, ed. David Shoemaker. Vol. 1. Oxford: Oxford University Press.

Einstein, Albert. 1929, October 26. What life means to Einstein: An interview by George Sylvester Viereck. *Saturday Evening Post* 17: 110–117.

Honderich, Ted. 1988. *A theory of determinism: The mind, neuroscience, and life-hopes*. Oxford: Oxford University Press. Republished in two volumes: *Mind and brain* and *The consequences of determinism,* 1990.

———. 2002a. *How free are you? The determinism problem*. 2nd ed. Oxford: Oxford University Press.

———. 2002b. Determinism as true, compatibilism and incompatibilism as false, and the real problem. In *The Oxford handbook of free will*, ed. Robert Kane, 461–476. New York: Oxford University Press.

———. 2004. *On determinism and freedom*. Edinburgh, UK: Edinburgh University Press.

———. 2013. Determinism, incompatibilism and compatibilism, actual consciousness and subjective physical worlds, humanity. In *Exploring the illusion of free will and moral responsibility*, ed. Gregg Caruso, 53–64. Lanham, MD: Lexington Books.

———. 2017. *MIND: Your being conscious is what and where?* Chicago, IL: Chicago University Press.

Kane, Robert. 1996. *The significance of free will*. Oxford: Oxford University Press.

Levy, Neil. 2011. *Hard luck: How luck undermines free will and moral responsibility*. New York: Oxford University Press.

Nichols, Shaun, and Joshua Knobe. 2007. Moral responsibility and determinism: The cognitive science of folk intuitions. *Nous* 41: 663–685.

Pereboom, Derk. 2001. *Living without free will*. New York: Cambridge University Press.

———. 2014. *Free will, agency, and meaning in life*. Oxford: Oxford University Press.

Pereboom, Derk, and Gregg D. Caruso. 2018. Hard-Incompatibilist Existentialism: Neuroscience, Punishment, and Meaning in Life. In *Neuroexistentialism: Meaning, morals, and purpose in the age of neuroscience*, ed. Gregg D. Caruso and Owen Flanagan. New York: Oxford University Press.

Russell, Paul. 2008. Free will, art and morality. *Journal of Ethics* 12: 307–325.
Sarkissian, H., A. Chatterjee, F. De Brigard, J. Knobe, S. Nichols, and S. Sirker. 2010. Is belief in free will a cultural universal? *Mind and Language* 25: 348–358.
Smeenk, Christopher. 2015. Empty out the drawer: Following Einstein's path to general relativity. *Western News*, November 19. http://news.westernu.ca/2015/11/empty-out-the-drawer-following-einsteins-path-to-general-relativity/
Strawson, Galen. 1986. *Freedom and belief.* Oxford: Oxford University Press.
Strawson, P.F. 1962. Freedom and resentment. *Proceedings of the British Academy* 48: 1–25.
Waller, Bruce. 2011. *Against moral responsibility*. Cambridge, MA: MIT Press.
———. 2015. *The stubborn system of moral responsibility*. Cambridge, MA: MIT Press.

12

Remarks on Papers on Determinism and Freedom

Ted Honderich

12.1 On Pereboom

When I arrived in the Philosophy Department of University College London in 1959, to be a graduate student of A. J. Ayer, which studenthood is included in an autobiographical record, it could not be said that the place was alive with the problem known as the freedom of the will. Still, something of what was to be called Ordinary Language Philosophy had arrived a little from Oxford in rural England. There was consideration of the problem of whether, if determinism is true, what could be meant by saying that somebody still *could have done otherwise* than he did. If what was much later also named "explanationism" by me, partly to avoid the implication of threat or the gloom of "determinism"—if consciousness and action were explainable as effects—could we still somehow do otherwise than we do?

After Freddie, under the inspiration of the drawing-room oratory of the next Grote, Stuart Hampshire, I got a good way forward with the

T. Honderich (✉)
University College London, London, UK

G. D. Caruso (ed.), *Ted Honderich on Consciousness, Determinism, and Humanity*, Philosophers in Depth, https://doi.org/10.1007/978-3-319-66754-6_12

question of Incompatibilism and Compatibilism. Whether determinism is logically incompatible and inconsistent with our freedom, or instead is compatible and consistent with it. That at bottom is the subject of or the beginning of the subject of these remarks and the following remarks on the papers of Russell, Timpe, and Caruso.

A whole history of philosophers, including Kant, said the first thing. Probably some ancient Greek and Latin predecessors too. They took our freedom to be what is most naturally understood by *free will*, a kind of origination of choices and the like, definitely not their just being effects of preceding causes—not having that fundamental kind of explanation. If determinism is true, we're not free. So, their tradition of philosophy is Incompatibilism.

But another sequence of philosophers, including Hume, held an opposite view. They took our freedom to be *voluntariness*, at bottom being able to do what you desire or want. *Not* being in jail or facing a man with a gun in the street or under your own internal compulsion, say to go on eating too much. So, if determinism is true, no problem. Determinism, they rightly said, obviously doesn't take away our desires and our satisfying them. Determinism is OK in this way. Thus, the tradition called Compatibilism.

All of that in a way ended a while ago in my life. You could a while ago look at the whole thing differently. Yes, if we have but *one* idea or conception of our freedom, either Incompatibilism or Compatibilism has to be true. But *do* we have only one conception? To ask the question was to get the answer.

No, we have both ideas. Obviously, we have both—a little proof will be offered, by the way, in the remarks after these on Paul Russell. So neither Incompatibilism nor Compatibilism is true of our situation. Incompatibilism is true with respect to our idea of origination, and false with voluntariness. Compatibilism is as true with voluntariness, and false with origination. I have been a little self-satisfied with that resolution of one problem of determinism and freedom, that resolution then, but since have wondered if it was the result of a certain simplicity, maybe a certain simplification.

The problem and the competing ideas, or similar or related ideas, come up with Pereboom and again in the remarks on the next paper to be glanced at here, Russell's. They are also the scene, or much of the scene, certainly the necessary backdrop, of the other two papers to be remarked on here, those of Timpe and Caruso. All four, despite their differences, fit together to that limited extent.

Derk Pereboom of Cornell University, definitely a leader of his subject, provides a paper that is an ordered line of exposition and argument—and one replete in questions, conceptions, arguments, and judgments. In these remarks, as in the cases of the remarks on other papers, I touch on some large things in the paper, without trying to reproduce that progress.

Pereboom was first, at least in recent times, indeed the predecessor of the three other contributors under consideration here, in taking it that a certain response to determinism or explanationism, say to the prospect of taking it to be true, has to do with morality, seemingly only or at least primarily.

More particularly, it has to do with one's own moral responsibility for one's actions. It has to do for them, still more particularly, with one's *deserving* things for one's actions, in general, deserving blame or praise, punishment or reward. Guilt or innocence. Desert as backward-looking, definitely not forward-looking or a matter of good consequences, as can be thought to be the case with punishment by the state. Pereboom might have added that this is a matter of experiencing or having assigned to us guilt or innocence. He is at least interesting on the subject of desert, and happier with it than I am with it, particularly in my writings on the supposed justifications of punishment.

But let me postpone for a while a further and final consideration of the large subject of desert here—indeed, until what I have to remark on the fourth paper here, that of Gregg Caruso, due additional consideration as the editor of this book you are reading.

Whatever we are to think about desert, and as you will be reading in the third part of this book, moralist in part I am and have been, taken up in part with right and wrong. In particular, taken up with what you will be hearing more about, the Principle of Humanity. It is, to the effect, very briefly indeed, that what is right is what gets people out of bad lives, these defined in terms of a lack of the great goods—decent length of life, bodily wellbeing, freedoms and powers, respect and self-respect, goods of relationship with others, goods of culture. Our moral responsibility is to take all and only rational steps to get people out of bad lives.

If I am on the right-and-wrong subject myself, not detached from it, the question comes to me of whether this particular philosophical concern with determinism nowadays, having to do with moral responsibility to the exclusion of other things, is confined to American philosophy? As distinct from English, French, and maybe German? I have given in for moments to the suspicion that determinism and freedom are now more alive in America than elsewhere because of the influence of fundamentalist religion, but I don't know. I do think and maybe know determinism isn't as black as it can seem just for a reason having to do with morality. Only that.

But to stick more to the present subject, I do indeed reject and once was first to have the good or bad repute of rejecting both Incompatibilism and Compatibilism as they were historically presented—as propositions about all of our concern with freedom, our beliefs, our human nature, our practices, or any way what naturally or necessarily governs our practices. Incompatibilism and Compatibilism share the view that our freedom as we understand it is *either* origination, free will in the most common use of that term, *or* it is voluntariness. As already implied, maybe Kant is the greatest philosophical exponent of the first view; that our concern with freedom is with free will. Certainly, Hume is the greatest exponent of the second view, that our thought and dealing with freedom is in fact dealing with voluntariness.

The idea of origination at bottom is that we come to our choices and decisions without their being effects, without being caused, without at all having explanations as events or states, things that happen in that fundamental sense. They are, we are to take it, just unlike all other events and states in the world—or maybe all but some supposed events of pure randomness or chance sometimes imagined to have been discovered in a mysterious part of physics, an interpretation of the mathematics of that physics.

With respect to voluntariness, one general understanding is that in our choices and actions we are not generally under any kind of *compulsion*. Obviously, we are not always doing what we don't want to do. To take into account both external compulsion, say being in jail, and internal compulsion, I have been inclined to say that what voluntariness or absence of compulsion comes to is *our acting out of embraced desires, desires that we desire to have*. Still sounds to me like at least a good starter and maybe a good finisher with respect to an analysis of voluntariness.

To come on to what Pereboom offers as a comparison between my views and those of an eminent kind of philosopher, there is Sartre's reported concern with determinism. Apparently, it is that that it is inconsistent with purpose for one's life, our life-defining plans, what is called meaning in life, maybe projects that achieve this so-called meaning. Being unable to recollect a word of Sartre, and having little time for further self-education now, I restrict myself to a brisk summary of myself.

In my view, if we contemplate the possibility or more of the truth of determinism, which in fact seems to me to follow from an overwhelming premise, in short, the premise of all of the reality of things that happen, we can make three possible responses, take and maybe keep to one of three possible attitudes.

One is what I have called the attitude or response of *dismay* to determinism. What is said here may be enriched or improved, I take it, by the use of Sartre. There is also the second possible attitude, *intransigence*—thinking or feeling at least assertively and without much reflection, maybe a kind of bluff, about our moral responsibility and whatever that somehow determinism just cannot or does not threaten it. Pereboom has more to say for it than I do, perhaps because he sees it somewhat differently. Here too, there is also consideration by another contributor to this book, Saul Smilansky.

The third attitude is *affirmation*. That is, arriving at, coming to have, a certain one of what are called philosophies of life. It is one in which we set out to accommodate ourselves to determinism, find help, look on the bright side, maybe somehow rise above determinism. Affirmation is a whole subject here, no doubt, whole subjects. One thing not contemplated by me in the past is the reassurance in affirmation that there is the general solace of truth. Truth *exists*, however difficult it is to find it and to hold to it. The fact of its being there, you can suppose, is a significant reassurance, better than religion, more than a crutch.

All of Pereboom's admirable first stage in a discussion of what is called my Attitudinism is carried forward by Russell, Timpe, and Caruso,

I repeat, proceeds from the proposition that we have the two fundamental ideas and indeed developed conceptions of freedom. You will be hearing more of this and hence of the impossibility of both Compatibilism and Incompatibilism, as understood. More, of course, of what each of us takes to be his reasonableness.

There is one more piece in this book partly on determinism and freedom, but in the third part of the book, on right and wrong, and so on. This, as already mentioned, is Smilansky's "Free Will, Understanding and Justification: Terrorism, Israel and the Palestinians."

12.2 On Russell

Professor Russell divides his academic time between the University of British Columbia in Canada and the University of Gothenburg in Sweden, where he is director of the Responsibility Project, and he has been a visiting professor in other good places. He has published strong books not only on free will and moral responsibility, but also about he who has a strong claim to being the philosophers' philosopher, David Hume.

Russell is concerned in his indubitably argued paper with my conclusion, of which you have heard already if you have read the remarks above on Pereboom, with respect to the long contest between the philosophical tradition that takes freedom to be compatible or consistent with determinism, and the tradition that takes the two things to be incompatible or inconsistent.

More particularly, he is partly concerned with my conclusion, with which you may have read me being a little pleased, and which he reports accurately—the simple truth that freedom is neither compatible nor incompatible with determinism. It is neither, since there is not one thing that is freedom but two. Reduced to phrases, one is choosing or deciding that is an uncaused event and one is doing what you want. The first is obviously incompatible with determinism, and the second can be as obviously compatible.

He specifies well what else on my recommendation is to be put in place of either Compatibilism or Incompatibilism, an attitude rather than a truth. This is not the attitude of dismay about determinism, or the attitude of intransigence, which is something like a kind of pretending that nothing changes, but rather *affirmation*. That is an attitude or indeed a philosophy of life that gives up what we have to give up, satisfactions having to do with what does not exist, origination—but an attitude that rightly values what remains, voluntariness or rather our kinds and extents of voluntariness.

Russell's most unique contention in his paper is an alternative to affirmation. This is not what he calls for his own reasons *free will skepticism*, which is that *fate* and *luck* serve to discredit our view of ourselves as free and responsible agents. Rather, his alternative to affirmation is what he calls *Free Will Pessimism*. It is to the effect that we *are* free and responsible agents despite being subject to fate and luck. And so, finally, Compatibilism is false, indeed false by way of something that Compatibilists do not and cannot reject. The argument involves fatalism as against determinism—that the future will be the same no matter what we do, that all choices are "idle" in that they cannot affect the future.

It is an argument that I will not try quickly to make plainer or easier than it is—maybe because in fact I cannot make it any of those things. In fact is an argument that I am not sure I really get into clear view. Over to you.

But there is something else I do get. It is an awful lot simpler. It is that Compatibilism as we have it is false no matter what arguments are offered for or against it. None of those arguments can have anything like the strength of the proposition that we have the *two* ideas of freedom, voluntariness and origination.

My simpler proof—yes, I guess there are a few proofs that turn up in philosophy, although not of its own main propositions—is of course what you can get out of a decent dictionary. Go to "free" and "freedom" in *The New Oxford Dictionary of English*, and sort the results into the two categories—origination and voluntariness. Or the *Merriam Webster's Collegiate Dictionary*, where being free is explicitly (i) kinds of voluntariness and (ii) not being determined. Or *The Chambers Dictionary* for (i) the welter of stuff under "free" and (ii) the entry under "determinism" as "the converse of free will."

You can also get to the falsehood of Compatibilism, of course, out of your conviction right now that (i) there is the want of freedom that is being in jail, hence, not doing what you want, and (ii) there is conceivable want of freedom that is conveyed by someone's assertive, forceful, aggressive, or punitive response that someone else, an offender of some kind, *could have done otherwise* right and then given things exactly as they were—of course, not just *could have done otherwise* in the funny sense that he *would have done otherwise if the past including his past had been different.*

Russell's paper may also be an excellent source of another proposition, an excellent instance of a certain state of affairs in philosophy, the one we are mainly concerned with. Compatibilism and Incompatibilism, you have just heard, are and have been taken as responses to what might be labeled linguistic problems, problems of language, problems of meaning. But is that right? As contemplated by me in the remarks above on Pereboom, are they instead problems themselves at least motivated by feeling, commitment, whatever else in affective consciousness rather than cognitive? Is that view better?

It is worth remembering that Kant's commitment to Incompatibilism, the understanding and assertion of origination, an understanding, as in the case of Russell, was of course somehow bound up with desert, and that Kant delivered himself of the judgment that if an island people were abandoning their island, their last obligation would be to execute any murderer left in jail—retribution having nothing whatever to do with deterrence or other prevention.

You can have the idea, too, that Hume in his affirmation of Compatibilism was also taken up with what does not go at all well with Incompatibilism, a consequentionalism in morals on the path to a Utilitarianism. I suspect my own writings on determinism and freedom, and those comments above, might be improved by this larger view of the problem—but certainly with the Principle of Humanity in place of Utility.

Russell, of course, if on present evidence, he is not to be tarred with the brush of retributivism in punishment, is also prompted and no doubt moved by considerations of desert. To say a few words of these considerations generally, without objection to or accusation against him, they all need reflection if not examination and conceivably need rejection.

My own ideas and feelings here include the proposition that it is very often difficult indeed to understand assertions of good or bad desert with respect to punishment or reward as other than just assertions of rightness or wrongness with respect to punishment or reward. Here, obviously, propositions to the effect that something is right because deserved are no more than circular—something is right because it's right. There are other adverse thoughts you can have about desert—say, as self-concern or indeed selfishness in our societies.

A first of three further remarks in passing. I welcome Russell's own welcoming of my resistance to the *illusionism* of Smilansky in the third part of this book. This attitude is to the effect that we should encourage belief in origination—support the illusion of it. I am inclined to think that this is not only something recommended by a philosopher but in fact an attitude or practice of importance and some salience in our own societies. Is it not more than suspected in some of our judges who resist pleas for leniency on the part of barristers appearing for defendants with childhood histories of deprivation or who have been subject to pressures toward breaking the law?

A second remark in passing. I am inclined to suppose that there is more than was said by me in the past about moral and other responsibility—both holding people responsible and crediting people with responsibility. There is of course a kind of these activities that is future-oriented. Its aim is to affect future behavior. The most familiar case is that of punishment by the state. In general, there is the consideration and fact of punishment, if not the only consideration and fact, that those punished are those whose punishment will affect the future—their own actions and also the actions of others, actions deterred or otherwise affected by the present punishment.

And one more remark. Maybe it is worth noting, for neophytes, that Russell seems to say what he knows otherwise than, that my view of causation is that effects are necessitated just by *causes*. He is aware that an effect is not something necessitated by a cause, where that is a singled-out thing within a causal circumstance or a sufficient condition containing more than a cause. Rather, an effect is necessitated by the whole causal circumstance. That is to say all too quickly that if or since the whole circumstance happened, whatever else was happening, the effect would still have happened.

Russell's paper is perhaps a candidate for the most difficult in the book, for pretty well all readers, on account of economies in style, labeling. A habit encouraged by my own? A paper sure worth your effort though. Keep concentrating and learn.

12.3 On Timpe

Kevin Timpe holds a chair of Christian Philosophy at Calvin College in the American state of Michigan, is a distinguished and ongoing philosophical author, and is also to his credit an advocate for children with disabilities.

He begins here by noting among other things that I have in the past defended a determinism of macroscopic events, including our choices, decisions, and actions, and taken this determinism as not put in question by the sometimes supposed possibility of some indeterminism at a micro-level of what exists—events that some interpretations of the quantum theory in physics take to be uncaused, truly random events. The idea was that either, in fact, there aren't any chance or random events down below or, if there are some, they don't translate upward to the level of our choices, decisions, and actions—to any of perceptual, cognitive, and affective consciousness and its effects.

I am now even less inclined than in the past to what in fact are those philosophical interpretations of the physics or its mathematics, which by the way carry the threat against all our responsibility for our actions that they are owed to chance or random events. I remember with some satisfaction one of the little past triumphs dear in the memory of any working philosopher. That was pointing out in a seminar at Yale, to another visiting professor from England, a philosopher of science, that his use of believed-by-him indeterminacy in physics could absolutely not save our moral responsibility, whatever was added. How could pure chance, randomness, conceivably issue in anybody's moral responsibility for something? In anybody's being imprisoned on account of the operation of a really uncaused roulette wheel in him?

Let us hurry on to the matter of the determinism of choices, decisions and actions, and the relation between it and freedom, and also the attitudes to determinism and freedom of three kinds.

At least as far back as the eighteenth century, and probably right now, as you may have read in these pages of remarks, there are philosophers who say that if determinism is true, then we are not free and there are philosophers who say that if it is true, then we can still be free anyway. Determinism and freedom are incompatible or inconsistent, or determinism and freedom are compatible or consistent. As you have read in my remarks on Pereboom and Russell, there has been Incompatibilism and there has been Compatibilism. Compatibilism between determinism and voluntariness, Incompatibilism between determinism and origination—the latter also spoken of by Timpe as *Free Will* as distinct from *free will* in accordance with a past usage of mine.

I say that there exists an understanding of freedom as voluntariness, which voluntariness is compatible with determinism. Timpe takes it or did take it that, therefore, my view is "properly labeled compatibilism." To which a first response might or must be that since my view is also, just as much, that there is an understanding of freedom as origination, and *it* is incompatible with determinism, my view is as reasonably labeled, Incompatibilism.

He is of course right to say that our thinking, talking and acting with respect to what I take to be freedom in general, including both kinds, involves various matters—phenomenology, responsibility, fairness, the law, moral development, and religious doctrine. Is he right in saying that it is implausible that we have a single general concept from all these sources and doing the same theoretical and practical work?

Well, he also shares another kind of conviction with me—and certainly goes beyond it. I have no doubt that our conceptions of origination and voluntariness have fundamental employments or applications in our societies, employments, or applications by those with the most standing and control in our societies. He speaks of these two concepts as "socially constructed," as concepts that "inhabit a social setting," indeed as being "tools."

This matter he considers by way of a certain way of thought, by way of concepts of a certain kind, called Ballung concepts.

These were named and considered by the philosophers of science Nancy Cartwright and Rosa Runhardt, then of the London School of Economics. Nancy, the author of *How the Laws of Physics Lie*, is well remembered by me as my own stern judge when we were conductors together of the postgraduate seminar in philosophy at the University of London. Ballung concepts, with which I have not been familiar, were so named by Otto Neurath, the German political economist and Logical Positivist exiled in England from 1940 until his death in 1945. "Ballung" is a German word for "a concentrated cluster." These concepts are sometimes described as "concepts with a fuzzy and context-dependent scope."

Further, Ballung concepts, with which I have not been familiar, have to do with measuring. According to *The Stanford Encyclopedia of Philosophy*, measuring is carried on not by way of a definite general property, but rather by way of a number of items that resemble one another in different ways rather than the single way that members of a family may do. Partial resemblances, some particular resemblances rather than complete uniformity.

More particularly, in part, Timpe's proposal is that the general concept of free choice or decision and action is somehow like the concept of "same family," which depends not on a single shared property but on extents of the same or like properties—maybe of heights, noses, and confidences. Ballung concepts are said to be multifaceted, some of these concepts being race, poverty, personal disability, social exclusion, and the quality of Ph.D. programs. In some sense there is "no right or wrong characterization of these Ballung, socially constructed concepts."

I do not have anything like a perfect grip of all that.

Is Timpe's line of thought to the effect that the general term "free" is or is of a Ballung concept in virtue not only of the various matters—that it has to do with phenomenology to religious doctrine to multifacetedness—but also the fact that "free" has to do with the two-part cluster that has in it origination and voluntariness?

Does this Ballung understanding of "free" and the associated reflection take us much further than we have got without it? Do we "better understand" my claim of our having more than one idea of freedom—see its mistake? Some mistake? Do we see that for us, freedom, in general, is not voluntariness and origination?

Well, to escape from the welter of ideas, propositions, terms, and whatnot, what the principal charge, or anyway contemplated objection, comes to is perhaps clear enough. To cut to the quick, or anyway near enough to the quick, the charge is that there is something or the other wrong with taking our idea of freedom as divided into the ideas of voluntariness and origination. There is some large and indeed fatal objection to that. It is indeed, in a sentence, that freedom in general is a Ballung concept.

Well, before having got to the explicit argument, but on the basis of my life and language and yours, and our dictionaries, I confidently assert that there is no fatal or indeed other serious objection to taking it that our idea of freedom is of voluntariness and origination—and of going on from there to conclusions about the facts of freedom, in general, voluntariness, and origination. That is my principal proposition.

The real argument here, I put it to you, must run the other way. From a false judgment against an indubitable genus and two species back to some false premise, some or the other false premise depended on the judgment. Resorting to Ballung concepts is an interesting move, but I trust you will agree, *interest* in philosophy is not enough.

It is my own reaction, then, that our thought and talk of freedom, general talk as in philosophy, is not in itself put in doubt by the proposition that it stands in connection with all of phenomenology, responsibility, fairness, the law, moral development, and religious doctrine—and is a Ballung concept. Can we think that our thought and talk of freedom, say in short their having to do with values, refutes the persistent division of freedom into origination and voluntariness? Although I am no linguistic philosopher, can we think that Ballungs dishes that little proof-by-good-dictionary?

Shall we also, by the way, give up and presumably begin again, somehow with the general concepts of right and wrong, justice, democracy, terrorism, and pretty much all else in moral and political philosophy?

It may be that I do not have exactly the right understanding of Timpe's main thesis. Certainly, my not being persuaded of it also rests on a further general premise. It has to do with philosophy and the rest of life being chock-full of general propositions. At least typically they have as their content less general propositions—categories and subcategories of things.

In fact, general categories in my sense are pretty much the stuff of intelligent life, certainly of philosophy. If they are to be discarded or doubted when they are in some way evaluative or connected with societies or whatever—matters of a kind of affective consciousness? Well, we will have to clear out a lot of libraries, close subjects in universities, to start out again with reflective life.

It is agreeable to hear that Kevin's present thinking has led him into doubt about his own past criticisms of my thoughts on determinism and the various attitudes. My present conclusion is that there is room for doubt about his new criticism. No, I have no proof on behalf of myself. As you have heard, there aren't proofs in philosophy. It's too hard for that. Just argument, or when brevity is called for, just nudgings in what is taken to be the right direction. In the present, just remarks.

There are impassioned or impassioned-on-one side disagreements between two philosophers, both of whom are at least respectable members of that line of life started by Plato and Aristotle—a line of life as defensible and also unavoidable and necessary now. Timpe's membership of the line of life, I end by saying, is in no doubt at all.

12.4 On Caruso

It is not a regularity in my life to find myself among philosophers or others of an inclination, tendency, or proclivity to determinism—people taking determinism to be more probably true or more arguable than denial of it, more arguable than its denial in any assertion of a freedom inconsistent with it. So already reassured I am by having made the acquaintance by chance, in so far as it exists, of Gregg Caruso, at least a strong thinker inclined to determinism—inclined, in his own less directly-to-the-point usage, to what he names *free will skepticism*.

He, like Chomsky, was a giver of one of the lectures on my stuff in a day given over to that enlightenment. His more ordinary employments include being professor in the State University of New York and being Co-Director of the Justice Without Retribution Network at the University of Aberdeen, School of Law in Scotland.

I compliment all of Pereboom, Russell, Timpe and Caruso. They are independent and, indeed, original philosophers who have gone on from my philosophical beginnings—and on in ways on such antecedents as the leader Peter Strawson on our personal attitudes of a reactive kind to one another in his paper "Freedom and Resentment." They seek to and, in ways, do more than take forward previous thoughts on determinism and freedoms.

I grant, certainly, that they have rightly complicated, and added to, and gone beyond, my own thoughts on dismay, intransigence, and affirmation—particularly affirmation. The contests between us, further, at least of emphasis, are not bouts that allow for knock-outs. There are only possibilities of winning on points.

I remind you that an Incompatibilist in the traditional continuing sense is somebody I am not—I do not suppose we have one idea of freedom or one fundamental idea, origination, such that it is inconsistent with determinism. Nor am I a Compatibilist in the traditional and continuing sense—I do not suppose our one idea of freedom is voluntariness, of course consistent with determinism. That I deny the existence of freedom as origination makes me a Compatibilist in only quite another sense, that I take our *only* existing freedom, voluntariness, of course, to be compatible with determinism.

As perhaps you guessed in reading my remarks on Pereboom and Russell, conceivably but with less reason on Timpe, and, as would not have been delayed until now by a perfect remarker, I am not at all keen on clarifying origination as being or involving a freedom that issues in the person in question *deserving* things—partly because of problems about all talk of desert.

It is typically the case, surely, that to take something as deserved, a punishment or a reward, maybe a reward for enterprise, sometimes called free enterprise, is to take the punishment or reward as *right*. That makes anything of the form "It's because he deserves it that it's right" just circular. Putting some meaning on talk of desert that avoids the circularity is not easy, to say the least. Added to those considerations is the general insecurity, to say no more than that, of any non-consequentialist idea of right and wrong whatever. At least I suspect the insecurity must be added.

To try to proceed by taking what is deserved to be what is *just*—a matter of *justice*—or *fair* or *fairness* is of course to have the problem of those terms and subjects. Quite as important, there is at least the possibility that our uses of talk of desert in our societies are best understood pretty quickly in terms of the self-interest of those taken as deserving.

It is my own preference that we concern ourselves with determinism and freedom by concerning ourselves directly with the sufficiently clear ideas of freedom as origination and as voluntariness. The idea of origination, of course, is the idea of choices and decisions as not effects—not effects of immediately preceding or earlier states of affairs. In particular, to make use of a fundamental and general clarification of causation, choices and decisions are taken as having immediate antecedents such that since those antecedents occurred, whatever else had been happening, the choices or decisions would still have happened.

Caruso's best but inexplicit expression of this proposition of determinism, I myself take it, is that our choices and decisions are the results of *factors beyond our control.* A useful or effective expression, but…

I find it hard to resist insisting here again that it is a remarkable fact about ourselves that we at least entertain the idea of origination or what occasionally was called *creative choice* about ourselves. It is a remarkable fact that except when desert or right and wrong or the like is in question, no one save for curious zealots doubts that choices and decisions *have causes.* And, inevitably and crucially, even if we are not all philosophers of causation, that those causes are members of sets of conditions, causal circumstances, or sufficient conditions, which necessitate the choices' conditions. Nor, as you have heard, is there any final obscurity about the conditional analysis of what it is for a causal circumstance to necessitate an effect.

There is another reason for at least reluctance about talk only of desert in connection with determinism. All talk of desert, in my judgment, as said or implied earlier, is ambiguous, obscure, partisan, selective, or prejudiced—the self-interest, or worse, of individuals or sets or classes of people. Punishment by the state is a first stop on a route to that conclusion. I brazenly recommend my old books on that subject to you. But desert is a larger subject than that, the subject of whole societies.

If we need an explanation of the upshot of determinism, the problem it poses, far better to take it with Caruso in other and better sentences, that determinism makes our choices and decisions, as already remarked, results of factors beyond our control. And then to explain that sentence, as its making our choices and decisions, as already remarked, unfree in exactly being effects of causal sequences. To remember one other way of putting the point, determinism is the proposition that in a certain sense, of course, in need of being made clear and capable of it, we *could never have chosen or decided otherwise than we did.*

What is said by Caruso and his allies in so much addition to and enlargement on my responses to determinism is new and strong. Perhaps more elaboration and indeed enrichment than refutation. Advances of qualification and nuance. As with some other papers in this book, there are thoughts and distinctions whose adequate consideration would require closer and longer attention than is in order in these remarks—and attention to other cited writings. Closer attention to Caruso's particular optimism about determinism, matters of control, meaning in life, intelligence and beauty, character, achievement, doxastic irrationality, my conception of embraced desires, the question of how much daylight there is between us.

His thoughts too on creativity and the testimony of Einstein—the father of modern physics, including quantum mechanics, and the perfectly clear-headed determinist—are remembered for the proposition about God's reality that He does not play dice. The absurdity of attempting to explain away Einstein's determinism by means of psychoanalysis was a nadir of that line of life.

Thoughts too on folk psychology being indeterministic about choices and decisions—to which can be added the further thought that that psychology and all of us are in agreement in what is yet more definite, the proposition that choices and decisions have causes. That proposition is the stuff of our lives.

But I give in passing something about consequentionalism with respect to right and wrong. Nothing else makes much sense to me—any sense except as special pleading, at bottom, kinds of self-concern or in fact selfishness, of deprivation and worse as against indulgence and surfeit, of all that rather than humanity. And I am as resolute about exactly the contrast between the mysterianism of origination as against the relative clarity of voluntariness in terms of consequences.

Was I, by the way, a philosopher owed to or instigated by an age that was already passing? Has now passed? How many philosophers are there now who are actually carrying forward the mission of asserting the mysterianism of origination, trying against the odds to make it into strongly argued sense?

But I add another hesitation true to the calling of philosophy, a hesitation against myself. Could it be, alarmingly, that determinism is owed to *personality* in the ordinary sense, where that includes kinds of attention-seeking, however well white-washed? It used to be said of my teacher, Freddie Ayer, that he thrived on the notoriety of his Logical Positivism in its most dramatic and false description of itself—as the philosophy that declared religious and moral utterances to be *meaningless.* I trust he would have agreed that in fact it was a philosophy much less dramatic, to the effect that the utterances in question do not have the standard truth values of utterances of fact or logic, these having to do with some correspondence to fact or such considerations as consistency and entailment.

So much, not enough, for remarks on my persuasive and productive critics, those may be rare things, these university examiners. My last word is again that the problem for us of the consequences of belief in determinism is evidently a problem to which only what can be called a local philosophy of life is a solution. Not a problem of at all the size or gravity of ones faced by others in other places. Not of the size or gravity of not enough life but instead multitudes of lifetimes cut short, or river blindness, or an existence where freedom and power are mainly *talk,* and only facts of other people's lives, exclusion by others who have the advantage of being able to read.

To come back to our present subject, do go to Caruso's books in support of his case: *Exploring the Illusion of Free Will and Moral Responsibility* and *Free Will and Consciousness: A Determinist Account of the Illusion of Free Will.*

Part III

Right and Wrong, Humanity, and Terrorism

13

Some Notes on the Principle of Humanity

Mary Warnock

Ted Honderich holds that there are six fundamental desires, shared by all human beings, desires that they actually have, and which form a factual basis for human morality or the ability to distinguish what is right from what is wrong. The six desires are for a reasonably long life, for reasonable physical comfort, for freedom and power, for good relationships with other people, for respect and self-respect, and for the good things deriving from culture. I have paraphrased his list not very accurately, but I do not want to quarrel with it, except that I would include security in the ownership of property (which might perhaps be already included under the heading of Freedom and Power). But this is a controversial matter to which I shall return in due course. However, the idea of such a list of common desires seems to me of great importance in the search for the origins of morality, and gives hope for a proof that morality and its nature cannot be relative to an individual, because of its basis in a shared humanity. However, I would prefer to compile my list, which would not differ much

M. Warnock (✉)
Lady Margaret Hall, Oxford, UK

G. D. Caruso (ed.), *Ted Honderich on Consciousness, Determinism, and Humanity*, Philosophers in Depth, https://doi.org/10.1007/978-3-319-66754-6_13

from Honderich's list, in terms of shared *needs* rather than shared *desires.* And I believe that such a list could be equally factual and objective.

Honderich mentions the possibility of compiling a list of needs rather than desires, but thinks that the factual nature of the list would thereby be obscured. I may have misunderstood him, but I think his objection is that a need must always be relative to some envisaged end, and that to specify such an end for all human beings would be arbitrary or meaningless through vagueness. Now I agree that generally to speak in terms of needs does entail an end (though often an end is so obvious that it does not need specifying, as when I come in wet and stiff from a day's hunting and say "I need a hot bath"). But sometimes the end can be specified quite precisely "If Eliza is to become a good violinist, she needs a decent instrument." When the Committee of Inquiry into "the education of handicapped children and young people," as it was first known, was set up in 1974, at our very first meeting we changed our terms of reference to include the phrase "special educational needs." I had a picture of education as a long road disappearing into the distance (rather like the old start-rite advertisement for children's shoes which some may remember), along which all children set out towards the far-off goals of independence, understanding and enjoyment. But for some the road was easy, for others it was fraught with obstacles. What these latter children objectively needed if they were to make even a little progress down the road was special measures to get them over the obstacles. And one could often identify the help needed quite easily. In the wider context of a whole life there is no specifiable goal, as we thought there was in the case of education, and vague goals such as "flourishing" (e.g., "This is what we all need if we are to flourish") are indeed lacking in factual content. But in the case of the needs that I would refer to in the Principle of Humanity, it seems to me no positive end is required. For the Principle is, as Honderich said, concerned with bad lives more than with good. What determines the need is the badness of the lives that people lead when their common needs are not satisfied, if their lives are cut short, they are living in extreme poverty without proper supplies of food and water and shelter, if they are forbidden to bring up a family, if they are not given equal respect under the law, and so on. These are the kind of conditions under which people live who live in countries which we say "have an appalling human rights record." Their lives are bad lives and the Principle of Humanity demands that we act to get them out of such lives. I do not therefore believe that the factual basis of the principle is diminished if it is couched in terms of needs rather than desires. And of course many of those whom we have a moral obligation to rescue from bad lives are children, who do not in fact yet experience all of the six fundamental desires, indeed whose poverty and ill-health and perpetual hunger may almost deprive them of desires at all; all they experience is misery without hope. All these considerations lead me to accept the Principle of Humanity, as amended, as crucial to the fundamentals of morality, part, at least, of the content of the idea of right as opposed to wrong.

I now move on, however, to less certain ground. I think Honderich holds that the human beings who experience the great fundamental wants or desires believe that their satisfaction constitutes a right or a set of rights. And, indeed, in what I have already said, I have linked the concept of the great needs, as I would have it, to our notion of human rights, such as that is. But I find myself sceptical about whether saying that the satisfaction of these basic needs constitutes a set of rights adds anything to saying that they are fundamental needs which no one ought, morally, to overlook and may actually be misleading. This is to raise the question whether the phrase "human rights" means the same as "moral rights." But what is a moral right? According to Bentham, it is "Nonsense on stilts." And I cannot cure myself of a somewhat outdated positivistic view of what it is to claim a right, namely that it is to claim that an entitlement or freedom has been conferred on you, which has thereby laid a duty on someone else not to stand in the way of your enjoying whatever it is that you claim as a right, or positively to provide the means to your enjoyment of it. And this is confirmed by what Honderich says: if those who are deprived of the great goods are deprived of their rights, then the rest of us (presumably) have a duty to supply the goods, the enjoyment of which they have been wrongfully denied. Indeed, he uses a stronger expression. He says that we *must* do so, as a matter of urgent practical intervention; the deprivation in question, the bad lives that are being led give us more than a good reason to intervene. Its force is stronger than that. I think, but am not sure, that Honderich will answer that the Principle of Humanity itself, just because it is a principle, but a principle with a special status, being based on undeniable facts, confers both the rights and the duty, in this case. But I may have misunderstood the force of his "must," and this is a crucial part of his argument. My difficulty is this: though a moral principle is law-like in some respects, it is not a law. Being a moral principle, it certainly deals in what ought to be done, perhaps what ought to become a law, in a better society, but is not a law in our society; think of the emergence of racial discrimination legislation in the twentieth century. Alternatively, a moral principle may be thought of as a "higher" law, with an authority that overrides the statutes of any particular country. Famously, Antigone appealed to such a law when the tyrant, Kreon, refused to allow her to throw earth on the body of her brother, in accordance with the proper rituals that her religion demanded. But unless one is prepared to assert the existence of such a hierarchy of law (a highly dangerous step, since it would be the step to be taken by any full-blown theocracy, within which the ruling priests and they alone can interpret what this higher law dictates), then it seems to me that to speak of moral rights is to borrow a kind of certainty and above all an enforceability that belongs to legal rights and to them alone. It may be a readily intelligible metaphor, but a metaphor it remains. I entirely accept the Great Goods and the human needs that, in my view, these point to; and insofar as these are also implied when people speak of Human Rights, and in terms of which they describe those regimes that have little or no respect for them, I accept the connection between these human needs and human rights. But I do not believe that the idea of a Right in this context adds anything to the thought that there are ways in which no human being ought, morally, to treat another.

And so the central difficulty remains. Granted that we know what constitutes a bad life, and that we know it would be bad for any human being who lived it, including, of course, ourselves, what motivates us to get people out of such lives, and keep them from slipping back? Our common humanity, certainly, and it is this that is the ground of our knowledge that such lives are bad for whoever lives them. But it is easy for everyone living in comfort and relative affluence, with no serious threat from famine, water shortage, or, for the most part, epidemic to forget the rest of the world. And how much should we ("we" as private individuals or "we" as essentially political animals living as part of a nation-state) think about these bad lives? How often should we remind ourselves that there are people living bad lives all around us not only abroad but also at home? (For we need not imaginatively move to the developing world to encounter poverty, poor education, or the gross injustice of having no access to the law.) I suppose the simple answer is that good people think of them quite a lot, less good people less often. But politicians or others involved in debating public policy should never have them far from their minds and should give good outcomes, under the Principle of Humanity, higher priority than most of their other goals.

And there is a difficulty here that encapsulates them all: I said earlier that I would add the ownership of property, and reasonable security in that ownership, to the list of Great goods. I believe that ownership, especially ownership of land and a house, is a Great Good, entangled as it is with the freedom to do as one likes with what is one's own, the power to improve it, the love one may bear it and the pride and satisfaction one may get from looking after it and using it. And yet it is increasingly obvious that one of the great moral demands upon us, one of the needs that society itself has, whether globally or domestically, is a redistribution of wealth. And perhaps this itself is enough to show that ownership has no place among the great goods because it may be necessary for it to be, at least in part, given up by some so that it may modestly, perhaps, be enjoyed by others. No moral principle should I suppose demand that anyone give up one of the Great Goods for the sake of others. So perhaps ownership should come out of my list and be relegated to a list of what we may desire but do not need. But I am not wholly convinced. To be insecure in the possession of one's house and land is surely a Great Evil. Moreover, since the Washington Conference on looted art works in 1998, Western countries that have such works in their museums and galleries have recognised the justice of hearing cases brought by surviving members of Jewish families who suffered during the war years, either from actual looting or from forced sale, and have set up bodies to look into such cases and recommend either restitution or compensation, if the case is made. They have, that is, recognised the rights of the family members, who have certainly come before the quasi-judicial bodies as the claimants of rights. Paradoxically, however, in this country and others, there is a time-limit, after which no claim for the wrongful acquisition of property can be heard (in this country it is 13 years). And so, in every case of alleged Nazi looting, it has to be made clear that the claimants have no legal rights whatever, but, if any right, a moral right. The museum or gallery is being asked to "do the decent thing." However, perhaps the evils perpetrated by the Nazi regime, not only on Jews but on other persons regarded as dispensable are unique; and if so, there is no general lesson to be learned and certainly none about the status of ownership as a need or otherwise.

My next point in this series of notes arises again out of the question whether the Principle of Humanity is experienced as a matter of rights by those who hold to it as a principle. If Honderich would agree with me that if rights come into the matter at all, they can be only moral, not legal rights, then would he further agree that this is only a more blustering way of saying that to be deprived of any (or of course all) of the Great Goods is a Great Evil, and no one can have any moral justification for so depriving a fellow human being. I prefer to use the word "evil," here, stripped of any religious flavour it may seem to have, because one cannot use the word "bad" as a noun, in the way that one can the word "good." I am aware that Honderich regards the upholding of the Principle of Humanity as a way of distinguishing Right from Wrong. But to say that people who live bad lives suffer a wrong, or many wrongs, seems to me to beg the question of rights, for to say that one has been wronged is generally, though not perhaps always, understood to imply that a right has been infringed. So is the Principle of Humanity, cast in its strongest form in terms of needs, not desires, strong enough to bridge the gap between the case where we ourselves are guilty, and that where other people, not ourselves, are guilty of inflicting intolerable evils on human beings?

Sometimes, the Great Evils are inflicted on a community, forcing all the members of that community for a time at least to lead bad lives, not by any human agency, but by natural disaster, floods, earthquakes, or volcanic eruptions. These days we are accustomed to hearing such events and their aftermath, referred to as "humanitarian Crises"; and this brings out the notion of common humanity and the demands that it makes on us all, so that we must take action. And indeed in such a crisis, wherever it occurs, the common reaction is usually astonishingly generous and spontaneous. Those who dig out their spare blankets, or dig into their pockets, are motivated by the Principle of Humanity. "I must" or "I cannot not" do something. Is this the "must" that motivates us, or should do so, to get people out of bad lives and keep them out? It was obviously the "must" that motivated the Good Samaritan to rescue the man who had been set upon by thieves and look after him at his own expense. But that story surely brings out the difference between wrongs and other misfortunes. The man in the ditch had no right to be rescued, only an acute need. If the Samaritan had been fulfilling the duty conferred on him by the victim's rights, then we should not particularly admire and love his behaviour. He would be doing what was "only his duty," and his motivation would have been quite different.

Now, I believe that the reaction to appeals in times of humanitarian crisis, and the reaction of the Good Samaritan that caused him to stop on the road are both of them natural, in that it arises in each case directly out of human nature, which dictates what we need if our lives are to be worth living or indeed are not to be cut short. There are also principles dictating what other animals need (and many, but not all of them, are the same). And this indeed is part of the reason why I do not want to say that the needs constitute or are identical with rights. For in my view, it is stretching the metaphor that I have argued is contained in the concept of "Human Rights" to suppose that other animals have rights, other than the general right under the criminal law not to be treated with cruelty, since cruelty to animals is a criminal offence. But the Principle of Humanity, though generating a reaction that is natural, and reflecting an aspect of human nature, does not reflect it all, as Thomas Hobbes well knew. The needs that we have, for sufficient means to supply us with food and shelter, for freedom, independence, and power, these needs may naturally become corrupted by another aspect of our common nature, namely greed. It is not appropriate within this essay to explore all the possible ramifications of the idea of the natural; but it is obviously relevant to call to mind Hobbes' belief that in their natural state human beings would tear themselves to destruction in the "war of all against all"; and this would be a war fired entirely by greed, the insatiable desire not only for resources, but for power. No one who considers the facts of human society, whether one thinks of individual societies or on an international scale, can deny that though the Principle of Humanity is recognised by some as the foundation for an imperative to action, it is not recognised as of any interest at all by others (and Honderich acknowledges this without, in my view, giving it due importance). Those to whom the Principle is of no concern remain morally in the condition of small children (see Sutherland 2014). They have no idea of the concepts of morally right or morally wrong, especially in the fields of domestic and foreign policy. There is an analogy to be drawn between those who believe that the concept of morality can be drawn from religious texts and those who believe they can be drawn from the Principle of Humanity. They can be so drawn only by believers. But, Honderich will say, that is no analogy. For religious texts are articles of belief without evidence, while the Principle of Humanity deals in hard facts, the facts of human needs, or of such a phenomenon as a Bad life, to accept the existence of which you need only look around you. But, I would reply sadly that I think the analogy holds, if only weakly. For Honderich and for me, what the sacred texts say is irrelevant as a foundation for morality (full of moral lessons as they may be), so for those who believe that greed is the only possible motivation for human action, the Principle has no relevance.

This is only to say again that I am not convinced that the principle is such that by itself, it can provide a motive for action. What is required is a separate foundation for an interest in distinguishing right from wrong, good from evil, a separate introduction of conscience into our thinking, especially in public as opposed to private matters, matters of policy, rather than day-to-day domestic life. And here I believe that the comparison between those who have no interest in other people's needs and small children is apt. And it has consequences. For it is only through the education of children when they are small that the generality of people can be introduced to the idea that other people exist and are as important as themselves, and that therefore it is always wrong for them to take more than their fair share of anything. And this enormously important educational step comes usually at school, which for most children is the first time they encounter people other than family members, within which closed circle the idea of fairness is often obscured (a child may be the youngest and expect special treatment or the oldest and expect a different kind of distinction). It seems to me, therefore, that moral education, if it deserves so grand a title, is of the very first importance in primary schools.

The habit of thinking of others can be completely ingrained in children by the time they are seven (the Jesuits knew this well though thinking of a less benign kind of indoctrination). Children must be taught that they will, by their nature, always be tempted by greed; and that also by their nature, they are capable of overcoming temptation. Without a recognition of both these facts, the fact of temptation and the fact that greed can be overcome by the thought of other human beings, I do not myself see that the Principle of Humanity can supply the imperative to action on which Honderich insists. It will do so only for those who already want to do good.

Reference

Sutherland, Stewart. 2014. Hume's problem and the nature of greed. *Dialogue* 43: 17–21.

14

Ted Honderich and Terrorism

Paul Gilbert

For 40 years, Ted Honderich has pursued the unpopular project of acting as an advocate for what he has called the violence of the Left—the violence involved in those terrorist campaigns which stand a reasonable chance of getting "freedom and power for a people when it is clear that nothing else will get it for them." These are his words on the notorious page 151 of *After the Terror* (2003), in which Honderich asserted that "the Palestinians have exercised a moral right in their terrorism against the Israelis," and thereby called down a well-known storm upon his head. It requires courage and perseverance to act as Honderich has, in a way that few philosophical projects can require them, and one of the questions I want to keep in mind in discussing his project is what might thus be required of us in our role as philosophers.

Honderich's own answer derives from his view of political philosophy as, indeed, advocacy. "Political philosophers," he writes, "are inevitably more like barristers, as distinct from judges, than is allowed by certain high conceptions of their subject, and it is best to admit it. No doubt

P. Gilbert (✉)
University of Hull, Hull, UK

G. D. Caruso (ed.), *Ted Honderich on Consciousness, Determinism, and Humanity*, Philosophers in Depth, https://doi.org/10.1007/978-3-319-66754-6_14

they are advocates more or less convinced of the rightness of their cases, but they are advocates nonetheless" (1989, p. 203). Barristers are, of course, confronted by opposing barristers, and we need to bear this in mind in considering Honderich's claims. They are not, as he is modestly conceding, magisterial. They are meant to present a case that stands only if the opposition to it falls, and they are to be scrutinized in this spirit.

In practicing philosophy as advocacy, Honderich stands in a long and honorable tradition that stretches through, among others, Bertrand Russell, John Stuart Mill, and Jeremy Bentham. Like the last two, Honderich is a consequentialist, basing his case for violence on its consequences for "getting and keeping people out of bad lives" (2006, p. 60). His Principle of Humanity, which Honderich is using here, is the fundamental principle which he believes is needed when we are considering questions of right and wrong in politics. It expresses, he thinks, "a morality to which we are all committed," and committed "by our human nature"—a nature which involves, on the one hand, "our great desires" for certain goods, and on the other, our rationality which requires us to acknowledge the general scope of the reasons such desires provide (2006, p. 58). Since bad lives are ones we would not wish to be plunged into, we are therefore obliged to try to keep others out of them. Terrorism is prima facie wrong because it does kill people and spoil lives, but it is possibly rightful if the Principle of Humanity would adjudicate in favor of using these means to get people out of their bad lives at the cost of these ills to others.

In formulating and employing his Principle of Humanity, Honderich shows that his interest in discussing various cases of terrorism, including the Palestinian one, is as much philosophical as political. The question he is addressing is the clearly philosophical one of how we can determine the rights and wrongs of terrorist acts. The principle gives us a general method to apply, so that, as with all consequentialist principles, we then need to look at the facts about likely consequences to see if an act can be endorsed or ought to be condemned. "What is hardest about morality," writes Honderich, "are questions of fact" (2006, p. 95). So, in endorsing Palestinian terrorism, one thing Honderich is doing is making a factual claim about the likelihood of its success in alleviating many bad Palestinian lives at the price of making a relatively small number of Israeli lives worse, including just ending them. Here, someone may think, Honderich has stepped out of his philosophical shoes. And yet, any consequentialist must do so on drawing specific conclusions. So we cannot say that in advocating a particular political position here that Honderich has somehow crossed a line that philosophers should not cross.

Honderich's interest is, however, clearly also political. After addressing the philosophical question of how to determine the moral character of terrorist acts and assessing the chance of Palestinian terrorism achieving its objective, he makes the judgment that it is morally justified. This is a political judgment because the intention in voicing it is to have an effect on public policy through affecting public opinion. The court in which Honderich acts as an advocate is, therefore, the court of public opinion. It is as citizens that we may hope to have an effect politically, in the first place, as citizens trying to affect policy in our own country, but, more broadly, through addressing also citizens in other countries so that they may have an effect on policy in theirs. We can see that this is what Honderich is aiming to do through the fact that he calls for changes in policy toward Israel and the Palestinians not only from Britain but from the USA and other Western countries too. As advocating the political position he does, Honderich is, I suggest, acting not only as a philosopher but also as a citizen.

On the face of it, there is no contradiction in performing the role both of philosopher and of citizen simultaneously in advocating political positions on philosophical grounds. Russell, Mill, and Bentham all did so, and, most famously, Socrates' argument for drinking hemlock is made in both capacities. There is, however, a potential tension between the roles. As a philosopher, Honderich formulates a principle which brings order and consistency to the judgments he makes on its basis. But, as an advocate in the court of public opinion, he surely needs to carry as many of the jury along with him as he can. It cannot be assumed that all of them will wish to subscribe to the Principle of Humanity or, indeed, to any consequentialist principle. Some may have deontological convictions despite Honderich's view that "all deontological morality is in fact lower stuff, dishonourable stuff, an abandoning of humanity, of the decent part of our nature, and an attempt to make that abandoning respectable to oneself and others" (2006, p. 78). Those with deontological inclinations are scarcely likely to give them up on being told this. Advocacy is the art of persuasion, and in persuading those whose initial instincts are to condemn Palestinian terrorism, the less general the grounds on which the advocate relies the better; for the more general they are, the more disputable they will probably be. Greater generality may, by contrast, suit one's philosophical urge for system.

Honderich does not rely only on the Principle of Humanity in arriving at his judgments. He uses it, rather, to organize and justify them. Thus, he says that "the wrong of 9/11 is to be taken as a kind of datum, a moral truth that has general moral principles as its possible consequences" (2006, p. 126). Most people would share his reaction. His task, then, in trying to convince them that Palestinian terrorism is not similarly wrong is to expose the differences between the cases. Here, Honderich has been criticized for distinguishing 9/11 as wrong because "there could be no certainty or significant probability, no reasonable hope, that it would work to secure a justifying end, but only a certainty that it would destroy lives" (2003, p. 118). But, as Gerald Cohen has observed, "The criticism that terror is counterproductive does not criticize it *as* terror" (as quoted by Meisels 2008, p. 35). It is not the fact that a terrorist act is counterproductive that horrifies people, but that it is the particular sort of act it is—an act that deliberately kills and wounds people like ourselves. Thus, Honderich acknowledges that "the killers of September 11 rightly have our revulsion" because "they violated the natural fact and practice of morality" by an attack that would have these savage consequences. His criticism of 9/11 is not, then, that it was counterproductive but precisely that it was that sort of act. His claim is that such acts are prima facie wrong because they have such consequences and they can only be justified if these are outweighed by beneficent ones. In the case of 9/11, not only are there no such countervailing factors, but the perpetrators could not rationally have thought that there would be. Honderich's criticism of 9/11 is, therefore, that it was solely destructive, which chimes in with the feelings of revulsion it excites as an act of terror. Yet, it is as terror that Palestinian suicide bombings and so forth do strike many as wrong; so it is some other aspect of them that needs to be shown if this judgment is to be overturned. I shall move, then, to discuss what Honderich has to say in his role as advocate to reveal this aspect which might justify Palestinian terrorism.

14.1 I

Honderich defines terrorism as "violence, short of war, political, illegal and prima facie wrong" (2006, p. 88). In thinking of it as short of war, he clearly conceives it as having the same aims as war, so when we look at his justification of Palestinian terrorism, by contrast with acts like 9/11, we can usefully employ the old just war notion of *jus ad bellum*. While Honderich regards just war theory as needing to be systematized in terms of the Principle of Humanity, he seems happy to employ its notions, which arguably do have a wider appeal. Thus, Honderich thinks that the Palestinians, unlike the 9/11 bombers, have a just cause which they can pursue by no other means than violence and that their violence is not hopeless. His view of the Palestinians' just cause is complex. In *After the Terror*, he seems to see it principally in terms of what looks like a right of national self-determination. "Peoples," he writes, "demand the freedom that the running of their lives in a place to which their history and culture attaches them" (2003, p. 28). Lives are bad if they lack this satisfaction, but also, according to the Principle of Humanity, if people lack respect and self-respect, adequate material goods, and opportunities for culture and for relationships, all of which applies to the Palestinians. Honderich sums this up and perhaps adds to it in *Humanity, Terrorism, Terrorist War*, writing that Palestinian terrorism has been "self-defence, resistance to ethnic cleansing, self-preservation, the preservation of the existence of a people" (2006, p. 110).

The various afflictions against which the Palestinians have been struggling seem to me to have very different weights in a possible justification of their campaign, and to my mind, Honderich lays too much stress on what I have termed the national self-determination argument. It is fair to point out that Honderich himself does not speak of the Palestinian cause in these terms. He speaks of the Palestinians as a people rather than as a nation, and this may be for one or both of two reasons. First, the idea of a nation may be taken to imply a distinctive cultural identity which seems to be lacking in the Palestinian case. They speak the same Arabic language as others in the Middle East, though there are colloquial variations. Thus, Palestinians have counted among Arab nationalists who think of speaking this language as a criterion of national identity much wider than any

Palestinian one. Religion does even worse than language in marking out a Palestinian nation since Palestinians include a large Christian minority who are equally committed to the cause. What is more, among the Muslims, many would reject the whole idea of nationhood, believing that "there can be no such thing as an individual and sovereign nation set apart from the rest of Islam" (Kiernan 1975, p. 200). Yet, this cultural conception of nationhood is not compulsory, and we can think of Palestinians as forming a nation in civic terms in virtue of their occupying a certain territory and having a consequent claim to it. By this criterion, speaking of a nation and of a people may be taken to be equivalent. A second reason why Honderich may prefer the latter formulation is that, as so conceived, "All peoples have the right to self-determination" under Article 1 of the United Nations International Covenant on Civil and Political Rights. But campaigns to claim this right are commonly termed nationalist and I shall follow this practice here, having duly noted the dangers of misinterpretation.

One reason why I question Honderich's emphasis on national self-determination as a justification for Palestinian violence is a very general one. It is that I am unconvinced by his claim that the value of a people's "freedom and power in their homeland" has been "better demonstrated historically than any other good," and that "our nature" is proof of it (2003, p. 120). A skeptical response would be that the sort of nationalism seemingly alluded to here is a comparatively modern phenomenon and a potentially dangerous one. Here, Honderich seems to come very close to viewing a people or a nation as a primordial aspect of human social organization, because it is rooted in "our nature." But any attempt to demonstrate this from history would surely be limited to citing comparatively recent and local events. People may indeed desire what Honderich says they do, but perhaps they are misguided to do so. Then, something much more ideologically modest in terms of the right of oppressed people to separate and autonomous government might guarantee them the other great goods they need in order to avoid bad lives. This much more restricted right may be what the United Nations was countenancing in acknowledging a right of self-determination to peoples, for the peoples it had in mind were those living under colonial or some similar type of domination.

Honderich, however, seems to place his greatest stress on what I have called the national self-determination argument in defending Palestinian terrorism, for he spends considerable time aiming to demonstrate that the Palestinians have "proved by their sacrifices" that prior to 1948, they were already a people with "the self-consciousness of a people" (2006, p. 109), rather than this being something that developed later. Again, there seems to be an alternative story that is at least equally convincing. Isaiah Berlin attributes nationalism to people being "like Schiller's bent twig, which always jumped back and hit its bender" (Berlin 2001, p. 131). He imputes German nationalism to the humiliation Germans experienced through being denied the respect accorded to the supposedly culturally superior French. A similar story could be told about the Palestinians in relation to the Jewish settlers who came to form and later expand the state of Israel, while often despising their Arab neighbors. It seems plausible to suppose that it is in response to the way they were thus treated that Palestinians came to think of themselves as a distinct people or nation. On this conception, resistance to a lack of respect is viewed as the engine for creating nationhood, contrary to Honderich's claim that the Palestinians already being a people is necessary to account for their resistance. On the alternative view, the resistance to humiliation staged by political organizations is what gets them to think of themselves as a people by gathering their support for restoring a sense of pride. Furthermore, the fact that the resistance is violent is what one might expect on this account of their nationalism as a reaction to being despised, for this will evoke indignation and will be overcome only by heroic deeds that humiliate the despisers.

Yet, does this alternative account weaken the Palestinian case for using violence? Not necessarily. Rather, it shifts the emphasis to all those other ills that the Palestinians have suffered and for which a separate and autonomous government may be the sole remedy, perhaps only to be achieved through violence. Then, a stronger case for it might be made by adverting to "self-defence, resistance to ethnic cleansing, self-preservation," in Honderich's words, than by concentrating upon "the preservation of the existence of a people," if this is conceived in nationalist terms. These aims will provide the *jus ad bellum* for Palestinian fighters and thus place their actions within a normal framework for the use of force that most people might accept, even for those with deontological views who reject Honderich's consequentialism.

14.2 II

The other element of the just war theory, though, is *jus in bello*, and its cardinal principle is that the innocent should not be targeted. Honderich regards the *ad bellum/in bello* distinction as artificial and raises some of the usual questions about who constitute the innocent and what sort of protection they can expect. However, even if it is accepted that Palestinians have a case for violence, the character of that violence will still need to be examined. Honderich does not, rightly to my mind, define terrorism in terms of attacks upon the innocent, but the suicide bombers he defends do kill and maim just such victims. How does Honderich justify this? It seems to be by assimilating these attacks to those in which civilians get killed and wounded in ordinary wars. The two sorts of cases are often distinguished by invoking the doctrine of double effect, whereby in the one, civilians are deliberately attacked and in the other, the harm to them is foreseen but not intended. Honderich is understandably skeptical of the way this doctrine is used to defend the infliction of so-called collateral damage, when it seems hard to deny that it is intended. But the point of the just war prohibition is independent of this doctrine about intentions. Its point is that civilians are not legitimate targets, so that if they are killed or wounded, it must only be as the effect of attacking a military target. So Palestinian suicide bombers who target civilians are not, as Honderich implies, in the same position as gunship pilots who kill civilians in the process of securing a military objective. The Palestinian terrorists may, perhaps, lack any military targets to attack, but that they would have attacked these in preference had they been available does not justify their actions in the way in which choosing targets with as little risk to civilians as possible may justify attacks involving such casualties.

Even if Honderich is right, and both the pilot and the bomber intend to kill civilians but intend to kill only those who need to be killed for them to secure their objectives, there is a crucial difference if the pilot's objective is a military one and the bomber's is not, as seems to be the case in Honderich's example (2003, pp. 172–174). Honderich might dispute the importance that the just war theory attaches to the distinction between properly military and merely murderous actions.

But the theory has resources for criticizing the pilot's action in killing as disproportionate to the significance of the objective achieved. Indeed, this may be the criticism underlying Honderich's observation that the pilot should be aware that there were "about three times as many deaths of more or less innocent Palestinians as against more or less innocent Israelis" (2003, p. 175).

It is, perhaps, possible that an oppressed people lack any properly military options so that all it can do is to murder civilians among its oppressors. Consequentialists may not want to rule out such actions, though I doubt if these have ever been the only options available to Palestinians. Honderich may be right that the Palestinians would often prefer other methods and regret the civilian casualties they cause. Indeed, this may originally have usually been the case. However, the problem with a group acquiring "the self-consciousness of a people," which Honderich ascribes to the Palestinians early on in their struggle, is that it engenders a politics in which their identity is set against the identity of those who resist their claim to self-determination. The identity politics into which nationalism may lead people is that the conflicts it causes are not, as on Rousseau's account of war, ones in which "the individuals who become involved ... are enemies only by accident" (Rousseau 1761, sect. 1.4). They are enemies because one identity group reacts against being despised, demeaned, disrespected, or denied due recognition by the other. This leads to hatred and anger against members of the other group, which readily spills over into communal violence and the targeting of ordinary civilians by militants. In these circumstances, the civilian immunity which *jus in bello* demands is no longer respected since the motivation required for it is lacking. Regrettably, this seems to be the situation which has arisen in the Palestinian/Israeli conflict, so the Palestinian bombers may well not regret killing their civilian targets.

The *in bello* rules, which apply to terrorism as much as to full-scale war, are in place to counter these attitudes and the evils they bring about when armed conflict arises. They need not be regarded as mysterious deontological edicts, but rather as principles governing the performance of a certain role, namely that of soldier or irregular fighter, acting on behalf of ordinary people. Principles regulating roles may be regarded as moral principles if the role is such that its proper performance can be viewed as morally good. Such principles are grasped by understanding the point and requirements of the role. In the case of soldiers, regular or irregular, the point is, in large part, the protection of civilians. The rule of civilian immunity recognizes this by acknowledging the special status they have on one's opponent's side as well as on one's own. This is partly a matter of expediency. If a soldier targets the other side's civilians, then his side's civilians are likely to be targeted too and his task of protecting them is made harder. But, the rule also limits the role to combat with other fighters in a way that makes possible pride in its performance, which is a very different thing from whatever grim gratification might be obtained by killing members of an opposing identity group.

Earlier, I suggested that the judgments one makes on the rights and wrongs of Palestinian bombings are made from one's position as a citizen. As citizens, we have a strong interest in maintaining the rule of civilian immunity and ensuring that those who fight on our behalf adhere to it, for general adherence should help to protect civilians, which most of us are. This will make us very reluctant to condone breaches of the rule. Arguably, adherence to it will reduce the overall amount of suffering that conflict would otherwise cause, and thus it can, in principle, be justified on consequentialist grounds. One way to argue for the rule of civilian immunity is to adopt the indirect consequentialism propounded by Richard Hare, in which guides to action, like this rule, are chosen as those that would minimize bad lives if they were followed (Hare 1981). This option seems to be open to Honderich who holds that it is not only the rightness of actions that is to be judged by their reasonably expected consequences but the rightness of policies and practices too. In particular cases, adhering to the rule might not produce the best results but overall it is the policy most likely to. In this framework, the question becomes whether the rule of civilian immunity best serves this purpose.

A commitment to civilian immunity does not, however, seem fully to explain the revulsion we feel at attacks upon civilians like those of suicide bombers, even when we may sympathize with their cause. This is due, I think, to the chilling experience of people being hated so much just for who they are, rather than for anything they do, as they would be if they were combatants who invited retaliation or posed a threat. And, this is especially disturbing if people are hated so much that those who target them are prepared to die themselves in the process. In the absence of adherence to the rule of civilian immunity, any of us is exposed to the risk of being treated like this, so that we become not "enemies only by accident," but through the hatred others have for us.

The wrong of 9/11 is taken as a moral datum, I think, partly because it has this background. However different Palestinian terrorism may have been at the outset, the concern is that it may have morphed into something where hatred rather than hope has become its moving force. International law, which seeks to enforce rules like that of civilian immunity, reflects the tragic view that even those with a just cause can, unless constrained, wreak havoc when bright designs fail and turn to vengefulness and indiscriminate violence. We have as citizens, I have suggested, a strong interest in supporting it. This may be reason enough for not following Honderich in endorsing Palestinian violence despite their cause. But, this is not to say that we should unreservedly condemn it. Like Honderich, when the Oxford Union debated the violence of the IRA, it is possible to acknowledge the complexities and sit upon the crossbenches (see 1989, pp. xi–xvi). The moderate skepticism that this reflects might be what is expected from us as philosophers. But, Honderich has demonstrated that conviction too is compatible with this calling, even if it must be bought at a considerably higher price.

Sometimes as citizens, if not as philosophers, it is demanded of us that we get off the fence and publicly approve or disapprove of political actions if we can conscientiously do so. We must, of course, consider the consequences, and publicly approving even what is right may conceivably sometimes do more harm than good. But if as philosophers we have any special expertise over and above that of the ordinary citizen in adjudicating upon political acts, it is because we may sometimes be more confident of the strength of our arguments. Whether or not one agrees with Honderich's conclusions on the issues discussed here, the clarity and force of his arguments shows what sort of thing is needed to justify that confidence.

References

Berlin, Isaiah. 2001. *The roots of romanticism*. Princeton, NJ: Princeton University Press.

Hare, Richard M. 1981. *Moral thinking*. Oxford: Clarendon Press.

Honderich, Ted. 1989. *Violence for equality*. London: Routledge.

———. 2003. *After the terror*. Edinburgh: Edinburgh University Press.

———. 2006. *Humanity, terrorism, terrorist war*. London: Continuum.

Kiernan, Thomas. 1975. *The Arabs: Their history, aims and challenges to the industrialized world*. London: Sphere.

Meisels, Tamar. 2008. *The trouble with terror: Liberty, security and the response to terrorism*. Cambridge: Cambridge University Press.

Rousseau, Jean-Jacques. 1761. *The social contract (many editions)*. France: Author.

15

Terrorism, Humanity, and a Plurality of Principles

Richard J. Norman

Honderich's book *After the Terror* (2003) managed to be both eminently commonsensical and highly controversial. This was a sure sign that it had touched a raw nerve and identified confusions and contradictions in conventional moral thinking which needed to be examined and clarified. The aspects of the contemporary world which he addressed in *After the Terror* and in its successor, *Humanity, Terrorism, Terrorist War* (2006), were:

(a) global poverty and the inadequate response to it on the part of the populations of the most prosperous societies;

(b) the Israeli occupation of Palestinian territories; and

(c) political terrorism, particularly Islamist-inspired terrorist actions such as the attack on the Twin Towers in 2001.

These he discussed in the light of his proposed ethical framework, the principle of humanity, revealing the inconsistency between the popular abhorrence of (c) and the prevailing complacency with respect to (a) and (b).

R. J. Norman (✉)
University of Kent, Canterbury, UK

G. D. Caruso (ed.), *Ted Honderich on Consciousness, Determinism, and Humanity*, Philosophers in Depth, https://doi.org/10.1007/978-3-319-66754-6_15

In this chapter, I shall be mainly concerned with philosophical questions about the principle of humanity, and its implications for moral attitudes to terrorism and political violence, but I shall preface that with a brief glance at the substantive practical concerns. Are things getting any better?

On global poverty, it is a mixed picture. There has been progress on many fronts. The World Bank's *World Development Indicators*—the data source used by Honderich—show, for instance, that:

- the number of people living in extreme poverty, as a percentage of the population, fell from about 44% in 1990 to about 13% in 2015;
- the share of the world's population suffering from hunger and undernourishment, whose food intake does not meet continuous dietary energy requirements, fell from 19% to 11% in the 25 years to 2016;
- the under-five mortality rate in developing countries declined by half from 99 deaths per 1000 live births in 1990 to 50 in 2013; and
- the maternal mortality ratio decreased in developing countries as a whole from 430 per 100,000 live births in 1990 to 230 in 2013.

Some of the Millennium Development Goals—the targets for world development from 2000 to 2015, now superseded by the Sustainable Development Goals—were met, but others were not, and progress continues to be slow in sub-Saharan Africa in particular.[1]

If there has been some progress in tackling global poverty and hunger, the plight of the Palestinians has become even worse. Israeli settlements in occupied territories continue to grow, making the two-state solution increasingly difficult and with no alternative route to justice on the table.[2] Palestinian resistance continues, though it involves only limited violence, and despite the publicity about Israeli casualties, the majority of the victims of violence are Palestinians.

Meanwhile, Islamist-inspired terrorism, and terrorist actions by other groups, continue. Such incidents rightly elicit horrified reactions—or at least they do if they occur in Europe or North America. Without minimising the horror, it is worth putting this into perspective. The statistics are problematic, in part because of the difficulty of defining terrorism, a question which I shall address in due course. However, available data sources suggest that from 20,487 deaths worldwide as a result of terrorism in 2006, the number fell to 13,186 in 2010. The breakdown by region in 2010 was:

South Asia 6172
Middle East 3750
Africa 2137
East Asia and Pacific Region 493
Europe, Eurasia 355
Western Hemisphere 279

The overall figure of 13,186 in 2010 should be compared with an estimated 8 million total figure for mortality rates for children under five from all causes in 2011, and an estimated 3.5 million infant deaths from under-nutrition in 2009. From 13,186 in 2010, the figure rose again to 32,763 in 2014 and 28,328 in 2015. In the first seven months of 2016, the number of deaths caused by terrorism in Western Europe was 143, the highest since 2004, but only 6% of deaths from terrorism worldwide in July 2016 happened in Western Europe, far fewer than the number in, for instance, the Middle East.[3]

In short, the facts cited by Honderich, including the disparities and the inconsistencies in popular reactions to them, are still with us, and still merit thoughtful consideration.

15.1 Humanity, Consequentialism, and Constraints

That thoughtful consideration should, according to Honderich, be guided by the principle of humanity:

> PH1. What we need to do morally is to try to save people from bad lives. (2003, p. 53).

Spelled out more fully, this becomes:

> PH1A. The right thing to do is the one that according to the best judgement and information is the rational thing with respect to the end or goal of saving people from bad lives. (2003, p. 53)

Bad lives are lives which lack some or all of the great human goods, the things which go to make up a good human life. These are:

1. a decent length of life;
2. physical well-being and the material goods needed for this;
3. freedom and power;
4. respect and self-respect;
5. private and public relationships with others; and
6. the satisfactions of culture and knowledge. (2003, pp. 1–5 and 52)

The principle of humanity is variously referred to by Honderich as a morality of humanity, fellow-feeling, or generosity, and the echoes of David Hume are both clear and deliberate. Honderich describes it as a "natural morality," which "arises out of" three fundamental features of human nature: first, our desires for good things; second, our capacity to be guided by reasons and their requirement of consistency; and third, our capacity for sympathy for other human beings (2003, pp. 31–32). This last is, as Honderich says, what Hume "made a foundation of his account of morality." The phrase "arises out of" seems to me to be the right way of putting the relationship between morality and the features of human nature. The phrase needs unpacking, Honderich does not elaborate it, and I shall not try to explore here how it could be unpacked. I can only say that it would be a mistake to look for a tighter logical relationship than is suggested by the words "arises out of." As Honderich says, the facts about human beings do not furnish a *proof* of the morality of humanity (2003, p. 57). He also, and rightly, eschews the position of many contemporary neo-Humeans—that moral utterances are to be construed as *expressions* of desires and feelings. In a perfectly good sense, there are "moral truths" and "moral facts" (2003, pp. 36–37).

Whatever "arises out of" amounts to, then, the important point is that the morality of humanity is grounded in our responsiveness to the lives of other human beings. I stress this in order to point out that there is more than one way in which such a responsiveness can issue in action. Honderich's emphasis is on *saving people from bad lives.* What seems to me to be warranted, however, is not the principle "*The* right thing to do is to save people from bad lives," but rather:

PH2. *One* right thing to do is to save people from bad lives.

The qualification is important because there are other ways in which our responsiveness to the goodness and badness of people's lives might be translated into action. In particular, another principle which could be regarded as "arising out of" our capacity for sympathy and humanity, together with our responsiveness to reasons and the facts about human desires, would be:

PH3. A wrong thing to do is to deprive people of good lives.

where "good lives" can plausibly be understood to mean "lives which they value as being lives worth living." In other words, our responsiveness to other people's lives would support a principle that it is prima facie wrong to kill people. Honderich says as much, but his inclination is to assimilate PH3 to PH1, by treating our refraining from killing people as one way of "saving people from bad lives."[4] That inclination is question-begging, and I want to resist it. In ordinary language, these are significantly different ways in which our concern for people may issue in action, and we need to take the differences seriously.

What is driving Honderich's inclination to assimilate the different formulations is, I think, his *consequentialism.* It is easy to see the attraction. On the face of it, the different applications of the principle of humanity may come into conflict with one another. The concrete practical dilemmas addressed by Honderich arise in part because depriving some people of their good lives—killing people—may sometimes be a means of saving other people from bad lives. How do we weigh the competing values—the concern not to end people's lives and the concern to improve the lives of other people? It is tempting to think that we can weigh them by considering them as means to the same end, the one goal of saving people from bad lives. The attraction is that we could then see the judgement we have to make, difficult though it may be, as essentially an assessment of *effectiveness*—of working out what will do most to save people from bad lives.

That is the appeal of consequentialism—but the appeal is spurious. We should first be clear what we mean by "consequentialism." Honderich sometimes seems to say that it is simply the requirement that when we are assessing the rightness or wrongness of actions, it is always important to look at their consequences. Of course, we have to take consequences into account. Of course, also, when considering whether we are acting rightly, we have to look not only at the consequences of our actions, but also at the consequences of our failure to act. If—to apply this to one of Honderich's main themes—other people are suffering and dying from poverty and hunger, and we have done nothing to help, then to that extent we have acted wrongly, and it is not enough for us to plead that we have not actively killed or harmed them. Of course also—to take another theme—one of the things that made the terrorist attack on the Twin Towers, like other comparable terrorist actions, morally appalling was that it was utterly futile. There was "no reasonable hope that it would work to secure a justifying end" (2003, p. 118). So yes, consequences are always relevant.

What does not follow is that the only rational way to assess the rightness or wrongness of actions is a *maximising* consequentialism. It is this that I want to question. If we focus on talk of good and bad lives, it may seem natural to suppose that the rational thing to do is always to maximise the good and minimise the bad. However, if we step back from that vocabulary, it is less self-evident. The natural way to think of the wrongness of killing would be not as a way of minimising the badness of bad lives, but as a *constraint*, a moral prohibition which sets limits to how we can treat people, and therefore also sets limits to the morally acceptable ways in which we can produce more good things and get rid of bad things. A response of humanity, fellow-feeling, can just as naturally issue in a refusal to do certain things to other people, in particular a refusal to take their lives, as in a concern to make their lives better. And, if the two conflict, it can be perfectly rational to try to resolve the conflict by saying "Well of course we want to save people from bad lives, but killing some people in order to save other people from bad lives is not an acceptable way of doing it." Honderich says that the appeal to reasons brings with it a requirement of consistency—but that can perfectly well be a rationally consistent position. It is no less rational than the idea that what needs to be done is to add up the total amount of goodness (whatever that may mean) likely to be produced by various courses of action, subtract the total amount of badness, and calculate which course of action will produce the greatest balance of goodness overall. A principle of humanity need not be just a principle of efficiency.

Three further observations may serve to dispel the appearance of self-evidence in the maximising approach. First, it is in any case not clear what the description "total amount of goodness" should mean in the light of Honderich's principle of humanity. He rightly offers a pluralist account of good lives. There is a plurality of human goods, and no single metric on which they can be compared and assessed. How do we weigh the value of longer or shorter lives against greater physical well-being? How do we weigh the value of loving relationships against the value of material prosperity? Honderich is right to avoid a simplistic utilitarianism which sees all human goods as quantities of one fundamental good, which is "happiness" or "well-being." In that case, however, there is no obvious way of weighing competing goods to arrive at a maximal sum.

Secondly, it is important also to recognise that the various goods are not free-standing items of value. They are the goods which go to make up good human lives, and what humanity requires of us is not the amassing of quantities of some impersonal commodity for which human beings are the bearers or vehicles. What humanity requires of us is that we *treat human beings* in the right ways. And the possible right and wrong ways of treating human beings consist of more than just the production of goods for them. Other human beings are more than just the potential beneficiaries of our agency. Along with a pluralism about human goods should go a pluralism about the right ways of treating people.

Thirdly, we need to bear in mind the moral significance of John Rawls' remarks about the separateness of persons. Rawls points out that maximising versions of consequentialism get their appeal from the principle of rational choice for a single individual. It is rational for me to forego certain advantages now for the sake of my greater future well-being. But it is a question-begging assumption that it is, in the same way, rational to sacrifice some people's well-being for the sake of the greater good of others. My own future gains may compensate for my short-term losses, but it is by no means self-evident that we can speak of *some people's* gains compensating for *other people's* losses. Compensate *whom*? "Utilitarianism," says Rawls, "does not take seriously the separateness of persons" (1971, p. 27). The same is true of other versions of maximising consequentialism, including Honderich's.

The appeal of the maximising view of practical rationality is therefore seductive but specious. Recognising this at least leaves open the possibility that some ways of treating people, even if they promote the goal of saving more people from bad lives, are morally ruled out, are off limits. Maybe there are some things that it would be morally unacceptable to do to people even if doing it might successfully promote that end. We therefore cannot dismiss the popular moral revulsion against certain ways of treating people. This is where we have to look at attitudes to terrorism and violence, and take seriously the possibility that they may be morally rational in setting limits to permissible ways of treating other human beings.

15.2 Terrorism

I turn, then, to the question of terrorism. I sympathise with Honderich's disinclination to make moral conclusions dependent on a precise definition of "terrorism" which distinguishes it from other kinds of political violence, but I do think that it is worth looking at the question of definition to see whether it points us to any features of particular kinds of violence which have a specific moral significance.

Honderich is reluctant to build a reference to "fear" into the definition of terrorism, despite the etymology of the word. As he rightly says, all violence induces fear, either in the victim, or in others, or both. Historically, nevertheless, the word "terrorism" appears to have been used typically to refer to the use of political violence to create *a general climate of fear*. What the fear is a fear of, who induces it, and who is made to feel the fear has varied from one historical instance to another. It seems to be generally agreed that the first use of the word "terrorist" in English was to refer to the use of violence by the Jacobin regime in the French Revolution, in the period referred to as "the Terror." That was one case of creating a climate of fear—in this case, by the agents of the state, not against the state. The killing of suspected opponents of the regime, on the merest hint of disloyalty, created an atmosphere in which no one could feel safe. A later use of the word "terrorist" in common parlance as a standard label was its application to the nineteenth-century Russian populists, who came to be seen at the time as the archetypal "terrorists." Their political violence was directed against rulers and state officials, but it could be said that it was intended to create a climate of fear insofar as it promoted a general sense of insecurity and unpredictable danger. Those two examples of "terrorism" coming to be identified with a particular political tendency do illustrate its imprecision, and the way in which its connotations can vary with the historical and political context. Their common feature, nevertheless, could be seen as the tactic of creating a political climate in which there is a general fear of who will strike next, where, and against whom.

There is a certain degree of continuity between these cases and those which have dominated the perception of terrorism in recent years. What has especially fuelled the idea of terrorism as something morally horrendous, I suggest, has been the *indiscriminate* character of the killings. The victims could have been anyone. The terrorist killing of the Charlie Hebdo journalists was perhaps an exception, and raises different questions about free expression, whether it includes the freedom to offend and whether finding something offensive could ever be a justification for repressive violence. In other notorious cases, however, the word "indiscriminate" seems entirely apposite. The people who were killed were simply carrying on with their daily lives. The 89 victims in the Bataclan theatre in Paris in November 2015 were young people attending a pop concert. The 86 victims of the lorry driven into the crowd on the Nice promenade in July 2016 were there to celebrate Bastille Day. The 12 people killed in the Berlin market in December 2016 were doing Christmas shopping. And the far more numerous victims of terrorist bombing in Iraq, Turkey, and elsewhere in the Middle East have typically been people going to work or to the market, or sometimes worshiping in a church or in a mosque of a different Islamic persuasion from that of the perpetrator.

At the intuitive level, this is a feature of terrorist violence which inclines many people to say that there is something especially appalling about it, even more so than other kinds of political violence. Can we make rational sense of this? One traditional way of doing so is to talk about the wrongness of killing the innocent, and to say that although there can sometimes be a moral justification for killing another human being, killing the innocent is morally impermissible. Terrorism, it may be said, characteristically targets innocent victims. I think that there can be mileage in that way of putting it, but there are also obvious difficulties.[5] Who is to count as "innocent"? How can we distinguish between those who are innocent and those who are not? At one level, none of us is morally innocent. For instance, as Honderich emphasises, we inhabitants of the more prosperous societies are all to some degree complicit in the perpetuation of global poverty and the failure to save people from bad lives. Does that mean that we are not "innocent" in the relevant sense, and does it make us morally legitimate targets for terrorist attacks, or is there some relevant sense in which most of the victims of terrorism are "innocent"?

There may be coherent ways of dealing with the difficulties, but for present purposes, I shall take a different approach. Let us look at the epithet "indiscriminate" itself. Thinking about the victims of terrorist attacks such as the ones I have mentioned, we might ask "Why them?" Why were they picked out as people to be killed? And we would be likely to ask this as a rhetorical question, knowing that there is no answer. There was no particular reason why these people were the ones to be killed. There was nothing about them that made them appropriate targets. They just happened to be the people there at the time. They were conveniently available to be used for a terrorist action, but anyone else would have served the purpose equally well.

A Kantian phrase may come to mind here. We could say that these people were used simply as means to an end—simply as objects to serve a purpose. That Kantian terminology is far from perspicuous, but by thinking about it in relation to our examples, we can form a clearer idea of why it might carry moral weight. Kant does not say that it is wrong to use people as means to an end, which of course we do constantly, but that we should treat persons "never *merely* as a means but always *also* as a end." What, then, would allow someone to say that although they had used someone as a means—killed someone, say, for the sake of the greater good—they had *also* treated that person as an end? A consequentialist might say that the condition is met provided the victim's interests have been taken into account in assessing the overall balance of goods and harms. If we kill one person to save 20, we are not treating the one person solely as a means if we have weighed the good of saving the 20 against the harm done to the one person by depriving them of the good of a longer life. That of course would not satisfy Kant. For him, to treat a person as an end requires respecting them as a person, treating them as someone with the capacity for rational agency and autonomy. So, though there can sometimes be a moral justification for ending someone's life, it would have to be justified by something about that person and about that person's agency.

Honderich might object that this is to take refuge in a morality of special obligations, a morality of relationship—something of which he is strongly critical. The idea that how it is right to treat someone might depend on something special about that person, or about that person's relationship to us, is a form of moral thinking which he initially contrasts with consequentialist moralities (Honderich 2003, p. 62). He then qualifies this, allowing that moralities of special obligation need not exclude the moral salience of consequences. His criticism then becomes the claim that moralities of special obligation, and moralities of relationship in particular, "boil down to a kind of selfishness." That is an odd way of characterising a moral commitment to give special care, or make special sacrifices, for one's child, or one's family or friends, or one's own community. Whether or not a case can be made for "special obligations" of this kind, it would hardly be a case for selfishness.

However, as Honderich says, moralities of special obligation are a mixed bag, and what concerns us here is a different candidate for being a "special obligation." It is the idea that killing or seriously harming a person can be morally acceptable only if there is something specific about that person, and in particular what that person is doing or has done, which justifies it. This is our possible explanation of why indiscriminate killing might be seen as especially wrong. Perhaps it would be better described as the idea of a "special permission": the fact that someone has acted in a certain way may make it morally permissible to treat that person in a way which would otherwise be morally impermissible.

I do not think that Honderich can dismiss such ideas since he wants to recognise the special moral status of killing in self-defence. He says:

> It has to be allowed, too, that the policy against killing and other violence has to be articulated so as not to prohibit self-defence and no doubt more than that. Even an ideal society would need to protect itself. (2003, p. 118; cf. p. 55)

And the concept of self-defence plays a key role in his remarks about Palestinian terrorism, which have been seen as so controversial.

> Are we to judge … that this terrorism of the Palestinians has been right? That this terrorism that has also been self-defence, resistance to ethnic cleansing, self-preservation, the preservation of the existence of a people, a humanly necessary opposition to the excessive self-interest of others, has been justified? That the suicide bombers have been morally permitted if not obliged to do what they have done? (2006, pp. 110–111)

These remarks could be construed in purely consequentialist terms—that their terrorism has been the exercise of a moral right if it has been the only way, or the only effective way, to resist a great wrong. But then why specifically mention self-defence? If that concept is to carry any moral weight, it must be the idea that I can have a moral right to kill or use violence against someone *because he is attacking me.* The details of what explains the right of self-defence are a matter for much debate but if it means anything at all, it means a right to defend myself by killing or violently resisting *the person who is the threat.* It is not, for instance, a right to use a passing stranger as a human shield so that he gets killed instead of me. In other words, it is a right to use violence against someone *because of what they are doing.*

15.3 Self-defence and the Morality of Political Violence

In the light of what Honderich says about self-defence, I want to return to the perception of terrorism as *indiscriminate* killing and to the idea that it is especially morally abhorrent because it is indiscriminate. If we interpret these ideas in Kantian terms, they may give us a way of thinking about the morality of political violence which avoids getting bogged down in arguments about the definition of terrorism.[6] What we can say, perhaps, is this: any moral justification for the use of extreme violence against some people in order to promote better lives for others would have to depend not only on showing that the desirable consequences would be sufficiently great and sufficiently likely, but also on showing that the potential victims of that violence are legitimate targets by virtue of something that they have done or are doing.

My formulation is deliberately vague and open-ended. What, exactly, would make someone a legitimate target? That is a matter which requires complex moral debate, and I do not think that any simple principle will do the work. We can, however, take simple cases of individual self-defence as the paradigm cases of justification. If you are directly and intentionally attacking me with lethal violence, I am justified in using violence against you to defend myself. At the other extreme, it would clearly not be a sufficient justification that you happen to be in the wrong place at the wrong time. Nor would it be a sufficient justification that you are a member of a certain social group or nationality. High-profile terrorist atrocities, which are typically seen as senseless and indiscriminate, would, I suggest, fall into that category, and we can recognise them to be morally indefensible without having to get into verbal disputes about what does or does not count as "terrorism" or about how much moral weight that label should carry.

Between those extremes, there is a whole range of cases which require careful moral discrimination. If violence in individual self-defence is a paradigm of permissible violence, what about collective defence? The switch from justifying individual self-defence to justifying collective self-defence is often made far too swiftly and glibly, for instance, in the just war tradition, and it requires careful scrutiny. And even if it is accepted that political violence in collective self-defence is, at least in some cases, morally permissible, that then raises familiar questions about who can be justifiable targets of such violence. Is political violence morally permissible when directed against armed forces which are currently engaged in attacking? Against occupying forces who are not currently engaged in military action? Against off-duty occupying forces? Against civilians who are directly supporting the occupying forces? These questions have traditionally been matters for moral debate. They are proper questions for debate. And the debate around them is, I am suggesting, an appropriate way of thinking about the concrete questions raised by Honderich in connection with Palestinian resistance. They are pertinent to an understanding of the moral differences between, say, self-defence against Israeli soldiers firing on unarmed demonstrators, using violence against illegal settlers, driving a bus into a group of off-duty members of the Israel Defense Forces (IDF), and planting a bomb in a Tel Aviv café.[7]

There are no easy answers to such questions. As Honderich recognises, the requirement of consistency can take us a fair distance—consistency between moral judgements about Palestinian resistance to occupation and, say, British defence against invasion, and the French Resistance and other European resistance movements, in 1940–1944. I have been suggesting that we can think them through without having to settle the question of the definition of terrorism and its relation to other kinds of political violence, but, at the same time, doing justice to some of our moral intuitions about particular terrorist actions. More fundamentally, we can think them through using the moral resources which arise out of our shared capacities for humanity and fellow-feeling. And that, as Honderich rightly says, is the kind of moral intelligence we need (2003, p. 154).

Notes

1. See http://blogs.worldbank.org/opendata/release-world-development-indicators015 (for *World Development Indicators 2015*) and http://databank.worldbank.org/data/download/site-content/wdi-2016-highlights-featuring-sdgs-booklet.pdf (for *World Development Indicators 2016*).
2. http://www.bbc.co.uk/news/world-middle-east-38421026.
3. See https://ourworldindata.org/terrorism/, https://www.statista.com/statistics/263275/number-of-deaths-due-to-terrorism-worldwide-by-region/, and http://www.bbc.co.uk/newsbeat/article/37085042/terror-deaths-in-western-europe-at-highest-level-since-2004.
4. In Honderich (2003, p. 19), he says that "to shorten lives or leave lives short is not the same as to kill," but on p. 54, he says that "a prohibition

on wounding, attack, killing, torture, sexual attack and violation, threat, intimidation, and other violence and near-violence is one of four 'policies' to 'reduce the number of bad lives.'"

5. I have explored this idea in Norman (2008).
6. Honderich suggests that "We can speak of one thing as either *terrorism* or *political violence*, making no difference between the two terms" (2003, p. 98).
7. See for instance: http://www.btselem.org/20160222_fatalities_from_unwarranted_gunfire, https://en.wikipedia.org/wiki/Palestinian_stone-throwing, http://www.bbc.co.uk/news/world-middle-east-38546740, http://www.cbsnews.com/news/3-dead-in-tel-aviv-cafe-bombing/.

References

Honderich, Ted. 2003. *After the terror*. Edinburgh: Edinburgh University Press.

———. 2006. *Humanity, terrorism, terrorist war*. London: Continuum.

Norman, Richard J. 2008. Killing the innocent. In *Israel, Palestine and terror*, ed. Stephen Law. London: Continuum.

Rawls, John. 1971. *A theory of justice*. Cambridge, MA: Harvard University Press.

16

Terror, Self-Defence, and the Principle of Humanity

Michael Neumann

Ted Honderich is no propagandist or advocate of terrorism. His judgements on particular cases seem reluctant. His purpose is not so much to judge acts of terror as to provide a framework within which to judge them. Nevertheless, he finds himself driven to at least one judgement that will shock many:

> I myself have no serious doubt, to take the outstanding case, that the Palestinians have exercised a moral right in their terrorism against the Israelis. They have had a moral right to terrorism as certain as was the moral right, say, of the African people of South Africa against their white captors and the apartheid state. Those Palestinians who have resorted to necessary killing have been right to try to free their people, and those who have killed themselves in the cause of their people have indeed sanctified themselves. This seems to me a terrible truth, a truth that overcomes what we must remember about all terrorism, and also overcomes the thought of hideousness and monstrosity. (Honderich 2003, 151)

M. Neumann (✉)
Trent University, Peterborough, ON, Canada

G. D. Caruso (ed.), *Ted Honderich on Consciousness, Determinism, and Humanity*, Philosophers in Depth, https://doi.org/10.1007/978-3-319-66754-6_16

This judgement guarantees that its framework will be subject—is subject—to hostile, almost enraged examination.[1] Central to this framework is the Principle of Humanity and its notion of lives—long, short, good, and bad. Actions of individuals, peoples, movements, and governments are to be assessed with an eye to the sort of lives led by those involved. Naturally, this requires some attention to subjective or psychological features that help determine the quality of these lives.

This essay suggests that the Principle of Humanity must reduce its subjective component if it is to gain acceptance as a context of assessment. Even among more measured reactions to his work, Honderich's version of the principle will encounter at least two problems. First, it is open to accusations of cultural and historical parochialism. Second, its breadth impedes its potential for justifying those terrorist acts of resistance that Honderich wishes to rehabilitate. Both problems prove surmountable when a Principle of Humanity is formulated in conformity with rights of self-defence.

16.1 Culture and Humanity

Honderich's Principle of Humanity is rich, or as Rawls puts it, "fat": fully explicated, its content is extensive. Here is a bare-bones statement of the principle:

> The Principle of Humanity has to do with bad lives. It is not well expressed, indeed not expressed at all, as the truistic principle that we should rescue those with bad lives, those who are badly off. It is the principle that we must actually take rational steps to the end of getting and keeping people out of bad lives. (2006)

The notion of a bad life and its complement, a good life, is defined in terms of "the great goods of our lives." Because these notions are crucial to the discussion, it is worth citing them at length.

> We all desire the great good of going on existing, where that does not mean a lot more than just being conscious, being in the world. As you can also

say, to the same effect, we want a personal world to go on longer. We have the same desire for those close to us, our children first. This desire can sometimes be defeated by others. It comes to mind that a lot of American men and women would have ended their own worlds, carried out suicide missions, to prevent the 2800 deaths on 9/11. Nonetheless, despite exceptions, this existence is something almost all of us crave. We crave a decent length of life. Say 75 years rather than 35.

A second desire we all have is for a quality of life in a certain sense. This is a kind of existence that has a lot to do with our bodies. We want not to be in pain, to have satisfactions of food, drink, shelter, safety, sleep, maybe sex. As that implies, and as is also the case with the first desire, we also want the material means to the end in question, the material means to this bodily quality of life. Some of the means are some of the consumer-goods, so-called, easier to be superior about if you have them. You are likely to lack these means if you are in poverty.

A third thing we all want is freedom and power. We do not want to be coerced by personal circumstances arranged by others, bullied, subjected to compulsion, unable to run our own lives, weakened. We want this voluntariness and strength in a range of settings, from a house, neighbourhood and place of work to the greatest and maybe most important setting, a society in a homeland. It is no oddity that freedom from something is what is promised by every political or national tradition or movement without exception and secured to some extent if it is in control.

Another of our shared desires is for goods of relationship to those around us. We want kinds of connections with these other people. Each of us wants the unique loyalty and if possible the love of one other person, maybe two or three. We also want to be members of larger groups. No one wants to be cut off by his or her own feelings from the surrounding society or cut off from it by others' feelings. This was a considerable part of why it was no good being a nigger or a Jew or a Paki in places where those words were spoken as they were.

A fifth desire, not far away from the one for relationship, is for respect and self respect. No one wants to feel worthless. No one is untouched by disdain, even stupid disdain. No one wants humiliation. Persons kill themselves, and others, because of it. We do not want humiliation for our people either. As in the case of all these great desires, this one for respect and self-respect extends to others close to us, and in ways to other people, and it goes with desires for the means to the ends.

> Finally, we want the goods of culture. All of us want at least some of them. Many of us want the practice and reassurance of a religion, or the custom of a people, or indeed a kind of society. We may want not to live in what we take to be a degraded society, maybe one that gives an ascendancy to buying and selling in its social policies and has a public preoccupation with sex. All of us with a glimmer of knowledge want the good of knowledge and thus of education. All with a glimmer of what is written down want to be able to read. We also want diversion if not art.
>
> A bad life, we take it, is to be defined in terms of the deprivation of some or all of these goods, the frustration of some or all of these desires. A good life is defined in terms of satisfaction of them. … A bad life, we will take it, quickly here, is one that lacks one or more of the first three goods—subsistence, a bodily quality of life, all freedom and power—or a life of subsistence that is only minimally satisfied with respect to the other five goods. Good lives are had by all other persons. (2006)

According to Honderich, the Principle of Humanity (supplemented by subsidiary principles making up a "morality of humanity") determines that some acts of terror are justified and some are not. These judgements would have no interest were the principle itself unacceptable, and they would have no weight unless the principle could plausibly stand as fundamental. In a political context, having this sort of weight requires very widespread acceptance or at least the potential to gain such acceptance. Only then can the principle acquire the authority it needs if it is to survive the attacks that, in discussions of terror, it is bound to provoke.

"Widespread acceptance" means something like "at almost all times and places." The idea is not that everyone subscribes to the principle. Stuart Hampshire (1982) helpfully suggests that moral principles or values are those which, even if they do not actually enjoy universal acceptance, may be expected to find it over time. Thus, sumptuary and sexual mores are not moral because they are not convergent in this sense. Norms about killing and inflicting suffering count as moral because we do expect convergence.

Though the Principle is obviously moral in its formulation, it does not seem to meet that standard. It expresses a concept of well-being characteristic of Western industrialized societies and the liberal-democratic ethos (or for that matter social-democratic; the two ideologies increasingly resemble one another) they spawned. This ethos may be highly desirable; for all I know it could solve all the world's problems. But it cannot claim either universality or the expectation thereof.

It is a problem that cannot be avoided by putting to one side, for example, the Hindu and Buddhist doctrines of self-abnegation. The difficulty for the Principle also arises in its divergence from the main Western ethos that preceded the liberal-democratic ethos: the Christian outlook. As little as 30 years ago, this ethos might have been expected to "converge" out of existence: no longer.

The difficulty arises when the Principle encounters what, despite Christianity's great diversity, remains a central message: it is the next life, not this one that should concern you. Nothing worldly, not secular freedom, not happiness, not solidarity or sexuality, is anything like a basic or fundamental good. Indeed the whole idea that man morally deserves some goods is quite foreign to Christian thought. Thus, Innocent III, an outstanding pope in an era when the pope could well be thought the chief spokesman of Christianity, states in his immensely popular *De Miseria Humanae Conditionis*:

> Man was formed of dust, slime, and ashes: what is even more vile, of the filthiest seed. He was conceived from the itch of the flesh, in the heat of passion and the stench of lust, land worse yet, with the stain of sin.

Two centuries later Thomas à Kempis applies the lesson to himself:

> I despise myself and cast myself before You in the depths of my unworthiness. Behold, You are the Holy of holies, and I the scum of sinners!

Things do not change with the advent of Protestantism. Martin Luther does not exactly rank himself among the advocates of human flourishing:

> God creates out of nothing. Therefore, until a man is nothing, God can make nothing out of him.

And, even the relatively progressive, socially minded John Wesley tells us that

> as soon as God opens the eyes of their understanding, they see the state they were in before; they are then deeply convinced, that "every man living," themselves especially, are, by nature, "altogether vanity"; that is, folly and ignorance, sin and wickedness.

Finally, Kant, the greatest Protestant philosopher, states that

> virtue (as the worthiness to be happy) is the *supreme condition* of whatever may seem to us desirable, and hence also of all our pursuit of happiness. (2002, 141)

In this context, a principle that offers all good things to all humans is simply out of the question. Yet, the problem is not confined to matters of religion. What of those simply pessimistic about human affairs, and cold to so ambitious an enterprise as the construction of good lives? The Chorus in Sophocles' *Oedipus at Colonus* proclaims that

> Never to have been born is best.
> Everyone knows that, and a close second,
> once you have appeared in this life, is a quick
> return, as soon as you can, to where you came from.
> In our light-headed youth we carry
> blithe ideas, not knowing what blows await,
> what hardships are bearing down, closer and closer.
> Murder, hatred, strife, resentment, and envy
> are lurking, and then, behind them, bitter old age,
> powerless, friendless, with evils our only neighbors. (Slavitt 2007, 202)

Nothing here suggests a quaint perspective, rendered obsolete by the technological growth and the expansion of productive capacity. When Honderich developed his principle, this sort of pessimism might have been consigned to an embittered few and never been expected to spread further. In the past decade or so, we can no longer be so confident: faith and trust in technology, in the economic system, in politics, and in the political will of well-meaning nations have all been severely undermined.

Even one of what Honderich terms an essential element of a good life, freedom, is not what it used to be. Perhaps, as he says, that freedom is promised by "*every* political or national tradition or movement without exception"—though one might wonder whether the collective freedom promoted by many past and present nationalist and religiously oriented political movements bears much resemblance to the individual freedom Honderich seems to have at least partly in mind. In any case, with the pervasiveness of surveillance and the growing sense of powerlessness, many may feel these are empty promises and that the pursuit of lives requiring freedom is pointless. Whatever the future, this is enough to suggest that the Principle of Humanity, as formulated, cannot claim widespread or emerging acceptance at any reassuring level.

This is by no means to say that the Principle is any less acceptable from a moral point of view. It is to say that its potential for providing politically satisfactory answers to questions about terror and related issues is limited.

16.2 Good Lives, Bad Lives, and Applying the Principle

The Principle of Humanity exhibits subjectivity when it departs from a somewhat limited cultural and historical perspective. This may not undermine its validity but it threatens its authority. There is another sort of subjectivity, one that is internal to the principle: it relies on the psychological criteria of good and bad lives. This reliance undermines its capacity to deliver clear judgements on actions or practices such as terrorism.

The problem is that as soon as immaterial, elusive "quality of life" factors are introduced, it becomes very difficult to say which political actions will promote good lives and diminish the number of bad lives. Take, for example, the Palestinian terrorism, which Honderich suggests is legitimate according to the Principle. How do these acts of violent resistance affect the "satisfactions of safety" of Israelis? Of Jews everywhere? Of Westerners who fear that terror will visit their nation—however unjustifiably, however unrelated the spread of terror might be to Palestinian acts? More broadly, just what will or would it take to calm the fears of certain large political constituencies about terror, crime, government encroachment, immigrants, and other *perceived* threats? To what extent do these fears make all these lives worse? And so far we have just explored potential effects relating to the first three criteria of good lives to which Honderich assigns greater importance. In the later criteria, there emerge, as elements of good lives, not wanting to feel cut off from others, experiencing the loyalty and love of others, not wanting to live in a degraded society, feeling self-respect and others' respect.

With all these goods weighing in—and especially with no weight assigned to each good—there is simply no telling whether the poor and oppressed have worse lives than, say, the lives of rich people subject to constant fear and terrible romantic disappointments. For all we know, the strength and solidarity among the oppressed, even amid suffering, bestow a better life than what the inhabitants of affluent societies experience. Even if it doesn't, the bad lives of the Palestinians must be weighed against the good lives of the settlers and anyone else who benefits from the occupation: the Principle of Humanity is not a principle of just distribution. With these internal, subjective elements introduced, the Principle of Humanity encounters a problem of interpersonal comparisons similar to the principles of utility.

If the Principle of Humanity were just another philosophical proposal, these difficulties would not seem devastating. The parochialism problem, in a purely intellectual context, might almost be dismissed: popularity, so to speak, is hardly a criterion of acceptability. But a principle applied to very controversial political issues needs something like political legitimacy, and for that, an appeal to near-universal normative foundations is highly desirable. There is a principle that offers this. It is very different from the Principle of Humanity, but, I believe, much closer in its spirit than in the letter.

16.3 Humanity and Self-defence

If there is one normative principle (and attendant right) that enjoys genuinely wide acceptance across time and place, it is self-defence. Honderich himself on occasion cites this principle (e.g., 2003, 93), but does not look into its relation to the Principle of Humanity. Yet, some discussion is desirable because if the Principle of Humanity is supreme, it may nullify the right to self-defence. In that case, little weight can be attached to the fact that "self-defence is in full accord with the body of international law" (2003, 93).

Revisit, for instance, the issue of Palestinian terror. Suppose Palestinian terrorism is legitimate according to principles of self-defence, but that, as is quite possible, it is counter-productive in the sense that it promotes bad lives rather than good lives. In that case, what is permitted according the principles of self-defence is forbidden according to the Principle of Humanity. So now, Honderich's defence of Palestinian terrorism is doubly weakened: first, because the subjectivity inherent in "good lives" makes it hard to show that the oppressors' lives are better than the oppressed's, and second, because it is hard to show that the oppressed's actions actually promote good lives rather than bad.

The conflict is not resolved by arguing that Palestinians *intend* in their acts of self-defence to promote good lives. Honderich refers to intentions in his exploration of our reactions to acts of terror, to suggest the moral picture is not so cut-and-dried as we might suppose. But in the end, the consequentialist Principle of Humanity cannot cite intentions in the justification of acts. Either the acts promote good lives versus bad or they don't. In the case of Palestinian terror, quite possibly they don't.[2]

But, what if the principle of self-defence is taken, not as a troublesome adjunct to the Principle of Humanity, but as the basis of a principle that will capture at least some of the Principle of Humanity's purpose? A number of problems disappear because, perhaps surprisingly, *principles of self-defence are not consequentialist.*

Consider two situations. First, I find three men blocking every escape route, advancing on me with clubs and knives. I have a right to defend myself against them. Second, suppose a hundred, or a thousand men, are menacing me in the same way. My right to self-defence is in no degree diminished. It makes no difference at all that, in the second case, my acts of self-defence are utterly futile. So, the consequences of the act have no bearing on whether it is justified according to some right of self-defence.

It is not even clear that principles of self-defence look seriously at intent. That someone poses a mortal threat has much more to do with that person's externally observable posture than with his intentions. That posture makes the threatened person's responses legitimate, whatever the actual intentions of the person deemed the aggressor. True, these rules presume a general link between posture and intentions. But you may also defend yourself against innocent threats, so the link seems to be inessential. Indeed, as long as you perform acts that *look* like self-defence, even the defender's intentions don't seem to be at issue.

If utterly futile self-defence is a right, that right diverges from self-interest. Futile actions are not in my interest and are not in most circumstances dictated by principles of rational behaviour. So, the right of self-defence seems far removed from the general normative principles prominent in modern moral thought. It is possible, however, to parlay that right into something like a moral good or ideal.

My suggestion here is that the right to self-defence expresses an aspect of some broader notion that might indeed be associated with a Principle of Humanity: the right to human agency.

When you defend yourself, you are not necessarily seeking to maximize your advantage or, indeed, to have any extensive effect on the world such as is considered in consequentialist ethics. Your act is one of self-preservation, however inconsequential when faced with overwhelming odds. In the case of futile self-defence, self-preservation cannot figure in as an *objective*, but rather as something *asserted*: it is not a consequence of the act, but something presupposed and exhibited in the act.

The right of self-defence, since it endorses the preservation of a living, acting human being, suggests a right to function as a human agent. Physical injury and death at the hands of attackers of course put an end to that functioning. But so do other things, which suggest that a right to human agency should be expanded.

The suggestion cannot simply be read into the right of self-defence. Unlike the American Constitution, we can't even try to guess the intention of the "original framers" of that right. Perhaps the intent was no more than to regulate combat. The notion that there is a broader right to human agency can, however, be seen as a matter of logic. Suppose I have a right to defend myself against attack on the grounds that such attacks are a threat to my life. Why would I have a right to defend myself against *that* sort of mortal threat and not *other* sorts? The right of self-defence doesn't just apply in some armed combat festival; it applies in society.

This means that society, implicitly, doesn't think it reasonable to expect someone to lay down their life when encountering a mortal threat from an adversary. But, it isn't the mere presence of the adversary that triggers the right; it is the (mortal) threat. If you allow that someone may respond to the adversary's threat, it makes no sense to deny him the right to oppose other threats to his existence.

In that sense, I think, a right to human agency is a reasonable extension of the right to self-defence in a *political* context. When considering the operations of a society as opposed to, say, a prison camp, there is a limit to what you can rationally expect people to put up with. And, one expression of that limit is that you cannot expect people not to oppose other sorts of moral threat, whether or not they come from an attacker.

It is not difficult to build a notion of human agency from the right to oppose mortal threats. Other such threats come from a lack of the traditional triad of "goods": food, clothing, and shelter. A trickier matter is to what extent medical care should be added to this list: perhaps to the extent of access to urgent care when such care is readily available. Another way of approaching the right is to suppose humans have a right to whatever the lack of which prompts the attention of disaster relief agencies. The details are beyond the scope of this essay. Suffice it to say that here is a bedrock "Principle of Humanity." Everyone, according to this principle, has the right to function as a human agent, and this means having the physical capacity to do so.

If that notion of human agency defines what is to be protected, what is to be taken as a *threat* to that status? To how much assurance of the means to life am I entitled? Within the limits suggested by the right to self-defence, the threat must be imminent. Just as I cannot roam the streets eliminating potential enemies, so I have no right to acquire the enormous sort of wealth that might make access to these necessities as close to absolutely certain as human endeavour can obtain.

However, there is potential for considerable controversy as to what sort of threats count as imminent. I'd suggest that in determining imminence, very strong probability trumps temporal remoteness. If a tyrant imposes an agricultural policy that assures my crops will fail in several months, that is an imminent threat to the extent that the results are "morally certain," even though the realization of the threat is remote in time.

On the other hand, the mere imposition of a dictatorship cannot by itself constitute an imminent threat because, even if the consequences are not remote, they may be uncertain. The right to human agency does not entail a right to political freedom, which these days may in any case seen unattainable in any substantive sense, at least for individuals rather than collectivities. Some sorts of dictatorship do infringe on human agency, for example if an occupation is severe enough to bear sufficient resemblance to kidnapping. Kidnapping-level occupations would trigger a right to self-defence.

Another issue is the relation of a right to self-defence or human agency to the rights of others to act on your behalf. It is plausible that if you have a right to defend yourself, it is because you may act to preserve something to which you have a right. It's hard to see why others might not have a right to rise to your defence as well. In a political context, these rights need to be interpreted with respect to whole populations. To apply the principle, there is no need to introduce controversial collective entities such as The Palestinian People or even "the Palestinians." It is enough to suppose a danger to some members of the population.

This has to do with the certainty of a threat. Suppose again the agricultural policy which will cause crop failures. I may not be certain that I personally will starve in such circumstances; perhaps I will find a way to get by. But I may be certain that some will not be so lucky; their right to human agency will be violated. If I can undertake actions opposed to the agricultural policy, my actions will count as justified according to the principle. It is sufficient that I am defending *someone* (or some people), even if I cannot identify *which* person that is.

Similar reasoning can be applied to the situation of the Palestinians. Arguably many innocents will die as the result of Israeli occupation, whether it is from lack of access to urgently needed medical care or as "collateral damage." Many, including children, will be imprisoned. Many will suffer, and are now suffering, from malnutrition. It does not matter if we cannot identify which individuals are subject to these mortal threats, and there is no need to posit a genocide against The Palestinian People. All these threats are violations of the principle that human agency is to be protected.

Do these circumstances justify Palestinian terrorism? Recall that an act of defence may be justified without being effective. However, there are cases where ineffectiveness raises questions about whether an act can be characterized as defence of any sort. I do not defend against the agricultural policy, and no one defends against Israeli occupation, by setting up an art exhibit. Such acts are less than futile; they are not anything a reasonable individual could expect to constitute, even an easily overcome defence of someone's agency.

The availability of plausible alternative acts of defence is probably the decisive issue when determining whether protection of human agency justifies Palestinian terrorism. The terrorists' view is that less bloody and dramatic acts, or acts directed against Israeli military positions, cannot plausibly be seen as self-defence, or defence of others' lives, because they carry futility beyond reasonable boundaries, into absurdity. Others, of course, will disagree.

My personal opinion is that this is the sort of discussion appropriate to terror. Debating consequences is inevitably tendentious; we typically don't know the full consequences of political acts. Invoking exalted values also seems unhelpful. We are not now in an age where anyone can pretend that any society does much to uphold such values. And since the realization of these values seems so terribly unlikely, we cannot even claim that political decisions should be made according to what enhances their pursuit. The more limited framework of attack and response offers opportunities to apply principles that at least have the merit of something like real-world acceptance.

More limited principles also seem better suited to the analysis of particular cases. The difficulties applying Honderich's Principle of Humanity arise partly from the application of an ambitious, wide-ranging principle applied to extreme cases, which require clear criteria of evaluation. The "fat" Principle incorporates broad concepts of well-being, so that it becomes unclear whether the oppressed are really so much worse off than the oppressors and justified in their violent reaction. The much more modest principle of human agency avoids these problems.

My proposed alternative to the Principle of Humanity may also play some role in defending Honderich's work on terror. The professional, even personal risk he has accepted in addressing these questions is perhaps unappreciated. There are many high-minded "public intellectuals"—Michael Walzer comes to mind—who condemn terror. Such condemnations seem to come from writers inhabiting a bubble. In Walzer's world, decades-long bouts of squeaky-clean political activism should be good enough for everyone, no matter how desperate; he sees terrorists essentially as psychopaths.[3] Opposed to these moralizers are the intellectuals who get snarky about terrorism out of, apparently, little but a desire for attention: Slavoj Zizek comes to mind.[4] Honderich stands out as someone who attends not only to general principles but to the world's realities. His venture is, I think, undermined by recourse to a principle too closely wedded to just those broad Western ideals which, in recent years, the West has done much to discredit. That is why I believe a more modest principle does more justice to his project.

Notes

1. See, for example, John Pike's review of *After the Terror* (2005).
2. I gloss over Honderich's qualification that acts are right or wrong when *reasonably believed* to promote good lives or bad lives, respectively. The doubts about whether acts of terror are self-defeating apply just as well to what may reasonably be believed as to what may actually ensue.
3. "It is not so easy to reach the last resort. To get there, one must indeed try everything … and not just once, as if a political party or movement might organize a single demonstration, fail to win immediate victory, and claim that it is now justified in moving on to murder. Politics is an art of repetition. Activists learn by doing the same thing over and over again. It is by no means clear when they run out of options." The sense of leisure, and the studied obliviousness to what it is like to suffer the relentless encroachment of an immensely powerful occupier, are striking. Walzer believes that hardly anyone justifies terrorism; they merely excuse it. Copied from: Excusing Terror: http://prospect.org/article/excusing-terror.
4. "The fundamentalist Islamic terror is NOT grounded in the terrorists' conviction of their superiority and in their desire to safeguard their cultural-religious identity from the onslaught of the global consumerist civilization: the problem with fundamentalists is not that we consider

them inferior to us, but, rather, that THEY THEMSELVES secretly consider themselves inferior (like, obviously, Hitler himself felt towards Jews)—which is why our condescending Politically Correct assurances that we feel no superiority towards them only makes them more furious and feeds their resentment." For Zizek, the problem of terrorism apparently consists in finding surprising things to say about it. Copied from Slavoj Zizek, "Some Politically Incorrect Reflections on Violence in France and Related Matters: The Terrorist Resentment": http://www.lacan.com/zizfrance1.htm.

References

Hampshire, Stuart. 1982. Morality and convention. In *Utilitarianism and beyond*, ed. Amartya Sen and Bernard Williams, 145–157. Cambridge, MA: Cambridge University Press.

Honderich, Ted. 2003. *After the terror*. Edinburgh: Edinburgh University Press.

———. 2006. *The principle of humanity, stated and defended*. Manuscript download from http://www.ucl.ac.uk/~uctytho/PofHSandD.html

Kant, Immanuel. 2002. *Critique of practical reason*. Trans. Werner Pluhar. Indianapolis: Hackett.

Pike, John. 2005. Review of *After the Terror*. *Democratiya* 2: 37–48.

Slavitt, David. 2007. Translation. *The Theban Plays of Sophocles*. New Haven, CT: Yale University Press.

17

Free Will, Understanding, and Justification: Terrorism, Israel, and the Palestinians

Saul Smilansky

In this piece, I wish to do two things: first, briefly explore the history of the interaction between the Israeli Jews and Palestinians in the last three generations, focusing on the question of why there is no Palestinian state, with a special emphasis on the role of terrorism. Second, combine this with some reflection on our attitudes regarding the free will problem and the role free will plays in understanding and in justification. This might at first be thought to be an odd choice. One reason why I wish to do this is that both Ted Honderich and myself have specialized in the free will problem, while also writing on terrorism in the Israeli-Palestinian context. A second, more important reason is that work on the free will problem has focused on the issue of punishment (another topic on which both of us have worked) but hardly at all on broad historical-political issues, so I think that we might gain from this new focus. I aim to explore the question as to why there is no Palestinian state (and the relevance of terrorism to this question), taking off from some comments by Ted Honderich; and in the process see what we can learn from this about the

S. Smilansky (✉)
Department of Philosophy, University of Haifa, Haifa, Israel

G. D. Caruso (ed.), *Ted Honderich on Consciousness, Determinism, and Humanity*, Philosophers in Depth, https://doi.org/10.1007/978-3-319-66754-6_17

free will problem. At the same time, I shall explore what reflection on agency, choice, and responsibility can add to our understanding of the Israeli-Palestinian conflict.

If I am to accomplish my aim I need to make rather broad stipulations and avoid a large number of topics. We need not enter into a discussion of the nature of terrorism. It suffices that the intentional targeting of civilians by Palestinians will be considered terrorism, and this Honderich acknowledges. Whether it is justified (as he claims) will be our focus. We will likewise not need to concern ourselves with questions of early history, for example about ancient rights and identities. Honderich acknowledges that it was morally right to establish Israel in 1948 (Honderich 2003, 169) and admits Israel's right to exist within the pre-1967 borders. Finally, the issue of individual versus collective responsibility is large and complex; like Honderich, I will assume here that this issue does not eliminate our ability to judge Israelis and Palestinians.

The focal point is Honderich's following clear (and often repeated) claim:

> [T]he terrorism of the Palestinians is a paradigm case of terrorism for humanity, terrorism with the aim of humanity. The most salient of these facts is the established necessity of this terrorism, the clear absence of *any* alternative policy whatever of dealing with rapacity. The terrorism of the Palestinians is their only effective and economical means of self-defence, of liberating themselves. (Honderich 2003, 170)

Palestinian terrorism is justified, he claims, since no other alternative is open for Palestinians to achieve a state of their own alongside Israel (in the West Bank and Gaza strip). I will first critically explore the merits of this claim, through an exploration of why there is no Palestinian state. Then I will turn to the free will problem.

17.1 Why Is There No Palestinian State?

Why is there no Palestinian state? Two striking conclusions emerge from any close look at historical and contemporary facts (I borrow here heavily from Smilansky 2004):

1. The Palestinians have had opportunities again and again that *could have* led to the establishment of a state of their own, but chose not to act to seize any of these opportunities.
2. On some occasions of these opportunities, the establishment of such a state *did not even depend on Israel.* It was up to the Palestinians to decide and to act. Israel was not the obstacle.

There is so much ignorance, and so much half-baked pseudo-knowledge and misinformation, that it is crucial to begin with some facts. Here is a list of the relevant ones:

1. Great Britain led a coalition of forces that won over the relevant territory from the Turks in 1917, during the First World War; and had been exercising, since 1923, the mandate Britain had received from the League of Nations to administer this territory, formerly part of the Ottoman empire. The British Peel Commission recommended in 1937 that separate Arab and Jewish states be established. The Jewish leadership was ready to consider and negotiate on this compromise, but the Arab leadership rejected it. The area that the British proposed for the Jewish state was very small, and much smaller than Israel as established after the 1948 war. But in the face of harsh Arab opposition in 1937, Britain did not implement the plan, choosing instead to radically curtail Jewish emigration to Palestine on the eve of the Second World War.

   In other words, as early as 1937—80 years ago—a large Palestinian state (covering by far most of the territory between the Jordan River and the Mediterranean) was on offer to the Palestinians, but the Palestinians turned it down.
2. In 1947, the United Nations confirmed, by a large majority, a resolution that partitioned what remained of the British mandate over Palestine (west of the Jordan River) into two independent states, a Jewish state and an Arab state. The Jewish leadership accepted Resolution 181 and Israel was established in 1948. But the official leadership of the Palestinian Arabs rejected the compromise partition plan, explicitly rejecting the very idea of an independent state for the Jews and insisting that only one Arab state be established on

the whole territory. The Palestinians began fighting, combining their forces with the forces of five Arab armies that invaded the just established state of Israel.

In 1948, therefore, the Palestinians could again have had an independent state alongside Israel; to be born at the same time as Israel.

3. During the 1948 war, Jordan captured the West Bank and East Jerusalem, and Egypt captured the Gaza Strip. During the 20 years between 1948 and 1967, the Palestinians could have called for and attempted to establish an independent Palestinian state in both of these areas, both of which were intended to be within the Palestinian/ Arab state according to the 1947 UN partition plan. The Palestinians made no such attempt. They aimed their political efforts at Israel, in tandem with continuous terrorist incursions into Israel. Their avowed intention was to provoke a war between Israel and the Arab states in order to liberate the territory on which Israel then rested. It is not certain that the Palestinians could have established a state for themselves in the West Bank and Gaza Strip, but they certainly did not try, and in any case the obstacle was not Israel, as these territories were not in Israeli hands.
4. After the Six Day War in 1967, in which Israel captured the West Bank, East Jerusalem, and the Gaza Strip, the Palestinian denial of Israel's right to exist continued until the late 1980s and the signing of the Oslo peace accords in 1993.
5. Israel signed a peace treaty with Egypt in 1979. In that treaty, Israel recognized the "Legitimate rights of the Palestinian people." One of the treaty's provisions was that Palestinian "full autonomy" was to be established in the territories, with further progress to be made after five years. That plan might also have led to the gradual establishment of a Palestinian state, but the Palestinians refused to join the talks when Egyptian President Anwar Sadat invited them. The Palestinians rejected the opening that the 1979 treaty between Egypt and Israel offered to them.
6. Israel, led by Yitzhak Rabin, and the Palestinians, led by Yasser Arafat, signed the Oslo agreement in 1993. This agreement arranged for the gradual withdrawal of Israel from territories in the West Bank and the Gaza Strip, in return for a commitment by the Palestinian

Authority to recognize Israel's right to exist, to end Palestinian terrorism, and to make every effort to combat terrorism by other Palestinian groups that continued to call for the annihilation of Israel. This conditional "land for peace" agreement was soon broken. Devastating terrorist attacks occurred within Israeli cities, almost always launched from territory controlled by the Palestinians. Although the Palestinian Authority was strengthened and well armed following the agreement, the Authority did little to stop the attacks or disarm the attackers, contrary to explicit agreements. The result was an unhappy equation, whereby the Israeli giving up of territory led to terrorism rather than peace. The incessant attacks were directly responsible for the Israeli right-wing Likud party victory in the 1996 elections, with Binyamin Netanyahu defeating Labor Premier Shimon Peres, Rabin's successor. Although Netanyahu continued to give further territory to the Palestinians, he did not implement the Oslo accords in good faith. By then, the Palestinians controlled fully or jointly approximately *40 per cent* of the territories in the West Bank and the Gaza Strip, including the major centres of Palestinian population. Palestinian terrorism once again derailed the establishment of a Palestinian state alongside Israel.

7. Labour candidate Ehud Barak was elected Prime Minister in 1999. Israeli voters gave him a sweeping victory for his platform of territorial compromise and an end to the conflict. At the Camp David negotiations in the summer of 2000 and in the Egyptian city of Taba during the following months, Barak made dramatic offers to the Palestinians. At Camp David, the offers that emerged (even from differing accounts) included all the Gaza Strip, about 90 per cent of the West Bank, and a capital in East Jerusalem, with the guarantee that most Israeli settlements would be dismantled. The Palestinians rejected the offers, made no counteroffer, and launched the campaign of violence including shooting known as the Second Intifada.
8. In the talks that took place in Egyptian Taba, the Israeli offers rose to nearly 97 per cent of the West Bank, East Jerusalem, and all the Gaza Strip. Barak even offered to hand over to the Palestinians some areas from within pre-67 Israel itself, in compensation for the missing 3 per cent (thus making it a roughly 100 per cent deal).

President Clinton also offered bridging proposals, which were rejected by the Palestinians. Palestinian independence, and the end to Israeli control, seemed imminent. However, "*like déjà vu all over again,*" the Palestinians rejected all these offers, made no counteroffer, and again resorted to violence, with systematic terrorism and suicide bombings. Not only the radical Islamic groups alone—Hamas and Islamic Jihad—but also the Palestinian mainstream, led by Arafat's Fatah movement, played central roles in the terrorist campaign. In a political backlash, the bitterly disappointed Israeli public elected Ariel Sharon.

9. Sharon, who epitomized the Israeli political right and was instrumental in establishing the settlements in the West Bank and Gaza, turned left when in power. It was under Sharon that Israel withdrew from the whole of the Gaza Strip in 2006, dismantling all the settlements and bringing all the settlers back within Israel's pre-1967 border, also withdrawing from two settlements in the West Bank (as a symbolic precedent). The emotional, economic, and political price was considerable. Sharon's decision to completely withdraw from the Gaza Strip (even unilaterally) was nevertheless so popular among Israelis that voters propelled to power Sharon's newly founded Kadima party, which had added even further pullbacks to its platform. The natural expectation would be for an establishment of a small Palestinian state in the Gaza Strip, along Israel. This could prove that a Palestinian state could co-exist with Israel, refute the Israeli right-wing's claim that the Palestinian's could not be trusted, and, with such a successful test-case, lead to negotiations concerning the West Bank. The Palestinians did not move to establish a state in the Gaza Strip that was now totally theirs. They elected the Hamas, which explicitly declared Israel's illegitimacy and the Palestinian aim to destroy it. Mortar fire and rockets were repeatedly and indiscriminately shelled from Gaza at towns and villages on the Israeli side of the border. Israel responded with a blockade of the Gaza Strip and recurring military action in response to the attacks.
10. Following Sharon's stroke, Ehud Olmert succeeded him. Olmert made offers that were said to be equal or better than any previous Israeli offer, getting to a complete 100 per cent deal (with limited territorial swaps), but the Palestinians have not been willing to budge.

11. In the country of Jordan, about 70 per cent of the population is Palestinian. The West Bank was part of Jordan till the 1967 war. The Palestinians are integrated into Jordanian society. Jordan's current queen is Palestinian. Yet, Palestinian aspirations for statehood have not focused on declaring Jordan illegitimate or on destroying Jordan. Palestinian efforts to found their own state are focused almost exclusively on Israel. Jordan has been an oasis of stability in the Mideast and a dependable ally of Israel and the West since the early seventies. However, even from the Palestinian perspective, surely one must wonder why the focus has been on Israel rather than on Jordan.

This is a long and very depressing list of opportunities to establish a Palestinian state that the Palestinians have rejected. No doubt, the narrative is more complex and might be interpreted in somewhat different ways at various points. But, what clearly emerge are both the number and the variety of opportunities. The outcome of all these rejected opportunities is that there still is no Palestinian state after all these years. The vast majority of the 200 or so states in the world were established in the last 70 years. National movements throughout the world have seized any half-chance that was offered to them to establish a state of their own. The Palestinians alone have refused each and every opportunity that has been handed to them.

We can formulate at least three compelling generalizations from the preceding list of historical events.

1. Whenever it was proposed that an Arab Palestine and a Jewish Israel be established *together*, the Palestinians declined the proposal. Note that in those early historical junctions, they did not accept the principle of the two-state solution while just proposing a *different* territorial deal, but rather rejected any sort of accommodation, the existence of Israel itself being unacceptable to them in principle.
2. The Palestinian's main grievance has always focused *only* on that part of the would-be Palestinian territory that happens to be in Israeli hands at any given time. Other areas where an independent Palestine could have been established have never interested the Palestinians unless such areas fell into Israeli hands, at which time those areas immediately become the centre of Palestinian interest.

3. Whenever Israel has offered to give up land that it holds (or has in fact withdrawn from that land), in which an independent Palestinian state could then be established, the focus of Palestinian demand has immediately shifted to factors that would disrupt matters (such as the "right of return" to Israel itself), and the Palestinians have directly sabotaged the plan through terrorism.

For three generations, *the Palestinians have repeatedly chosen not to have the independent state that they manifestly could have had. Why*? Here we enter more into the sphere of interpretation and speculation, rather than facts. My conclusion is this: the Palestinians have continuously said No to the establishment of a Palestinian state because that would have required them to *accept an independent Israel*, a homeland for the Jewish people, alongside Palestine. The conditions of the offers have varied. In 1937 and again in 1947, the offers to the Palestinians were presented as a two-state deal, so the Palestinians could not have accepted it without agreeing to the establishment of Israel. Sometimes the establishment of a Palestinian state has depended on Israeli withdrawal from territory that Israel held, and hence on Israel's agreement. And at other instances neither of these conditions was present (as when the West Bank and/or the Gaza strip were not even in Israeli control, between 1948 and 1967; and from 2006 concerning Gaza).

The size of the Israeli state that would have been the Palestinians' neighbour if the Palestinians had acquiesced varied over time. But it was not the particular circumference of the border within which Israel existed as it was the *principle* that Israel would exist that mattered. The one theory capable of explaining the historic facts is that the Palestinians have repeatedly cut off their own heads so as to spite Israel's nose.

This is not to say that the Israelis have been saints or to deny that Israeli actions have often contributed to the deteriorating situations. But, to recall, our question is not who has been historically well-or-ill-behaved (surely a reply here would be complex and context specific), but why there still is no Palestinian state, after all those years and all those opportunities. So the focus is on the Palestinians. After all, the Israelis took *their* opportunity some 70 years ago, and already have a long-established, flourishing democratic state.

Someone could argue that I have been ignoring the fact that the Palestinians recognized Israel in the 1993 Oslo agreement, a recognition implying that, at a certain stage, the Palestinians were ready to accommodate an independent Israel alongside their own state. What are we to make of those declarations? Perhaps some prominent Palestinians even believed them. But Palestinian actions speak louder than these words that seemed to promise peace. The Palestinians have acted in ways that would resist or terminate any agreement for them to live peaceably alongside the Israelis—although accepting and keeping to the agreements would have put the pressure on Israel for compliance, arguably resulting long ago in Palestinian statehood.

Traditional Just War Theory, the foundation for the prevalent ethical thinking as well as contemporary international laws of warfare, emphasizes the "necessity condition" as one of the conditions for justifying violence, whereby it is required that no other alternative be available. The violence of terrorism, of intentionally targeting Israeli non-combatants, surely requires even stronger justification than would the targeting of Israeli soldiers. In the Palestinian case, the "necessity condition" has not been met, for there were (and are) repeated opportunities to gain a state without having recourse to violence, let alone to the indiscriminate targeting of civilians through terrorism. Not only has the necessity condition not been met, but matters stand in the exact opposite direction. Often, as following the Oslo agreement or more recently in choosing violence over the Camp David/Taba proposals of 2000 and later similar offers; or still later, following 2006, when Israel withdrew from the Gaza strip, pulled out its army and evacuated all Israeli settlements, handing over the Gaza strip to the Palestinians—it is the Palestinian leadership's choice of terrorism that has blocked the establishment of a Palestinian state.

So, not only is Honderich's claim (that the Palestinians have had no other choice but to resort to terrorism in order to establish a state alongside Israel) false, but it gets things backwards: *the Palestinians have repeatedly chosen terrorism when they could have chosen a state instead, and their resort to terrorism has repeatedly hindered the quest for a Palestinian state.*[1]

Some might still suggest that the fault lies with the Israelis because there was some point at which peace would have ensued if only the

Israelis had acted differently. But this suggestion is not very illuminating. Palestinian leaders themselves could have proposed the offers that they rejected in the past: if they would be willing to accept Camp David or Taba 2000 or more recent proposals now (suggesting changes, if they want), give up the demand for a "right of return" into Israel in exchange for a Palestinian state, and renounce violence, then negotiations would have had an excellent chance of success. The Israeli public today is reasonably sceptical of the intentions of the Palestinians, and hesitant about giving up control of the West Bank in the light of the history detailed above, particularly the grim consequences of giving up "land for peace" in Gaza in 2006. The Palestinians are reasonably sceptical about the right-wing Netanyahu's declarations that he too favours a two-state-solution, but then they have not done anything to call his bluff, if it is indeed one. In any case, centrist candidates willing to give up something like 100 per cent of the West Bank (or equivalent land from within pre-67 Israel in exchange) have repeatedly been elected in Israel; however, they have never found partners on the Palestinian side.

Alternatively, Palestinian leaders could even have begun piecemeal: they could have established a Palestinian state in the part of the territory they control, declaring it to be demilitarized and non-terrorist, as a way of beginning to build confidence between themselves and the Israelis. The "Gaza first" option, that is, the establishment of a Palestinian state in the Gaza strip, could even today be completed within weeks, for there are no longer any Israeli settlements nor an Israeli military presence there. Constructive options are always available, if one is open to options.

17.2 Why Have the Palestinians Chosen to Not Establish a State of Their Own (Alongside Israel)?

We have a fundamental question here: why do the Palestinians follow this route so consistently and so seemingly irrationally?

Many Palestinians seem focussed on the need to revenge and reverse the results of the establishment of the state of Israel in 1948 by asserting the rights of the 1948 refugees to return to where they came from within today's Israel. Of course not many of the refugees of 1948 are still alive anyway; the claim includes their offspring.[2] The emphasis on reversing history and on retribution dominates much of Palestinian discourse and education, precluding accommodation, moreover precluding even the provisional adoption of a forward-looking attitude of living and letting live.

When we compare Palestinian behaviour to the behaviour of other peoples, the full impact of how anomalous it is emerges. Tens of millions of people—Greeks, Turks, Germans, Czechs, Romanians, Finns, and indeed Jews both from Europe and from Arab countries (among still others)—were displaced in the twentieth century. Of all those, only one population has not yet solved its problem. Despite the fact that most Palestinians sit on Palestinian land and could many times have established a Palestinian state, after three wasted generations, the Palestinians still do not have their own state.

The demand for a "right of return" contradicts the two-state solution by eliminating Israeli sovereignty. It also blocks from the outset any agreement with Israel, since it basically says "what's mine is mine, and what's yours is also mine." Yet, no prominent Palestinian leader has ever openly declared that that demand is void; that is the simple idea that Palestinians who are not currently Israeli citizens (or live in territories to be annexed by Israel) could have a right to live in an independent Palestine but not in Israel. Many Palestinians support this "right of return" demand with an irrational estimate of their chances for success.

Incredibly enough, in many Palestinian eyes victory is imminent; it has been imminent for three generations. Each period sees a new dictator (Hitler in the 1930s and 1940s, Nasser in the 1950s and 1960s, Sadam Hussein in the 1990s, and most recently the Hezbollah's Nasrallah and the Iranians) as their saviour. Therefore, there is no reason to betray the cause by accommodating the existence of Israel.

The historical and contemporary data is so striking that we can speculate that deeper factors may be at play. It is difficult to resist the impression that Palestinians have resisted compromise and statehood also because that would have entailed active *agency and responsibility*, and an acceptance of the need to run their own lives and solve their own problems, by contrast to the attractions of continued dependency and helplessness, when one can blame Israel, the West, and indeed everyone but themselves. The attractions of violent struggle and of striking a revolutionary pose in themselves seem to play an important role with many, but violence is also a distraction from the challenges of the mundane and from the prospects of struggling with Third World difficulties. The reality of statehood and the disappearance of the common enemy also risk bringing about internal confrontation along political and religious lines and threaten fragile Palestinian unity. The reality of statehood would mean giving up the illusions of the restoration of some pre-1948 era or of a golden future not connected to reality and to the need to confront it.

Compare what other Arab countries have concluded about the existence of Israel. Both Egypt and Jordan also initially tried to prevent the establishment of Israel, being intent on preventing the establishment of a state for the Jews, however, small. Indeed, they were the leading military powers attacking newly born Israel in 1948, their openly declared aim being to smother it at birth. No *territory* was in dispute: their struggle was with the very existence of Israel. Both countries again schemed to destroy Israel in 1967, only to be soundly defeated. But a decade later, in 1979, Egypt recognized Israel's right to exist, as did Jordan in 1994. Both countries established diplomatic relations with Israel, and continue to live in peace with it.

Perhaps this direction is too limited, and focused on the near term. Perhaps, the continuous Palestinian resistance to the idea of a state of their own (alongside Israel) *does* make sense—if one takes a longer view. Palestinians often speak about Israel as a recurrence of the Crusader presence; saying that, as with the Crusaders, continuous resistance will pay off in the end. On this view, accepting some generations of chosen statelessness is a small price to pay for ultimate victory. This is not completely irrational: were the Palestinian to have accepted a Jewish state alongside a Palestinian one, then at some stage that would have resulted in a stronger Israel. In 1937, millions of Jews could have escaped the Holocaust and come to Israel (no other country would have them, and they were stuck in Europe, to be murdered within a few years). After the Second World War erupted, the Germans and their helpers went about annihilation enthusiastically and efficiently, but in 1937 millions could have been saved had they had a place that they could call their own. So from that perspective, Palestinian negativity in the 1930s on the establishment of two states played an important role and paid off. On a smaller but still significant scale, there is little doubt that were there to be peace between Israel and the Palestinians (in a two-state solution), many hundreds of thousands of Jews who would otherwise wish to live in a Jewish state, but are deterred by the risks of terrorism and war, would come over; as well as hundreds of thousands of former Israelis who left the country and live abroad. Not only would Israel grow more populous, but clearly if much less would need to be spent on security, and if Israel's international status would improve greatly, then it would flourish even more than today. So in this way as well, if the Palestinian aim is ultimate victory and non-accommodation with Israel, then the sacrifice of the present generations, the choices not to establish a state of their own, not to solve the conflict and not to cease terrorism, perhaps make sense.

Further support to scepticism about real Palestinian intentions seems to me to follow reasonably from the "Cultural Genocide" prevalent in even the more moderate Palestinian circles, including the old establishment of Fatah. The denial of Jewish national (rather than merely religious) identity, of major elements of Jewish historical national continuity, of Jewish connection to Jerusalem and The Land of Israel/Palestine in general, and widespread Holocaust denial, all these are unnecessarily vicious attempts to erase the other, rather than what one would expect if a Honderich-like interpretation were reasonable. It is one thing to demand a few more percent of, say, the West Bank than Israel is perhaps willing to give at a certain time and quite another thing to deny the very legitimacy and identity of the Jewish side.

But whether one interprets Palestinian resistance to stateship as a manifestation of irrational hopes and beliefs or sees it as part of a long-term strategy that is not necessarily irrational, all this has no relationship with the purported justification given by Honderich.

We have asked three questions:

(1) Why is there no Palestinian state? The reason, in large measure, is that the Palestinians have again and again *chosen* not to gain a state. The data repeatedly points to that conclusion.

(2) Why have they made *that* choice? Here, it seems to me, the central reply is that Palestinians are not willing to accept the existence of Israel alongside a Palestinian state.

(3) And why has *that*—national existence alongside Israel—been perceived with such horror, horror that suffices to make one deprive oneself of a state of one's own? Here, we largely need to enter the deep and murky world of fanaticism, hatred, and self-deception. Accommodation with Israel is perceived as being an acquiescence to historical injustice, or a religious or national sin, or unnecessary in the light of Israel's imminent collapse. More speculatively, perhaps it is the very fact that the issues are not resolved that has psychological advantages for many Palestinians: the continuation of the state of juvenile irresponsibility, where one can blame everyone but oneself, and maintain a fantasy world. Alternatively, a long-term view is taken, where anything is better than acquiescence in Israel's existence. This harms the Palestinians of present generations but harms Israel's growth and flourishing—thereby keeping alive the hope that it will one day be overcome. Today's underdogs will not be underdogs in the long term, if they have enough patience. There are indications in internal Palestinian discourse supporting these different interpretations. None of them, however, support Honderich's view, that the Palestinians have been merely engaging in terrorism since they have no other choice, with the aim of establishing a state of their own alongside Israel.[3]

17.3 Free Will and Moral Responsibility

The literature on the free will problem is immense, yet, as I noted at the beginning, conspicuously missing are discussions of it in the context of considering issues like the Israeli-Palestinian conflict. I will make some tentative first steps.

Ted Honderich has done distinguished work on the free will problem (see primarily Honderich 1988). Yet notice, first, that although Honderich is of course well aware of the free will problem, and is quite sceptical of free will's existence, this does not appear in his discussion of terrorism in the Israeli-Palestinian context. Honderich does not shy away from using the language of choice, moral responsibility, and blameworthiness. He speaks, for example, about the "wrongful actions" of the Jewish people, and about "our responsibility for what has gone wrong" (Honderich 2003, 29). This is a problem for someone like Honderich, who is a determinist and not a compatibilist. I cannot discuss the complexities of his position here in detail, but arguably his "emotivist" meta-stand on free will does not suffice to solve the difficulty.[4]

Perhaps the lesson is, rather, that scepticism about the language of free will and moral responsibility is not sustainable since it would impoverish our moral and political evaluation and discourse too greatly (this line follows in the direction of P.F. Strawson's (2003) classic paper "Freedom and Resentment"). One cannot seriously discuss the rights and wrongs without assuming that, say, many Israelis are responsible and can be candidates for blame for some of the settlements after 1967, or that many Palestinians are responsible and possible candidates for blame concerning their choice of the Hamas and their support of attacks on Israel following the 2006 Israeli withdrawal from the Gaza Strip. Refraining to discuss the rights and wrongs here in a way that treats human beings as accountable and blameworthy (or praiseworthy) agents would be a huge price. This in itself is an argument against positions such as hard determinism that disallow such discourse.

In any case, Honderich clearly engages in free will-and-moral responsibility-assuming discourse. I have criticized above his discussion of Palestinian choices and responsibilities. Partly the fault lies in a narrowing of focus: he begins the justification of Palestinian terrorism in the aftermath of the 1967 war, avoiding repeated and persistent earlier terrorism and, more importantly, repeated Palestinian negativity as to establishing a state of their own alongside Israel in response to the Peel Commission recommendations in 1937; the UN Decision to establish Arab and Jewish states in 1947; and (when the West Bank and Gaza Strip were in Jordanian and Egyptian hands between 1949 and 1967) the absence of any attempt to strive for a state in these territories, and the exclusive focus on pre-1967 Israel. Partly, the fault lies with the denial of the wealth of possibilities in the post-1967 era for the establishment of a Palestinian state, in nearly all the West Bank and the Gaza Strip.[5] One might see here a depreciation of Palestinian agency and implicitly of their capacity for control and responsibility. But this would probably be unfair, it is more likely merely a (false) claim that the Palestinians "have no choice" to engage in terrorism, not in the strict free will sense, but in that he holds them morally justified in doing so. It is not free will-based exemption, but an attempt at moral excuse.

Yet, on a deeper level, perhaps there is something in this last thought. In light of the points I made above, Honderich's discussion invites a search for an "error theory."[6] It is so implausible to deny the repeated, manifest Palestinian rejection of opportunities for establishing a state of their own, now for three generations, in a way that has often not even depended on the good will of Israel that one should look for a different sort of explanation for such views. Although there are certain romanticized views of violence in his writings (even beyond our issue), I do not think that Honderich supports terrorism for its own sake. There are unfortunately occasional anti-Semitic expressions and tropes in his writings, but I also do not think that he is an anti-Semite. (I would not agree to participate in this volume if I did. I state this explicitly because he has been publically charged with anti-Semitism.) I think that the most likely explanation is a fairly typical Western guilt complex, which (largely unconsciously) requires that the overwhelming *Palestinian responsibility* for their plight be denied and Israel blamed instead. And that is, deep down, a depreciation of Palestinian ability, responsibility and maturity, capacities and traits of the sort that Honderich clearly attributes to Israelis and himself.

One interesting point that can be learnt from the Israeli-Palestinian conflict concerning the free will problem is about the significance of the role of repetition and continuity. If we would be speaking about some single distant Palestinian choice, then perhaps doubts related to the free will problem might gain traction. Yet, I have shown a consistent, repetitive picture of Palestinian intransience, of *repeated choices*, over many generations, and given very different conditions and options, not to accept the idea of a Palestinian state alongside Israel, but to engage in terrorism. This lends support to compatibilist views about the evaluation of character and dispositions rather than merely distinct unrelated actions. I will not enter into a discussion of complex technical matters from within the free will debate, but this seems also to lend some support to the "real self" variety of compatibilist interpretations of the nature of free will.

Even more significant is the fact that choices are still present. Israeli's have a choice, for example, whether to withdraw from the West Bank as they did from the Gaza Strip; Palestinians have a choice, for example, whether to agree to some of the proposals made by American presidents, and the like. When we are speaking about the present, arguably hard determinism becomes quite impotent, and empty. How can one deny, in such situations, one's personal or collective ability to choose? And the concomitant moral responsibility for what one does or does not do? The reality of control and choice over our decisions, the phenomenological "ability to do otherwise," seems undeniable at the present time, when deliberating and choosing how to act.

What if we assume hard determinism, that is the "hard" interpretation according to which the implications of determinism (or absence of libertarian-metaphysical free will irrespective of determinism) are that there is no free will, moral responsibility, desert, and blameworthiness? In that case the language of moral evaluation would primarily need to be transformed in a future-oriented, consequentialist, or contractual direction (see, e.g., Pereboom 2014). Instead of asking what the Israelis or Palestinians are responsible for, whether they (say) deserve condemnation or have themselves or others to blame for their situation, we would then turn towards the future. This would involve a price for both sides. Israelis have wanted to hold responsible and put the blame for much of the plight of individual Palestinians at the choices of the Palestinian leaders and to explain the absence of a Palestinian state and the recurrent violence through Palestinian intransience. The Palestinians have wanted to hold responsible and blame the Israelis for both individual hardship and collective plight. Both sides often believe and say that the other side deserves condemnation, violence, and so on because of their choices and actions. Giving up free will and moral responsibility-related evaluations would be a radical change.

Would it be a change for the better? I am in general sceptical about radical eliminativism concerning free will, and hold a fairly conservative view according to which we would lose much more than we would gain by giving up free will-related beliefs, attitudes, and practices (see, e.g., Smilansky 2000, 2005). And in our present context, I think that the price would also be considerable. The Israelis need to be more rather than less aware of their responsibility, for how the choices they can make may improve the daily living conditions of Palestinians under Israeli military occupation in the West Bank. They also need to choose to curtail the construction of new settlements, particularly in areas which are to be within Palestinian hands in any future two-state solution. The Palestinians in turn need to be more rather than less aware of their agency and responsibility, and of how their choices and actions have been and still are a main factor determining their statelessness. Free will-based excuses, and the shedding of moral responsibility, would be the wrong direction to take.

However, in moderate form, a forward-looking, consequentialist or contractual approach could be useful. Palestinian discourse in general has focussed on the perceived grievances of the past and on the purported injustice of Israel's very existence. Most Israeli Jews, and Palestinians, living between the Jordan River and the Mediterranean were born there and are not going anywhere. Israel has a right to exist, and the Palestinians have a right to a state of their own, if they will be willing to live alongside Israel in peace. Moving on to pragmatic accommodation and compromise would be an improvement.

So, perhaps a mixed conclusion is in order at this point. A decline in belief in free will and moral responsibility would not be helpful for either side or for any acceptable solution. Indeed, greater awareness of choice, agency, and responsibility would be positive. Nevertheless, a forward-looking approach that does not give up the recognition and awareness of choice-related rights and wrongs, but still seeks to replace the grievances and condemnations of the past with a pragmatic compromise, would be more helpful for everyone.[7]

Notes

1. It seems that when the West Bank and Gaza Strip were in Israeli hands, Israel became a classic target for non-violent resistance, as practiced by Gandhi in India. The fact that Israel is a democracy, the moral traditions and sensibilities of Jews who themselves were continuously persecuted when non-violent, and Israel's dependence on support from similarly open and morally principled societies, could have made such a non-terrorist campaign (if aimed at establishing a Palestinian state alongside Israel rather than instead of it) particularly successful (this point was suggested to me by Jeff McMahan). But this direction has never even been seriously attempted, while the opposite course has been repeatedly taken.
2. I bracket here the relevance of the Parfitian "nonidentity problem," the fact that nearly all of these offspring depend for their existence on Israeli actions in 1948; for a general discussion of this issue, see Smilansky (2013).
3. One cannot but be struck by the prevailing widespread Shia-Sunni indiscriminate violence in the Muslim world, by murderous anti-Western hatred and terrorism in Al-Qaeda and Islamic State of Iraq and Syria (ISIS), and by the general failure of democracy and civil society in the Arab world; all of which has little or nothing to do with Israel. Perhaps the failures of the Palestinians, whether interpreted as a form of repeated irrationality or as not necessarily irrational long-term planning, are to be better understood as expressions of these monumental cultural and social weaknesses, rather than as being inherently concerned with the Israeli-Palestinian conflict. But of course my denial of Honderich's basic claim does not depend on these further interpretive options.
4. One could try to turn this argument towards myself. But on the compatibility question, I combine hard determinism with compatibilism, and in any case hold that we must stick with the practical belief in free will, moral responsibility, and related reactions and practices. See, for example, Smilansky (2000).
5. As far as I can see, Honderich says nothing about the option of establishing a Palestinian state in Jordan, joined by a large part of the West Bank and the whole of the Gaza Strip—all areas where the Palestinians are a majority.

6. The notion of the "error theory" was first introduced by J.L. Mackie in Mackie (1977).
7. I am grateful for the invitation to participate in this volume, and am very grateful to Gregg Caruso, Iddo Landau, Ariel Meirav, Daniel Statman, and Alexander Yakobson, for helpful comments on drafts of my paper.

References

Honderich, Ted. 1988. *A theory of determinism*. Oxford: Oxford University Press.

———. 2003. *After the terror*. Expanded, revised ed. Edinburgh: Edinburgh University Press.

Mackie, J.L. 1977. *Ethics*. Harmondsworth: Penguin.

Pereboom, Derk. 2014. *Free will, agency and meaning in life*. New York: Oxford University Press.

Smilansky, Saul. 2000. *Free will and illusion*. Oxford: Oxford University Press.

———. 2004. Terrorism, justification, and illusion. *Ethics* 114: 790–805.

———. 2005. Free will and respect for persons. *Midwest Studies in Philosophy* 29: 248–261.

———. 2013. Morally, should we prefer never to have existed? *Australasian Journal of Philosophy* 91: 655–666.

Strawson, P.F. 2003. Freedom and resentment. In *Free will*, ed. Gary Watson. Oxford: Oxford University Press.

18

Remarks on Papers on Right and Wrong, Humanity, Terrorism

Ted Honderich

18.1 On Warnock

Mary Warnock has been first among Englishwomen in giving the great and good of England the good name they have. She has by her philosophy enlightened her fellow members of the House of Lords and various Royal Commissions of inquiry about large questions. In her philosophy book *Ethics Since 1900*, she introduced and judged all of it. In *Existentialism*, she was an acute examiner for England of that philosophy of France. She has also informed the Royal Institute of Philosophy on the subject of *What Is Natural and Should We Care?*

T. Honderich (✉)
University College London, London, UK

G. D. Caruso (ed.), *Ted Honderich on Consciousness, Determinism, and Humanity*, Philosophers in Depth, https://doi.org/10.1007/978-3-319-66754-6_18

Desires and Needs

It is a satisfaction to me to have her welcome, if qualified, support for the Principle of Humanity. As with most other chapters in this book, there is too much and too much of interest in her paper, various conceptions, for me to make remarks here on all of it.

In various writings of mine consulted by Warnock on the Principle of Humanity, outlined in the introduction to this book, I have as the first step of the argument for the principle our six greatest *desires* for things—rather than taking them as *needs* for things. Warnock, in my own endeavour or in her alteration of it, would rather think of *needs*. I was taken aback for a while by her proposal with respect to the Principle of Humanity that *must* from the beginning be taken as having to do with needs.

It is easy enough to slip into that habit, as in the introduction to this very book but, in a way, mistaken. If other contributors to this book had not been supplied with the introduction, I would change it now.

This has to do with some of the content in the use of the term "needs." Needed things are generally taken to be necessary to the satisfaction of desires that are *somehow justified*. One American dictionary defines a need as what we cannot well do without. *The Oxford Companion to Philosophy* partly says needs are what are needed for flourishing, not merely surviving.

But, if we start with such needs, we are indeed starting partly with the disputability of valuing, subjectivity, cultural relativity, relativity to an individual, one man's opinion, and the like—we are starting not just with fact, the truth that is correspondence to fact. First, a thing referred to being as it is described to be. With needs we are starting, in my general terms, with affective rather than cognitive or perceptual consciousness.

I note in passing here that the second stage of my argument for the Principle of Humanity in a different way is also a premise of fact. It is that each of us takes himself or herself to have the six desires but also to have *reason* for being satisfied with respect to them. And the third stage, quite as much a matter of truth as against subjectivity, is that all reasons, all reasons worth the name, by their very nature, are *general*—applying to everybody else as much as to me or you.

A pity it would be to miss this support for a principle that it is an explicit form of what is surely the most accepted thing in ordinary morality—the Golden Rule. Do unto others as you would be done by. Is it also the best content to be given to Kant's Categorical Imperative—Treat every other person not only as a means but also as an end? I don't know about that.

Desires and Rights

What has now been said about needs also has to be said about something else. Warnock is perhaps inclined to taking the first premise of the argument as being that each of us has *a right* to the six great things. No. In order to get started safe from objection about subjectivity, and so on, stick to the indubitable fact of desires.

Come on now to something different, some talk of rights that I *do* absolutely go in for. Having got by the line of argument to the conclusion that is the Principle of Humanity, I do speak of rights owed to *it*. I speak of particular judgements that *follow* from the Principle as assertions precisely of rights. Given that the Principle is the great principle of right and wrong, analogous to the great constitutional or other law of a society, there is, in my mind, quite as much ground for speaking of what follows from the principle as moral rights as there is for speaking of what follows from a society's law as legal rights.

Warnock mentions a famous objection to such non-legal rights, by the Utilitarian philosopher and philosopher of law, Jeremy Bentham, his auto-icon still on display in the cloisters of University College London. His objection is, of course, that there are legal rights, which fact we understand, but that there are only said to be moral rights, which are not merely nonsense but nonsense on stilts. Putting aside the different kind of moral nonsense of Utilitarianism itself, the greatest-total-of-happiness philosophy, which justifies a slave class in a society if the result is a greater *total* of happiness in the society than without the slave class, Bentham's mere legalism about rights cannot conceivably bar talk of rights as obligations owed to the fundamental principle of right and wrong.

And, I bravely take it, too, as a result of the existence of the three-stage argument for humanity, that our greatest philosopher, David Hume, was wrong in declaring "Reason is, and ought only to be, the slave of the passions, and can never pretend to any other office than to serve and obey them." Not so. As you have heard, rationality can really get into right and wrong.

Private Property

I have the idea that Warnock's welcome, if qualified, support for the Principle of Humanity has most to do with the argument for it, but there are also questions she asks about it. One is whether the great goods at the beginning should include the ownership of property, say land and a house. Is that a step on the way to the private ownership in what we know as capitalism, better named profitalism, private ownership of great things in national economies for profit? I doubt that it is a step to the nonsense of another Englishwoman, Thatcher, of the great but not the good, to the effect that great concentrations of wealth result in a little of it trickling down to little lives down below? That the wealth results in something else than what is to me the monstrous inequality of our societies?

Despite my politics, I am more than inclined to join Warnock in including in the great good of freedom and power for everyone a certain security in the place in which they live, a lifelong use of a place of living. Here, I can say no more than that. Something else comes to mind. The Principle of Humanity is further explained by speaking of various policies in which it issues. As so far thought about, they do not settle the question of private ownership of living places and no doubt smaller and larger enterprises in a society's economy. There is a kind of secondary philosophy of decency undone here. Certainly undone by me. Philosophy—not something hobbled by a convention or consensus from economics or anywhere else. More to be done, maybe by you.

Goodness, The Left, and So On

Warnock finishes by touching on the moral education of children and, in a phrase, an emphasis on coming to *want to do good.* She remarks that she cannot see that the Principle of Humanity can provide the imperative or imperatives to action on which I insist. It will do so only for those who already want to do good.

Let me remark in connection with this only that to be moved by the Principle of Humanity *is* to be moved to doing good. If this is stated in terms of what it is *right*, it is in its content entirely concerned with the good of others. It begins with the subject of the great goods, enjoins us to act now with respect to the great goods of all. That it is an assertion of what is right owed not to any consideration *separate* from that of the great goods. It is owed, rather, to the necessity of affirming the moral necessity, not so to speak the mere goodness, of acting to secure the great goods for all. The principle, so to speak, asserts the necessity of wanting to do good, a well-defined good, the greatest good. No blab.

Quite a lot in her paper has now been left unconsidered by me. Say greed. Also evil, which I myself would be inclined to define in terms of both understanding and then resisting or condemning the Principle of Humanity. What way of living can be worse? Also unconsidered by me, embarrassingly, has been animals other than ourselves. They too have desires. Over to you.

The Principle of Humanity, in my view, is the principle of the Left in politics—when the Left is true to itself. Does Warnock at least see the great decency of the Left, the temptation she does not give in to? Read her again. And how is the principle related to what we know of under the name of *humanitarian crises*? In our generous responses, in so far as they exist, is there a further kind of support for the entirely general principle we have been considering about more than crises?

Finally, several questions to all sceptics and condemners of humanity. If not humanity, what is the principle or general stand or outlook that is to be relied on by you? And, what is it based on? Politicians? Could it conceivably be that no such principle is needed, that you just bumble on, and that reason and consistency are not required? Could reference just to goodness left unexplained be enough? Anything a democracy does? Reference to hierarchic or oligarchic democracy? If in terms of consequences of action, of course and necessarily, what consequences? Something else from the history of ethics? Kant's imperatives finally made clear 200 years later? Intoning about duty? A society's law whatever it is? Intoning by a careerist political class? Just habit?

* * *

18.2 On Gilbert

Gilbert's course of reflections has my respect not only for its conclusion among others that despite his various critical arguments, we should not unreservedly condemn Palestinian terrorism. He upholds in this and other ways the standing of the resolutely distinguished University of Hull. One of his books, written in the aftermath of 9/11, is *New Terror, New Wars*.

Advocacy and Moral Rights

He does not dispute that political and some other philosophy consists in a kind of advocacy. If later he characterizes this as the art of persuasion, he also does not dispute that all philosophy is also concentration on the logic of intelligence, a greater concentration than that of science—whether the philosophy is addressed to fellow citizens or just other philosophers. Neither of the two of us faces the challenge here of defining advocacy more closely in terms of the three sides of consciousness—cognitive, affective, and perceptual, the first and second parts consisting in representations concerned with truth and what is good.

Gilbert does not dispute the existence of moral rights in my sense, these as you have heard being understood as having a moral basis that is a counterpart to the legal basis in the fundamental law of legal rights. More particularly, moral rights have the moral basis of a fundamental principle of right and wrong action rather than anything else, the Principle of Humanity. It is not here disputed by him.

Facts

He does not dispute either, perhaps despite discomfort with it, the idea that factual questions about terrorism, war, and other things are harder than the question of right and wrong. If he notes that any consequentialist must answer questions of fact, he does not suppose either that any other moral philosopher can avoid doing so in answering questions of right and wrong.

Does he half-imply later, in saying truly that consequentialism requires us to look at facts about likely consequences, that questions of fact pose *less* of a problem for deontology than consequentialism? Not much less, I'd say. Not enough to be nearly decisive in any comparison with consequentialism.

Take what is surely the best kind of example in favour of deontology or non-consequentialism, whatever it is, an example of a human relationship, think of a mother who defends her being right in caring for a particular child on the non-consequential ground that it is *her* child. She comes to face no less difficulty about the comparative effects of different alternatives of care. It cannot be that deontology frees her from factual inquiries, assumptions, judgements, probabilities, and so on. So, the philosophical deontologist also has to step out of his philosophical shoes.

Nor, by the way, does the mother weaken at all a purely consequentialist argument—the argument from the effective *division of labour*—for her caring for her own child in particular.

Deontology as Lower, Dishonourable

I have in mind and stand by my dismissive judgement not on mother and child but, say, on whole social classes. We, many or most readers of this book, continue to live in surfeit while other classes or peoples exist in privation here—or in suffering in Syria and thereabouts, or enduring misery, as in much of Africa and Asia. Our whole social classes defend themselves by much stuff exemplified partly by some dim proposition, typically a circularity, to the effect that they *deserve* their lives, say that there is a *return* for what they do, but the others do not deserve an escape from theirs.

I take it that any consequentialist among us about privation, suffering, and misery can be or should be persuaded to escape a *lingua franca* that, in effect, is lies about privation, suffering, and misery. I do not accuse Gilbert of such a membership, but stand by the necessity, as often as is effective, of declaring the vileness of societies and in particular a political class that is commonly against humanity for all. In Britain, it has included the New Labour Party and the blokey moral dimwit Blair as distinct from the Labour Party. Worse than that. Academic restraint, parliamentary language, and so on would serve the end of those societies and political classes.

9/11

I stand by what was said of right and wrong with the terrorism of 9/11 as against the terrorism of neo-Zionism in taking from a people, the Palestinians, at least their liberty in the place of which they indubitably are the indigenous people. It was easier to stand by what was said on hearing the vicious lying of Netanyahu to the American people after the American government, in the last days of President Obama, rose to the challenge of joining the world by acting at the United Nations to condemn neo-Zionism. Netanyahu spoke not as a friend but as an enemy of one great moral tradition of Jewry, of course, the greatest tradition of it.

Jerry Cohen's Objection

With respect to my condemnation of 9/11 by means of the Principle of Humanity, Gilbert agrees with Jerry's gnomic verdict that this condemnation does not criticize it "as terror." That is, especially as causing fear? Well, my condemnation most certainly criticizes it as having all the effects it had and more importantly also the effects of success it contemplated but which could not reasonably be anticipated and certainly did not have.

All the effects include anything of sense that can be included or implied in talk exactly of *terrorism* as against, say, other *political violence*, of which there arguably has been at least some by our democratic states, including terrorist war. Was Cohen's inexplicit objection that my condemnation was not on what Gilbert calls deontological grounds? That is assumed by Gilbert, maybe rightly. We now come to that matter or matters.

Terrorism and the Just War Notion of Rightness in *Going to War*

What is near enough Gilbert's main line of argument, or what might fairly enough be called speculation, is to the effect that my attempted defence of Palestinian terrorism, against neo-Zionism as distinct from Zionism, proceeds from the premise or anyway one premise variously referred to by him. My defence of the Palestinians is spoken of by him in terms of nationalism, national self-determination, nationhood, citizenry, identity politics, identity groups perhaps united by hatred against another group, something like German nationalism in the view of Isaiah Berlin.

Gilbert has of course written fully and well elsewhere of nationalism, national self-determination, and so on. I cannot enter into that subject—but no doubt would learn from doing so.

What is to be said here is that my essential view of the Palestinians and their justification, despite what you might call some adjacent words, is not in sum anything like nationalism but *is* that they are moved and justified by their resistance to neo-Zionism. What is concluded by me is based on the six great goods of which you have heard specified in the Principle of Humanity. These are decent length of life, bodily well-being, freedoms and powers, the goods of relationships, respect and self-respect, the goods of culture. Nationalism, national self-determination, and the like are specifically or in the first instance a part of the third good.

But, in my common view, certainly, control by an indigenous people of a homeland is the principal means to progress towards the other great goods, including other freedoms, as indeed a sentence by Gilbert implies. He rightly reports that I have written that the value of a people's freedom and power in their homeland "has been better demonstrated historically than any other good." That was quick, not clear enough, and in need of more reflection. But it does not make a principal means to humanity into nationalism.

For what it is worth, I note that what the Palestinians are against, neo-Zionism, is a better candidate for being nationalism or something close enough to it. Listen to Netanyahu. Its being a candidate includes the fact of the race-prejudice of Semitism, a stupid condescension arguably greater than the prejudice of anti-Semitism on the part of any Palestinians.

Note in passing here that the term "terrorism," its condemnation sanctified or made tolerable by habit even in the better newspapers and other media, will when used with the automatic implication of wrong or unspeakable or worse remain in the wide category of cant. Is cant as distinct from the rest of advocacy within the role of philosophers?

It is for me also cant, as you will have gathered, to indulge in the piety with which some of us regularly engage in self-praise of our Western democracies, our freedoms both political and economic. The practice forgets so much.

It forgets, for a first example, the plain and fundamental relationship of equalities and inequalities to freedoms and lacks of them. Equalities are necessary conditions not of general geniality or whatever in societies, but of basic freedoms. We live not in hierarchic democracies, as used to be said by me, but in oligarchic democracies. The inequalities of them, facts allowed by all of us, at least in some contexts of thought and talk, are things that should restrain all our newspapers from our easy contrasts between free societies or democracies and what our newspapers follow most of the political class in naming as *regimes*. What is the relation of oligarchic democracy to regime?

Terrorism and the Just War Notion of Right Conduct in War

Deontology with respect to terrorism is explained by Gilbert in terms of what is called the double-effect consideration. This has been exemplified in war rather than terrorism, not by cases in which civilians are deliberately attacked. It is exemplified, rather, by cases where the harm to civilians may be called a side effect. It is a harm foreseen but not intended—which, incidentally, may not be the case in actually intended "collateral damage."

Deontology is explained or spoken of as the proposition that in war and terrorism, civilians are not "legitimate" targets. These are targets most obviously not armed and seeking to kill. Persons not being legitimate targets are spoken of as their being attacked in accordance with the principles of moral goodness with respect to the roles of soldiers or terrorists. Does that boil down to the targets being wrong? I have difficulty in coming to any other idea.

My resistance to this includes its contained mistake about intention—intention in almost all contexts, certainly including this one. To intend is not to act with some desire, to have any pair or bundle of desires. It is not to perform some funny act of will, origination. To intend something in the fundamental sense, certainly the sense that principally informs our legal systems, is to act with the knowledge that the action will have a certain effect or effects.

That is the intention that is relevant to the attempted distinction between terrorism and killing, and so on in war. It is simply not the case, whatever else can be thought about, that there is a prompt condemnation of terrorism to be got by way of the proposition that killing of civilians in war is not intended and killing of civilians in terrorism is intended.

Something else. Evidently, we need a reason for the judgements about the killings, an explicit general reason—that is exactly what we need, in particular, in order to go on to condemn terrorism's "illegitimate" targets.

It would be more reassuring if Gilbert had been able to give the general principle, presumably other than humanity, that must underlie right conduct in war and whatever else and, thus, given further support for what is said of conduct in war and terrorism. It cannot be that what is right is what is owed to good intention, as in the case of Kant and the pure good will, or that in all circumstances whatever it is wrong to kill. We as societies do a lot of killing, reassuringly distinguished as not barbarous or savage. That doesn't make a lot of difference to the dead or those left behind who lack them.

Hatred, Contempt, Absence of Regret, and the Like

These matters of emotionality, whatever their importance, must be regarded as complicated by there being no great difference in the given respects between neo-Zionists and Palestinians, in particular, Palestinians in concentration in Gaza and periodically attacked by the Israeli army.

To return to the opening of Gilbert's essay and his mention of the well-known storm upon my head, in my view a particular case of the prejudice of Semitism contributing to the false accusation of anti-Semitism, there is a recollection of it all on the website http://www.homepages.ucl.ac.uk/~uctytho/ that brings to mind again, to return to the end of Gilbert's essay, that we need to get off fences not only as citizens but also as philosophers.

* * *

18.3 On Norman

An Empiricism

Richard Norman is of the risen new University of Kent in the cathedral city of Canterbury and is the author of the books *The Moral Philosophers* and *Hegel, Marx and Dialectic: A Debate*. It is more than reassuring that he uniquely begins his objections to me in a certain way. He gives proper attention to ongoing matters of fact that in connection with terrorism are in a proper sense inescapable but ordinarily escaped. Not the facts of terrorism that rightly engender a horror with respect to it, of course. But the misery, wretchedness, and suffering, whatever they justify or fail to justify, that are a cause of terrorism and raise the question for me of whether societies themselves are lower forms of life.

If there is a necessity of an empiricism in philosophy having to do with consciousness and the mind, there is a still greater necessity of an empiricism in political philosophy. Almost all of it, certainly as good as all Conservative and most of Liberal politics political philosophy, gives itself the help of leaving at the edge of its consumers' minds, or right out of their minds, the conditions of multitudes of lives that justify or fail to justify terrorism, say by way of the Principle of Humanity.

The Argument for the Principle of Humanity

Norman goes on to note rightly that in the past I took the Principle of Humanity to "arise out" of features of our human nature—primarily our great desires, and hence good and bad lives. This was succeeded by the three-stage argument sketched above in my remarks on Mary Warnock. That argument is not a proof of the principle, but a little closer to a proof than earlier efforts.

As for the principle itself, I still do take it to be tolerably expressed as Norman does in his version PH1A as follows: The right as against the wrong thing to do is the one that according to the best judgement and information is rational with respect to the end or goal of saving people from bad lives as defined.

Yes, this humanity is a consequentialism about right and wrong, if entirely different from, say, Utilitarianism or the Greatest Happiness Principle, lately resurrected at the London School of Economics in the form of a proposition about making people happy by something like psychoanalysis. Also, however, humanity is not that what is right is what may be suggested by "the ends justify the means."

Rather, what is right is what is rational, taking account of *both* means and ends in terms of effects, of getting or keeping people out of bad lives, including its victims. It cannot possibly ignore bad or worse effects with respect to means themselves—say deaths of victims. And, of course, it is a maximizing principle—it is for the largest number of people possible not left in or put into bad lives. I come back to this after what is more important.

Norman reports correctly, more fully than mentioned above, that I have not in the past had much more to say, in general, in advocacy of the Principle of Humanity than that it arises of human nature—our desires, our capacity to be guided by reasons and hence consistency, and our capacity for sympathy with others. I hope better has since been done or can be done now. To be quick and crude, such a fact of human nature as our capacity for sympathy with others seems very likely to be of at least less use in argument for the Principle of Humanity. For a start, there are other facts, wants of sympathy with others, say, desires and characteristics cited by Conservative thinkers in the history of attempts to justify that politics, in a sense to moralize it.

The better that I hope can be done in advocacy of the principle, touched on in the introduction to this book, is that argument in three stages.

(1) We all share certain desires, maybe rightly called primal desires or evolutionarily selected desires whose satisfactions we put ahead of the satisfactions of all other desires. These stand in relation to the six great goods given in the Principle of Humanity—length of life, bodily well-being, freedoms and powers, respect and self-respect, relationships with others, goods of culture in a wide sense, including literacy, several memberships, and knowledge. We desire these things for ourselves ahead of the objects of other desires we have.
(2) Each of us does more than desire them. Our psychology, the reality of our lived lives, is such that we take it is *right* that we have these things. It is *right* that we should have or get them if we lack them. A general fact nearly as good as any other around here.
(3) What is to have such a *reason* for anything? In fact, any reason? In particular, what is it to have a reason as distinct from a desire with respect to the great goods? Well, plainly all reasons are *general*. That is their very nature. Whatever the further complexities, you can't have a fact that is reason for X's being right that is also a fact of Y but is not a reason for Y's being right. So there is the conclusion that each accepts it as right that others, all our fellow humans, also have lives in which there are the six great goods—or anyway the greatest approximation possible to that state of affairs.

Change of Mind

That is not to say that Norman has not really changed my mind about anything. He has—certainly more so than any other objector to my use of my principle with terrorism.

I have in the past, until now, weighed both the immediate terrible effects of terrorism, say deaths of victims, and the terrorism's anticipated or possible further effects, its aim, and its effects of getting many people out of bad lives. Certainly, as you have heard already, and may excuse my repeating, there was not the slightest possibility in my mind of not considering the immediate effects, not counting them. The idea was, of course, that the end and the means considered together could in some cases justify the means. The total of good and bad consequences could be better than the alternative of no terrorism.

Yes, of course, this was what Norman calls a maximizing consequentialism. What other kind of arguable consequentialism could there be? Who says, whatever else is to be said, that what is really more of a good is not better than less?

Yes, there would always be difficulty in judging the matter. Uncertainty. Uncertainty not affected, not made less, by the biased judgements of familiar adversaries of all terrorism. Uncertainty not made less by at least the uncertainty of *all* large judgements about societies and human life, not made less by the mere or dim assertiveness of almost all democratic politicians. But my uncertainty has not saved me now from more concession right now than with any other objection to my position of asserting a moral right of Palestinian terrorists against neo-Zionism. That is not to say that nothing remains, nothing that can be regarded as a moral right.

The choice for me, and conceivably for you, is between what it is safe to call the known and, indeed, patent inhumanity of our oligarchic democracies, of such policies as tacit support of neo-Zionism and the possible inhumanity of some terrorism—some terrorism for which a case in terms of humanity can be attempted. Can you have a moral right to a *chance* of success as against a policy or policies other than terrorism, policies of which history has proved—yes, proved—to be a failure in terms of humanity? I take it or anyway suppose that the Palestinians can have such a right.

So I defend myself finally or anyway for now by my seeing, along with many others, conceivably Norman, at least an appalling difficulty—a more terrible counterpart of the certainty of the inhumanity of those in control of our societies.

Indiscriminativeness

You will gather or guess, rightly, that this change of mind is not owed just to what Norman makes so much of, terrorism's extent of *indiscriminateness* in its choice of victims. Yes, of course, questions of indiscriminateness arise, if to my mind not the liberal John Rawls' of "the separateness of persons." The principle, in its way, exactly does not separate persons, say in terms of the circularity of rightness taken as desert—or in terms of relationships where those are not results of the principle but defeats of it.

These remarks, however, cannot be the place for the contention that it is exactly the denial of consequentionalism, remarked on already as known in the past as *deontology*, that is to me spurious. The ideas of desert that are the basis of most Conservatism in politics are also at bottom tools of self-interest in societies. To that must be added the overwhelming proposition that the means of oligarchic democracy are both in ways indiscriminating and in ways all too discriminating, both of them offences against humanity. Many automatic condemners of terrorism, those of the tradition of Conservatism, are discriminating to a fault, discriminating in favour of themselves, discriminatory against those to whom they absurdly condescend.

"Terrorism"

Norman's consideration of the history, and so on of the word "terrorism" is typically instructive. If his characterization of it as indiscriminate killing is not true of all of what we call terrorism, it is a decent generality. So, too, with the characterization of it, although maybe less true, that it targets innocent victims. It does not do so uniquely, of course. What is still rightly called our "terror bombing" or "carpet bombing" of German cities in World War II in effect did the same, and was in effect admitted in much of its justification, as it has been.

Norman allows that his formulation "legitimate targets" is vague and open-ended. Yes, it is at least that. It will not have escaped him that what is also known as carpet bombing did not do any *selecting* of victims other than Germans of a whole city.

Self-defence

There is a simpler thought or impulse, one having to do with self-defence, that very likely has been expressed by terrorists themselves. It is of course that their terrorism *is* a form of self-defence. Their terrorism is a justified use of force against those, perhaps a society as well as those in control of it, attacking the people of the terrorist. The thought or impulse, of course, cannot conceivably be to the effect that the terrorism is action called self-defence in virtue of being sanctioned by the law of the society. That cannot distinguish it.

Can the thought or impulse be to the effect that the terrorism is sanctioned or also sanctioned by some principle of morality? The thought or impulse is unlikely to be to the effect that the attacking terrorist himself or herself is under attack. Is some kind of identification of terrorist and people contemplated? A reply to the thought or impulse of course is that terrorism called self-defence has as much need or explicit justification as standard legal self-defence on our own parts. That, patently, has to be more than mere assertion of self-justification.

But I leave more reflections on this sort of thing, and also on the mention of agency in connection with self-defence, until my resolute consideration of the objector to follow, Michael Neumann, who also concerns himself with self-defence and a kind of agency.

Conclusion

Norman is impressive and in a smallish class of philosophers in seeing that there are not easy answers to the question of some terrorism—if perhaps less difficult answers to the particular questions having to do with terrorism related to millions of horrific lives in Asia and Africa and what is understated as the plight of the Palestinians. There *are* articulated answers, necessarily general. The Principle of Humanity is the basis of one. I stand by the principle about as much as any such thing can be stood by.

Norman's piece of philosophy is about as clear as a bell despite the perfect attention to the complexity of questions and the necessary hesitation in answers. He avoids complication unnecessary to an effective mission.

His piece is advocacy that briefly and cogently informs and contends. Using no more than is necessary to a clear and reasonable end. Not like all philosophy. Maybe not like every paragraph or distinction of every piece of philosophy in this book. In its economy not like, as it comes to mind to add, a book of mine, one on consciousness that leaves *nothing* out.

With Norman, it is worth remembering that a whole definable class or category or categories of persons in our own societies are in bad lives that cannot conceivably be explained by causal circumstances that do not include another definable class or category of persons in our societies. Nor can judgement here have to do with intentional action in any other sense than action being in its essential relevant nature only a certain thing—action with the foreknowledge of the probability of a certain result, nothing other than that.

* * *

18.4 On Neumann

Michael Neumann's paper is to me original, combative, baffling in parts, and more than replete. Its originality, in no way, lets down the University of Trent in Canada—or his own book, *What's Left? Radical Politics and the Radical Psyche*. My remarks here, as inadequate as brevity must make them, follow the course of his paper. They are not greatly more than retorts to most of his principal propositions.

Principle of Humanity Doubly or Triply Subjective

One general judgement by him is to the effect that the Principle of Humanity is *subjective*. That might be taken as the proposition that the principle is not a matter of ordinary factual truth, or not sufficiently of this truth, but of personal or other feeling or inclination—in the general category not of cognitive consciousness or of course perceptual but rather in the category of affective consciousness. My main reply as you know is that the principle is supported by the facts and logic of the main argument for it.

That the principle is subjective, however, might be taken as meaning two more particular things considered. One is to the effect that the principle in its essential content having to do with certain desires or great goods is in an albeit large sense parochial in terms of space—of our Western moneyed societies. Another more particular sense in which my moral and political philosophy is subjective is that it and more particularly the desires or great goods affirmed in it are parochial in time, of our time—the account of good things does not derive from the past as well as the present. It owes little or nothing to the past.

My reaction to the general judgement of subjectivity was surprise. There has existed and does exist that argument based in factual truths. Certainly, it consists of or adds up to *an* objectivity about right and wrong. Neumann raises no question about the argument, the foundation of my stuff.

My reaction to the proposition of parochialism in place, Westernness, was astonishment. Whatever else is to be said, the Principle of Humanity is different from, indeed what you can call a world apart from, our Western values. Some guardians of those values may be inclined to burn my books that deny them. These values are formed against the wide tradition of Conservatism as it can be defined. The Principle of Humanity is indeed what can be argued to have been the principle of the Left when it had not lost its way. The ideology of the Left is certainly not now our leading or most-effective Western ideology.

My reaction to my second parochialism is less confident. Yes, it is true that the forming and defence of humanity has not drawn on the past, despite mentions of it. The largest mention has been what is perhaps most fundamental or inescapable in our whole history of morality—the Golden Rule in its various expressions. If you press the question of where the principle came from philosophically in my case, the best answer, despite my condemnation of this source, was Utilitarianism. Its clarity, consequentialism, and so on do not save Utilitarianism from its mere generality about satisfaction, happiness, utility, or the like—or, more than that, save it from its absurd consequence of justifying, say, a slave class in a society when that serves the best total of satisfaction or the like for the society.

Of course, the Principle of Humanity is in a familiar way or ways of its time. Is any such thing not at all of its time? Would it get any attention if it was?

More Problems with Humanity

To come on from subjectivity and the two parochialisms, it is objected to humanity that it is not a principle of such strengths as fundamentality, weight, what is called something like political effectiveness. One of my several responses here is that my stuff is indeed philosophy, not any other more ordinary immediate engagement in politics, not the first thing usually meant by talk of ideology and the like.

You have heard my account of the nature of philosophy—a concentration on ordinary logic. Political philosophy as such has had some effects. I bravely take Marx, a philosopher of whom I know so little, to have had some effect. So do you. Maybe few readers of these words will need to put "political philosophy" into Wikipedia in order to think of more effects—or fail to think of Hobbes, Locke, Rousseau, Mill, and so on, up to the smaller fry Rawls, Nozick, and so on.

Is someone of strong and clear political attitudes rightly spending his time with philosophy as distinguished from politics, that political effectiveness? It's a little late for me to be opening that question. Will try division of labour as an answer sometime. We need thinking as well as acting.

I pass by much in Neumann's paper that is so different. One proposition that is his own is to the effect that in terms of my expression of the Principle of Humanity, which for a start includes a lot more than the six great goods and the definition of bad lives, there is more than the possibility that the poor and oppressed have lives no worse than those of the rich subject to fear and romantic disappointments. The privation, suffering, and enduring misery with us and conceivably to the Middle East of us and in much of Asia and Africa, may be in worse shape than our own well-heeled. A little more realism and empiricism please.

A Principle of Self-defence or Human Agency

I come now towards one of several remaining main questions. What we are given as superior to humanity is a principle of *self-defence*—as you remember also at least touched on by Richard Norman. Self-defence is ordinarily and reasonably taken at first to be the subject of a response to *attack*. Self-defence is a response, I think taken as justified, to some or other aggressive action, most familiarly physical force or the threat of it. What comes to mind first in this whole context is self-defence against terrorism. But it transpires that self-defence as we are considering it can be and mostly is against what again in accurate brevity can be what terrorism may be taken to be against, what can be called social and economic conditions. In my abbreviation, bad and good lives.

All of that includes argument—about both terrorism and the social and economic conditions. It includes, more particularly, an answer to the question of what *is* right and what *is* wrong with respect to social and economic conditions, what is right and wrong with our own and other societies. Our own form of life. Maybe our own lower form of life?

Neumann's progress—it *is* progress—is not impeded, certainly, but rather made more official, by what also happens, which is to say a transformation, maybe what is now unkindly called a morphing. The subject and principle of self-defence becomes the subject of what is called *human agency*. The activity of self-defence traditionally conceived becomes, I take it, the subject and recommendation of engaging in a higher/superior category or side of human existence.

I don't know, but does human agency by any chance have to do with what you have heard of from me, what traditionally has been *free will*, where that is an undetermined freedom different indeed from *voluntariness*, being able to do what you want, for example not being in jail? Certainly, we are to give the meaning of interest and importance to what is suggestively spoken of as human agency.

Attack and Humanity

To come back to attack, or the like, could it be understood by Neumann as merely action that is prohibited by the existing law of a society—positive law, the law of the land, legislated or enacted or courtroom law, law of the state or government, maybe a democratic kind of state? Is attack in Neumann's case to be more generally understood? There are sentences, I take it, where attack can be taken that way. In effect, attack, which here asks for some other name, is an offence not against positive or state law but against right and wrong, against that fundamental content of morality.

Well then, we need to hear about that morality, some principle. What is Neumann's right and wrong that issues in a necessarily enlarged idea of attack, which idea then issues in an idea of self-defence of which he approves? I put it to you that we don't really hear.

So, you may anticipate what I have to say hereabouts. The Principle of Humanity, in effect in one unattended part a principle of attack and defence, is the principle of the effect that what is right is what serves the end of getting people out of bad lives, whether they have got into that condition by themselves or by the acts or omissions of others.

Might it be that Neumann, evidently of a kind of sympathy or generosity, evidently of the Left rather than the Right, should on further reflection be a philosopher dependent and celebrating the Principle of Humanity? The fundamental, weighty, non-subjective, non-parochial principle of right and wrong? He can't do without some such principle if he wants to tell us about attack in a general sense and self-defence. It still won't be easy. We should all think about it.

One other remark here. Is his understanding of attack or whatever a kind of compound? For him, is it action understood somehow *both* in terms of being against state law and also right and wrong? You might be excused for wondering that on the basis of the piece of writing with which we are now concerned. If he has some richer conception of attack or whatever, we do still need to have his sense of right and wrong, maybe its relation to humanity.

My own position with respect to self-defence, as you will have guessed, can be made clear enough. What is ordinarily called attack or whatever is one kind of violation of the Principle of Humanity. The response to it that is justified self-defence is whatever, in rationality, serves the end of humanity.

Certainly, Neuman and I could not be in much more disagreement about so much of the subject in hand, whatever the rest of our philosophical and committed lives. It is not plain to me that the thinking in his paper, as he supposes, may play some role in defending me in connection with the moral right of the Palestinians to their self-defence. We disagree, certainly, about the possible justification of self-defence known in advance to be futile.

The two of us are birds of a feather. Reddish or pinkish, you might say. For the badly off somehow understood? Evidently, birds of a feather don't always flock together.

Another thing—larger and not only comradely. Neumann's self-defences of himself, I am sure, are in his books *What's Left? Radical Politics and the Radical Psyche* and the more particular *The Case Against Israel*, including its pp. 79–86 on self-defence. Read both books, more thoughtfully than I have been able to do in the course of making the remarks in this book you are reading.

* * *

18.5 On Smilansky

Broad Historical-Political Issues

Saul Smilansky is rightly known for his conviction that we have illusory beliefs about our freedom. His paper here, despite its title "Free Will, Understanding and Justification: Terrorism, Israel and the Palestinians" and despite an earlier expectation that it would best fit the second part of this book, the one about determinism and freedom, is three quarters about Palestine and Israel. Perhaps understandably since it comes from the University of Haifa.

It is in accord with Smilansky's idea, still, that possibly we can advance thinking on determinism and freedom, which has always and naturally been concerned with ourselves as individual men and women and our actions, if only occasionally in connection with punishment, by also doing something else. We can advance by thinking of determinism and freedom in connection with "broad historical-political issues," Palestine and Israel, in particular.

There has of course been a consideration of political freedom as one kind of freedom in such general and fortitudinous works on freedom as Mortimer Adler's *The Idea of Freedom*, and political freedom has been given attention in works on kinds of government, and considerable attention has been paid to political liberty and some to collective liberty. But, Smilansky's idea is his own, partly because it concerns free will or origination—uncaused decisions and choices excluded by determinism. It is this mystery that is to be inquired into by way of Israel and the Palestinians.

But, to leave all that, the paper is in fact not so much taken up with the broad historical-political issue in question with free will. Most of the paper is four propositions.

(1) There is no Palestinian state because the Palestinians themselves in their actions have chosen not to have one.
(2) They themselves are to be held overwhelmingly or mainly morally responsible or deserving or blameworthy with respect to their lack of a state.
(3) They have so chosen no state for themselves by way of being unwilling to accept the existence of a state of Israel alongside a Palestinian state—despite their entering into the Oslo Agreement of 1993.
(4) The explanation of their stance of not accepting a state of Israel has been largely their uniqueness among peoples. This is their deep and murky fanaticism, hatred, and self-deception—related to juvenile irresponsibility, blaming everyone but themselves, a fantasy world, preferring helplessness, and a mad hope.

Of course with respect to (1) to (4) I cannot join him in the seeming implication of one condition, or one uniquely explanatory condition, in the causal circumstance for there being no Palestinian state, and, certainly I remark that his by implication leaving out neo-Zionism is extraordinary.

It also ignores the historical truth that the Palestinians are the *only* indigenous people of the land in question, and that Jewish people were intruded on them after the Holocaust—however rightly intruded, as in my own view.

There is also no adequate consideration in his paper of such explanatory facts of disproportion as that in 2014 following the killing of three Israeli teenagers by the Palestinian terrorists Hamas, there was the onslaught on Gaza by the Israeli army and air force in which 2200 Palestinians were killed, including 1462 civilians, 551 of them children, 1500 children were orphaned, and 18,000 homes were destroyed.

Smilansky's given explanation of there being no Palestinian state also ignores the fact that Israel could indeed have been expected and surely was expected to overcome or deal with the historic Palestinian stance of not accepting in negotiation Israel's right to exist. No doubt, this was, at least, unwise on their part, but, given the overwhelming power of Israel, it was, in reality, no threat at all. Acting on it by neo-Zionism was essentially a pretence.

Those negative remarks of mine do not prompt me to read through my past works on our subjects to defend myself from the objection that I engage in moral judgement with neo-Zionism but do not do so with the Palestinians. In all my stuff on terrorism including Palestinian terrorism I have always faced and considered the prima facie wrong of terrorism, however few the victims.

Determinism, and So On

In passing, I remark that it is or would be absurd to suggest that I take what Smilansky calls hard determinism, historic and ordinary full determinism or explanationism, which I am at least inclined to believe, to rule out all moral praise and blame of anyone, holding people responsible, and so on. It is patently obvious that we praise and blame morally as much or even more on the basis of the freedom that is voluntariness of action—in a phrase or two doing what you want, not being in jail, not subject to an inner compulsion—as against the origination that has not been given much more than the content that it is inconsistent with determinism.

I also need to remark in passing, although this too is no great matter, that he speaks of me as "a determinist and not a compatibilist," thereby allowing the careless reader to suppose I am an incompatibilist. But presumably as he is aware, I have always been and I remain *neither* a compatibilist nor an incompatibilist about freedom in the established philosophical sense. That is because it is indeed my view, so widely shared, indeed shared by all decent dictionaries, that we do not have one idea of freedom, but two—one being incompatible and the other compatible with determinism. Is this what he can be taken as referring to as a complexity of my position?

Maybe it is worth remarking, also, that I have no "emotivist" stand on anything in the sense of an attitude or doctrine or principle or philosophy like any of A. J. Ayer in his Logical Positivism or C. L. Stevenson on "persuasive definitions" in his *Ethics and Language*.

To revert now to the beginning of these remarks of mine, thinking on determinism and freedom has always concerned itself with ourselves as individual men and women. That has still been so even when there has been some general subject in hand, say the practice of punishment by the state or the provision of incentives or rewards for entrepreneurs or some other higher category of members of a society. Smilansky proposes to correct this concentration, as you have heard, by thinking of determinism and freedom in connection with "broad historical-political issues," in particular the issue of Palestine and Israel.

I doubt that there is the slightest gain, and feel no reason to believe it as a result of Professor Smilansky's endeavour on behalf of his people. Partly because in my recollection of all that has been written on determinism from the ancient Greeks to Hume and Kant to the present day, his idea must count as not only absolutely original but also unreasoned and conceivably a kind of pretext having to do with Palestine and Israel.

How could particular freedoms or responsibilities or deserts in a broad historical-political context be of different and additional use with respect to the general philosophical question of what it is to act freely and how this is related to determinism. But leave that.

Anti-Semitism, and So On

I deny, and would resent more in the absence of past experience, Smilansky's report that there are occasional anti-Semitic expressions and tropes in my writings. Tropes, Shmopes. There would be as much sense in my attempting to make something of the Semitic prejudice brought to mind by Smilansky's paper. There is in fact good feeling for Jews in my writings, including my philosophical autobiography and, it comes to mind to add, there is the real relevance of my past marriage to a Jewish woman and of one of my two closest philosophical colleagues having been Jerry Cohen. Still, I quote two paragraphs from *Humanity, Terrorism, Terrorist War: Palestine, 9/11, Iraq, 7/7*.

> 'But that is perfectly consistent with something else, quite as large a fact.It is that Israel is now also the homeland of the Jews. A half-century has passed since 1948. A homeland has come into being. Its human existence is a reality entirely independent of whatever can be said of an ancient past. It has come into being and lives of Jewish people are in it, including the lives of many so honourably and courageously opposed to the neo-Zionism of their state. They have human rights there. They can weep too. Something of the lives of many Jews who are not there is also there.' (2006, 104)

For more thinking relevant to Palestine and Israel, look at Smilansky's paper "Terrorism, Justification and Illusion" and at more of his work. Perhaps you will find that he has something that serves his line of argument in his paper here. The most useful thing would be a kind of test for consistency, a constraint on special pleading. I mean a general principle of right and wrong, a counterpart to my Principle of Humanity. There is no indication in his present paper that it exists.

Resolute self-interest instead is what the paper brings to mind, put into sharper definition by the other Israelis who are indeed moved at least to protest by what is or is close enough to the Principle of Humanity.

In my view too if you are in danger of being impressed by Professor Smilansky, you need to look at things by Professor Chomsky, one of so many Jews who condemn neo-Zionism to one extent or another. Look in particular at *The Fateful Triangle: The United States, Israel, and the Palestinians* and at *Israel, The Holocaust, and Anti-Semitism*. To which can be added, perhaps most relevantly, another work by a Jewish author, Ilan Pappe's *A History of Modern Palestine: One Land, Two Peoples*.

Finally, with respect to Smilansky's own general idea that we as philosophers advance our thinking on determinism and freedom by thinking of them not in connection with individuals but in connection with "broad historical-political issues," one in particular—that general claim that in my opinion has not worked out. No, if your subject is kind of freedom and its relation to determinism, how do you shed more light on the subject by thinking of more people as having the freedom, whatever else unites or does not unite them? Is *being tall* itself defined or given more definition or clarified by the number of men who are it?

Nor, of course, does Smilansky's single-mindedness of taking the question of our freedom to be that of the causelessness of our choices throw any light at all on that freedom owed to mystery beyond explanation. Does the idea persist essentially because of its usefulness in such contexts as punishments in our societies—and the broad historical-political issue of Palestine and Israel?

Conclusion

In these remarks on the four pieces on right and wrong, and in the remarks on the previous pieces about mind and consciousness and about determinism and freedom, I have been philosophical too in the common use of the term where it is keeping calm. Keeping calm in the face of the exigencies of space and time—word limits and deadlines. You too have kept calm, I hope. *Ave atque vale*.

Index[1]

[1] Note: Page numbers followed by "n" refers to notes.

G. D. Caruso (ed.), *Ted Honderich on Consciousness, Determinism, and Humanity*, Philosophers in Depth, https://doi.org/10.1007/978-3-319-66754-6

M

N

Printed by Printforce, the Netherlands